Curtis captures the apostle Paul's way of life, attack against the gospel, and false theology on conversion before his conversion and his zeal to preach the gospel and true conversion with all boldness after his conversion. This is a must-read book which is written with clarity by Curtis and encapsulates Paul's statement in Philippians 1:21: "For to me to live is Christ, and to die is gain."

—Paul Patterson

The Apostle Paul's Theology *on* Conversion

And His Refutation and Condemnation of Sacramental Conversion and Salvation

CURTIS BRAUN

LUCIDBOOKS

Dedicated to Laura, Pax, and Keryx. Trust and follow the Lord Jesus Christ no matter the cost.

If anyone comes to me and does not hate his own father and mother and wife and children and brothers and sisters, yes, and even his own life, he cannot be my disciple. Whoever does not bear his own cross and come after me cannot be my disciple. . . . So therefore, any one of you who does not renounce all that he has cannot be my disciple.

—Luke 14:26–27, 33

But that is not the way you learned Christ!— assuming that you have heard about him and were taught in him, as the truth is in Jesus, to put off your old self, which belongs to your former manner of life and is corrupt through deceitful desires, and to be renewed in the spirit of your minds, and to put on the new self, created after the likeness of God in true righteousness and holiness.

—Ephesians 4:20–24

I appeal to you therefore, brothers, by the mercies of God, to present your bodies as a living sacrifice, holy and acceptable to God, which is your spiritual worship.

—Romans 12:1

Stand Up, Stand Up for Jesus

Stand up! stand up for Jesus! Ye soldiers of the cross;
Lift high his royal banner, It must not suffer loss.
From victory unto victory His army shall he lead,
Till every foe is vanquished, And Christ is Lord indeed.

Stand up! stand up for Jesus! The trumpet call obey;
Forth to the mighty conflict in this his glorious day.
Ye that are men now serve him against unnumbered foes;
Let courage rise with danger and strength to strength oppose.

Stand up! stand up for Jesus! Stand in his strength alone;
The arm of flesh will fail you, Ye dare not trust your own.
Put on the Gospel armor, Each piece put on with prayer;
Where duty calls or danger, Be never wanting there.

Stand up! stand up for Jesus! The strife will not be long;
This day the noise of battle, The next the victor's song.
To those who vanquish evil, A crown of life shall be;
They with the King of Glory Shall reign eternally.

George Duffield, Jr. 1858

Contents

Part 3:
The Apostle Paul's Theology
on Conversion

Preface

A great burden has been laid upon my heart to both defend and proclaim the gospel. My first book, *The False Gospel of Baptismal Regeneration in the Lutheran Church and Christ's Call to Saving Faith*, was written to address the conservative Lutheran Church and the false gospel they were proclaiming and defending. That was the church and denomination that I was raised in, and it is where many of my family and friends remain. Therefore, my burden was to write a book addressing this gospel issue.

In that book, I addressed the specific doctrinal issue of baptismal regeneration by distinguishing between water baptism and the baptism with the Holy Spirit. I also explained how baptismal regeneration corrupted, twisted, and destroyed the doctrines of regeneration, conversion, and the baptism with the Holy Spirit. Most importantly, that book exegetically explained how baptismal regeneration is a condemning false gospel, which clashes with the true gospel of the Lord Jesus Christ.

In *Apostle Paul's Theology on Conversion*, I attempt to exegetically demonstrate the Apostle Paul's understanding and theology on conversion (e.g., repentance and faith in Jesus Christ) and display his utter rejection and denunciation of sacramental conversion. There is much false teaching about conversion within Christendom, and it burdens my heart to see how many churchgoers are deceived by false teachers and false gospels, especially when it comes to sacramental conversion. Additionally, it troubles me to see how Paul's letters and teaching in Scripture can be twisted in such a way that it portrays the apostle Paul as teaching sacramental conversion.

This book is organized into three parts: Part 1 Jewish Rituals, Ceremonies, and Religious Life; Part 2 The Apostle Paul's Conversion; and Part 3 The Apostle Paul's Theology on Conversion. In part 1, we will do a close examination of the Old Testament Jewish rituals and pay particular attention to how God used signs, ceremonies, and rituals to teach His people. We will also look at the historical background and setting in which Paul lived to understand how Jewish signs, ceremonies, and rituals became twisted and perverted during his lifetime. This discussion will help us understand God's intended meaning for the most prominent signs, ceremonies, and rituals in the Old Testament and trace how they became corrupted during Paul's lifetime. As we correctly understand the signs, ceremonies, rituals, historical context, and Jewish cultural daily life during the Apostle Paul's life, it should be clear why Paul would never put hope in sacraments or rituals for salvation.

In part 2, we will explore the apostle Paul's conversion account, which includes the external events in Acts 9, 22, and 26 as well as his internal conversion experience in Philippians 3. By detailing the external events and understanding his internal thoughts at conversion, we will be able to understand Paul's repentance and how he wholly put his faith in Jesus Christ for salvation.

In part 3, we will review the Apostle Paul's doctrine on conversion in his epistles and missionary work. In writing the book, my goal is to help the reader understand why Paul would never teach sacramental conversion and why he condemned such teaching as false.

In the final chapter, we will briefly review how Paul dealt with teachers who taught a works-based salvation or a ceremony, sacrament, or ritual-based conversion or salvation. Though the last chapter will be brief, we will be able to see how Paul dealt with false teachers. For example, how did Paul deal with those that would teach a works-salvation, ritual-salvation, or sacramental-salvation? Answer: He taught that they were accursed (Galatians 1:8–9). Did Paul ignore false teachers, or did he confront and deal with those who taught a false gospel? Answer: He identified (Philippians 3:2), confronted (1 Timothy 1:3), sharply rebuked (Titus 1:13), warned (Titus 3:10), silenced (Titus 1:11), taught when possible (2 Timothy 2:24–26), and shunned false teachers when necessary (Romans 16:17, 2 Timothy 3:5, Titus 3:10). What kind of things did Paul say about false teachers that taught such things? Answer: He said they were evildoers and dogs (Philippians 3:2), warped and sinful (Titus 3:11), self-condemned (Titus 3:11), and accursed by

God (Galatians 1:8–9). Was Paul seeking to appease the false teachers, compromise with the false teachers, or see what he had in common with false teachers? Answer: He sought to please God, not men (Galatians 1:10).

We should ask ourselves some tough questions on how pastors and believers should approach such false teachings and false teachers. Are we trying to please men or God? Have we compromised on the gospel by aiding and abetting false teachers who give a false gospel? Is it easier to thin down the gospel and not identify those who have a corrupt gospel or to preach the gospel and identify those that have a corrupt gospel? When reflecting on Scripture, the gospel, and sacramental conversion, perhaps the best exhortation would be simply as follows from Paul in 1 Corinthians 11:1: "*Be imitators of me, as I am of Christ.*"

To compromise with false teachers who give a false gospel is to be unlike Christ and unlike Paul. Not confronting, addressing, or warning of the dangers of a false gospel is to be unlike Christ and unlike Paul. Sadly, there are many pastors who do not imitate Paul and Christ; there are many pastors who fear men more than they fear God. There are even many reformed pastors who know of the widespread sacramental false gospels that exist in false Christianity but refuse to stand firm and speak the truth in love.

John Macarthur described how a true man of God acts:

Men don't give in to fear. Men don't give in to pressure. Men don't give in to intimidation, and they don't give in to temptation. They don't seek the easy way. They will take the pain, they will invite the risk, they will confront the challenge, and they will not bow to the pressure to compromise the commandments of God. Strength of a man is that he lives on principle, that he lives on conviction, that he has the courage of those convictions, stands strong against everything that comes at those convictions, bravely faces the challenges in a fortified way. Manly fortitude means contending with difficulty, facing every enemy, meeting the enemy head on, bearing the pain, maintaining self-discipline, upholding truth, pressing on to the goal. That's what defines a man.[1]

Finally, this book is designed to make the reader aware that many churches teach sacramental conversion. Whether sacramental conversion is through water baptism, chrismation, or any other ritual, sacrament, or ceremony, it amounts to a false gospel. Below is a list of churches that unrepentantly, consistently, and deliberately hold to a false gospel of sacramental conversion. There are likely more churches that teach sacramental conversion, but please note that these churches account for a vast majority of the churchgoing population in the world.

- Roman Catholic Church
- Lutheran Church
- United Methodist Church

- Episcopal Church
- Eastern Orthodox
- Oriental Orthodox
- Assyrian Church
- Churches of Christ
- Some Anglican Church denominations
- Many other churches

Part 1

Jewish Rituals, Ceremonies, and Religious Life

Chapter 1

The Abrahamic Covenant Sign of Circumcision

And the Lord your God will circumcise your heart and the heart of your offspring, so that you will love the Lord your God with all your heart and with all your soul, that you may live.

—Deuteronomy 30:6

For we are the circumcision, who worship by the Spirit of God and glory in Christ Jesus and put no confidence in the flesh.

—Philippians 3:3

Understanding circumcision was critically important in the Old Testament just as it is in the New Testament. A false and tragic understanding of circumcision would lead one to believe that they have right standing with God when, in fact, they do not. A true understanding of circumcision helps an individual grasp the necessity of having a circumcision of the heart, through God's Word and by the power of the Holy Spirit. Thus, having a biblical understanding of circumcision clarifies God's purpose for this sign, which was not properly understood by the teachers of Israel during the life and times of Jesus and Paul, and this led to disastrous spiritual consequences. We will begin by explaining the true meaning of circumcision before exploring how circumcision was misunderstood by many Jewish leaders in the first century.

Circumcision was practiced as early as 2400 BC for various reasons such as ritualistically preparing boys for manhood and preventing diseases that can be found in the folds of the foreskin of the male organ. However, when the Lord made the covenant with Abram, He instituted circumcision as a sign of that covenant, and thus, He gave circumcision religious meaning as it says in Genesis 17:9–12:

> And God said to Abraham, "As for you, you shall keep my covenant, you and your offspring after you throughout their generations. This is my covenant, which you shall keep, between me and you and your offspring after you: Every male among you shall be circumcised. You shall be circumcised in the flesh of your foreskins, **and it shall be a sign of the covenant** between me and you. He who is eight days old among you shall be circumcised. Every male throughout your generations, whether born in your house or bought with your money from

any foreigner who is not of your offspring, both he who is born in your house and he who is bought with your money, shall surely be circumcised. So shall my covenant be in your flesh an everlasting covenant. (emphasis added)

Before I introduce the sign of circumcision, I should first explain the Abrahamic Covenant. Without an understanding of the Abrahamic Covenant, we would not be able to fully grasp the meaning of the sign of circumcision, and we would be left with a truncated understanding of both the sign and the covenant. Therefore, we will need to start with Genesis 12 and move through Genesis 17 to understand the Abrahamic Covenant and how circumcision became a sign of this covenant between Abram (later called Abraham) and the Lord. In Genesis 12:1–3, we see the start or the unfolding of the Abrahamic Covenant.

Now the Lord said to Abram, "Go from your country and your kindred and your father's house to the land that I will show you. And I will make of you a great nation, and I will bless you and make your name great, so that you will be a blessing. And I will bless those who bless you, and him who dishonors you I will curse, and in you all the families of the earth shall be blessed."

When the Lord called Abram to move away from his father's house he was seventy-five years old. We immediately see the manifold blessings that the Lord promised to Abram in Genesis 12:2–3:

- Abram would become a great nation (Genesis 12:2).

- Abram's name would be great (Genesis 12:2).

- The nation that would come from Abram would be a blessing (Genesis 12:2).

- Those who blessed Abram would be blessed, and those who dishonored Abram would be cursed (Genesis 12:3).

- All people and families would be blessed through Abram (Genesis 12:3).

This covenant included the promise of land—a very specific piece of land that the Lord promised he would give to Abram; the land that was inhabited by the Canaanites (Genesis 12:6–7, 13:14–17). In fact, in Genesis 13:15, the Lord says that this land would be Abram's possession forever: "*For all the land that you see I will give to you and to your offspring forever.*"

So not only do we learn that a nation will come from Abram, but his name will also be great; he will be a blessing, and others will be blessed through him. We also come to understand that this Abrahamic Covenant will give him and his offspring land that they will possess forever. In Genesis 15, we begin to learn even more about this Abrahamic

Covenant. As Abram remained childless and believed that the heir to God's covenant will be Eliezer of Damascus, the Lord made the following promise to Abram in Genesis 15:4–6:

> *And behold, the word of the Lord came to him: "This man shall not be your heir; your very own son shall be your heir." And he brought him outside and said, "Look toward heaven, and number the stars, if you are able to number them." Then he said to him, "So shall your offspring be. And he believed the Lord, and he counted it to him as righteousness."*

In this portion of Scripture, we learn of the Abrahamic Covenant that the promised nation to come from Abram will be from his own body, not come from Abram's servant (Genesis 15:4). We also learn that Abram's descendants are going to be many. In fact, Abram's descendants are going to be as innumerable as the stars in the heavens (Genesis 15:5), which is another way of saying that Abram's descendants would be as innumerable as the dust of the earth (Genesis 13:16). After the Lord promises these blessings to Abram, we find that Abram believed in the Lord and in His promises, and the Lord credited this belief to Abram as righteousness as it says in Genesis 15:6: *"And he believed the Lord, and he counted it to him as righteousness."*

At this point, Abram was made right and justified before the Lord. Up until this point, Abram was not justified by faith and did not possess a right standing with the Lord.

Abram had been led out by the Lord and had been following the Lord, but he had not yet come to a saving faith in the Lord. Abram saw the deadness of his body, and he saw the deadness of Sarai's womb, but against all hope, he trusted in the Lord (Romans 4:21). At this point, he took his eyes off his ability to have a child. He took his eyes off the doubt that a great nation could come from him, and he looked to the Lord and put his trust in the Lord. Abram saw what was impossible for him, and he trusted what was only possible with the Lord. Abram's non-saving faith in the Lord turned to saving faith in the Lord. At this point, Abram trusted the character and promise of Yahweh as it says, *"And he believed in the Lord, and he counted it to him as righteousness"* (Genesis 15:6). Paul tells us that Abram was *"fully convinced that God was able to do what he had promised;"* Abram grew strong in his faith; he gave glory to God, and this faith was *"counted to him as righteousness"* (Romans 4:20–22).

It is good to remember that up until this point, Abram did not have a saving faith and right standing with God. Although we read that Abram had left his country to go to the land the Lord promised by faith, this was not a justifying faith (Hebrews 11:8). Although Abram had listened to the Lord, left his father, and was being led by the Lord, he did not yet possess the righteousness of the Lord. Up to this point, the Lord had promised Abram that he would be a great nation (Genesis 12:2), that he would be blessed (Genesis 12:2), that his name would be great

(Genesis 12:2), that he would be a blessing (Genesis 12:2), and that all peoples of the earth would be blessed through him (Genesis 12:3). The Lord had protected Abram from a famine in the land (Genesis 12:9); He gave him many possessions even after he lied to Pharaoh's officials and claimed Sarai was his sister (Genesis 12:11–20). The Lord continued to bless Abram when he and Lot split (Genesis 13:1–18), and He gave Abram victory over King Kedorlaomer and the kings allied with him (Genesis 14:1–17). However, it was not until Genesis 15:6 Abram trusted in the Lord and His promise that he was made right before God. Both in Romans and Galatians, Paul makes a point of identifying this as the moment when Abram had a saving or justifying faith (Romans 4:22, Galatians 3:6). James uses this same moment to identify when Abram had a saving or justifying faith in God (James 2:23). Abram trusted God and His promises and, at this point, God reckoned and imputed to Abraham the Lord's perfect righteousness. Up until this point, Abram had an unbelieving heart and a non-saving faith. Most importantly, and as we'll see, until Abram believed in the Lord, he had an uncircumcised heart.

One additional point should be made regarding Abram possessing a non-saving faith up until Genesis 15:6. It would be advantageous to understand at what age Abram possessed saving faith (see diagram below). We know that Abram was seventy-five years old when he left Haran to go to the land the Lord had promised (Genesis 12:4). We also know that he left by faith (Hebrews 11:8). We also know that several events took place between Abram leaving Haran and being justified by faith (Genesis 12:4–14:24). We now know that this faith was not a saving or justifying faith because Abram was justified by faith in Genesis 15:6. Additionally, we can see that Abram was eighty-six years old when Ishmael was born, which means that he could have been eighty-five or eighty-six years old when he came to saving faith, but this cannot be said for certain. So, why make this point? Scripture warns that there is a saving faith and a non-saving faith (James 2:14–26; Hebrews 4:2–3; Matthew 7:21–27, 13:18–23). It is far too common for pastors, denominations, and professing Christians to announce that someone is saved when they believe facts about the Lord Jesus Christ or the gospel. While the doctrine of justification by faith is vital and must be upheld, we must also listen to Christ when He commands men to agonize and strive to enter through the narrow gate (Luke 13:24, Matthew 7:13); we must listen when He says the kingdom of heaven is taken by violence and force and that there are few who find eternal life (Matthew 7:14, 11:12). Let us keep in mind that Abram was not justified by faith the moment he left Haran, but rather, he was justified the moment he trusted that God was able to do what He promised—when he trusted the character and promise of the Lord; this could have occurred months to years after leaving Haran (Genesis 15:6, Romans 4:20–22).

Age 75
Abram Leaves
Haran by Faith
[non-saving faith]
(Genesis 12:4,
Hebrews 11:8)

Age 85-86
Abram Conceives a
Child with Hagar
(Genesis 16:4)

Age 75-85
Abram justified by
faith
(Genesis 15:6,
Romans 4:3, 4:22,
James 2:23)

Age 86
Ishmael is born
to Abram
(Genesis 16:4)

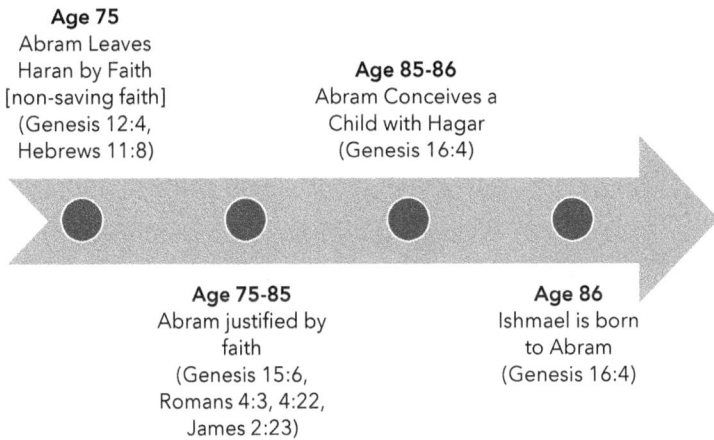

In Genesis 15:7–17, the Lord ratified His covenant with Abram. Abram wanted the Lord's assurance that the promise to inherit the land would be fulfilled, so Abram asked this of the Lord in Genesis 15:8: *"But he said, 'Lord God, how am I to know that I will possess it?'"* The Lord then had Abram bring a three year-old heifer, a three-year-old goat, a turtledove, and a young pigeon and cut them in two and lay each half opposite the other except for the birds (Genesis 15:9–11). As Abram fell into a deep sleep, the Lord appeared to him in a dream as a theophany, or a visible manifestation of God, and ratified His covenant. Genesis 15:17describes how the Lord ratified the covenant He had made with Abram: *"When the sun had gone down and it was dark, behold, a smoking firepot and a flaming torch passed between these pieces."*

When a person made a covenant in the ancient world, it was customary to cut animals in half and then have both pledging parties walk between them to affirm that if either party broke the covenant, the guilty party would agree that they should be torn in two. However, in this theophany, only God passed through the dismembered animals. God was saying that if He didn't uphold this covenant that was made with Abram, He should be torn apart in two and dismembered. The Lord still exists today, and He has not been torn asunder. The Lord is faithful to keep His covenants; this speaks of the Lord's truthfulness and faithfulness to do what He says He will do. There are many explanations for the flaming torch and smoking pot, but perhaps the best explanation is that these theophanies represent the all-consuming presence of God. Deuteronomy 4:24 captures this idea where it says, *"For the Lord your God is a consuming fire, a jealous God."* In this exchange, we also see that the specific dimensions of the promised land are given in Genesis 15:18: *"On that day the Lord made a covenant with Abram, saying, "To your offspring I give this land, from the river of Egypt to the great river, the river Euphrates."* Thus, Abram was justified by faith for believing God; and God ratified His covenant with Abram.

As we move through Genesis 16, we learn that Sarai, Abram's wife, had prompted Abram to sleep with Hagar so they could have a child, and Hagar conceived (Genesis 16:1–4). Afterward, Sarai despised Hagar who fled to a spring in the desert (Genesis 16:5–7). The Lord then promised Hagar that the son she had conceived would be named Ishmael and that many descendants would come from him, but that Ishmael would live in hostility toward everyone (Genesis 16:8–12). Hagar eventually gave birth to Ishmael; Abram was eighty-six years old when Ishmael was born (Genesis 16:16).

As we transition to Genesis 17, we see the Lord giving the sign of circumcision to Abram when he was ninety-nine years old. It had been a long thirteen years, and there is no evidence that the Lord had spoken to Abram during that time. The long wait before Abram heard from the Lord may have caused him to doubt the promise. Prior to giving the sign of circumcision to Abram, the Lord said, *"I am God Almighty; walk before me, and be blameless, that I may make my covenant between me and you, and may multiply you greatly"* (Genesis 17:1). The Lord told Abram that he was El Shaddai or God Almighty. Abram had a son by his own sinful doing, which was not how God was going to bless Abram and make him a great nation. The Lord reminded Abram that He was God Almighty and that nothing was impossible with Him. Finally, the Lord reminded Abram that He was mighty and powerful to do everything He had promised.

So the LORD commanded that Abram walk before Him blamelessly. Although Abram had been justified by faith for believing God and His promises, the Lord still required Abram to walk before Him with full devotion. This is not to say that Abram would never sin, but it is to say that the Lord

commanded Abram to live a life of faithful obedience to
Him. Again, the Lord gives the following promises to Abram
in Genesis 17:4–8 (NASB):

> *As for Me, behold, My covenant is with you, and you
> will be the father of a multitude of nations. No longer
> shall you be named Abram, but your name shall be
> Abraham; for I have made you the father of a multitude
> of nations. I will make you exceedingly fruitful, and I
> will make nations of you, and kings will come from you.
> I will establish My covenant between Me and you and
> your descendants after you throughout their generations
> for an everlasting covenant, to be God to you and to
> your descendants after you. And I will give to you and to
> your descendants after you the land of your sojournings,
> all the land of Canaan, for an everlasting possession,
> and I will be their God.*

Let's review the following promises that have been made:

- Abram would become a great nation (Genesis
  12:2).

- Abram's name would be great (Genesis 12:2).

- The nation that would come from Abram would
  be a blessing (Genesis 12:2).

- Those who blessed Abram would be blessed, and
  those who dishonor Abram would be cursed
  (Genesis 12:3).

- All people and families would be blessed through Abram (Genesis 12:3).

- Abram's descendants would be as innumerable as the dust of the earth, and he would receive a very specific plot of land (Genesis 13:14–17).

- This nation to come from Abram will be from Abram's body, not from Abram's servant (Genesis 15:4).

- Abram's descendants are going to be as innumerable as the stars in the heavens (Genesis 15:5).

- Abraham will be the father of many nations (Genesis 17:4).

- Abraham would be fruitful, and many nations will come from him (Genesis 17:6).

- The covenant is to be an everlasting covenant (Genesis 17:7).

- Abraham is to possess the land of Canaan (Genesis 17:8).

Thus, the Lord promised that He would be the God of Abraham and his descendants:

I will establish My covenant between Me and you and your descendants after you throughout their generations as an everlasting covenant, to be God to you and to your descendants after you. And I will give to you and to your

descendants after you the land of your sojournings, all
the land of Canaan, for an everlasting possession; and I
will be their God.

—Genesis 17:7–8 NASB

This statement about the Lord being Abraham's God and a God to his descendants is very important. In fact, this statement is used very often in New Covenant language later in the Bible. When the Lord gives His covenants, He commonly says "*I will,*" which notes that He is the one who will act to fulfill the covenant, not man. The Lord also commonly says, "*They shall be my people, and I will be their God.*" This is a way of saying that there will be a relationship with God and His chosen people. Genesis 17:7–8 certainly contains this language, but below is a demonstration of the Lord using this language in New Covenant promises. For demonstration purposes, I will highlight the statements "*I will*" and "*They shall be my people, and I will be their God,*" but it's also important to take note that this New Covenant promise will change the inner man's heart, will, and spirit. This New Covenant will change man's thoughts, affects, desires, and will by changing the inner man. This New Covenant includes a new heart, a devoted heart, a God-fearing heart, a new spirit, internal cleansing, and the promise of the Holy Spirit indwelling God's people:

*And **I will** give them one heart, and a new spirit **I will***
*put within them. **I will** remove the heart of stone from*

their flesh and give them a heart of flesh, that they may walk in my statutes and keep my rules and obey them. **And they shall be my people,** *and* **I will** *be their God.*

—Ezekiel 11:19–20 (emphasis added)

I will *take you from the nations and gather you from all the countries and bring you into your own land.* **I will** *sprinkle clean water on you, and you shall be clean from all your uncleannesses, and from all your idols* **I will** *cleanse you. And* **I will** *give you a new heart, and a new spirit* **I will** *put within you. And* **I will** *remove the heart of stone from your flesh and give you a heart of flesh. And* **I will** *put my Spirit within you, and cause you to walk in my statutes and be careful to obey my rules. You shall dwell in the land that I gave to your fathers, and* **you shall be my people,** *and* **I will** *be your God.*

—Ezekiel 36:24–28 (emphasis added)

I will *give them a heart to know that I am the Lord, and* **they shall be my people** *and* **I will** *be their God, for they shall return to me with their whole heart.*

—Jeremiah 24:7 (emphasis added)

Behold, **I will** *gather them from all the countries to which I drove them in my anger and my wrath and in great indignation.* **I will** *bring them back to this place, and* **I will** *make them dwell in safety. And* **they shall be my people,** *and* **I will** *be their God.* **I will** *give them* *one heart and one way, that they may fear me forever, for their own good and the good of their children after them.* **I will** *make with them an everlasting covenant,* **that I will not** *turn away from doing good to them. And* **I will** *put the fear of me in their hearts, that they may not turn from me.* **I will** *rejoice in doing them good, and* **I will** *plant them in this land in faithfulness, with all my heart and all my soul.*

—Jeremiah 32:37–41 (emphasis added)

"Behold, the days are coming, declares the Lord, when **I will** *make a new covenant with the house of Israel and the house of Judah,   not like the covenant that I made with their fathers on the day when I took them by the hand to bring them out of the land of Egypt, my covenant that they broke, though I was their husband, declares the Lord. For this is the covenant that* **I will** *make with the house of Israel after those days, declares the Lord:* **I will** *put my law within them, and* **I will** *write it on their hearts. And* **I will** *be their God, and* **they shall be my people***. And no longer shall each one teach his neighbor and each his brother, saying, 'Know the Lord,' for they shall all know me, from the least of them to the greatest, declares the Lord. For* **I will** *forgive their iniquity, and* **I will** *remember their sin no more."*

—Jeremiah 31:31–33 (emphasis added)

It is true that this covenant began with the Lord taking one man out of his home country and making him into a nation, giving him a multitude of descendants, and giving him a land to possess, but it is critical to understand that this covenant promised that the Lord would be Abraham's God and God to Abraham's descendants. The covenant would allow Abraham and his descendants to have right standing with God and to be reconciled to God. It allowed Abraham and his descendants to have a relationship with the Lord. Later in this chapter, we'll see how it was possible for Abraham's descendants to be blessed through Abraham.

After the Lord further clarified His covenant with Abraham, He commanded Abraham to keep the covenant as it says in Genesis 17:9–14:

> *And God said to Abraham, "As for you, you shall keep my covenant, you and your offspring after you throughout their generations. This is my covenant, which you shall keep, between me and you and your offspring after you: Every male among you shall be circumcised. You shall be circumcised in the flesh of your foreskins, **and it shall be a sign of the covenant** between me and you. He who is eight days old among you shall be circumcised. Every male throughout your generations, whether born in your house or bought with your money from any foreigner who is not of your offspring, both he who is born in your house and he who is bought with your*

money, shall surely be circumcised. So shall my covenant be in your flesh an everlasting covenant. Any uncircumcised male who is not circumcised in the flesh of his foreskin shall be cut off from his people; he has broken my covenant." (emphasis added)

The sign of circumcision would certainly be considered a sign, which had *progressive revelation*, meaning that more truth about the sign would be revealed throughout Scripture. However, it is important to note in Genesis 17:11 that circumcision was to be a sign of the covenant. The word for *sign* carries a connotation of being a symbol or a banner. A sign simply indicates or acts as a token of a fact. The sign is intended to convey information or a command. The reality is not the sign itself but the truth that the sign conveys. For example, if you saw a sign that read, "Highway 405 – 200 miles to Los Angeles, California," it would be a colossal mistake to think that you had made it to Los Angeles, California, just because you had reached the sign. The reality is that the sign simply points you to Los Angeles, California; you are still 200 miles away. In the very same way, circumcision was meant to be a sign of the covenant between the Lord and Abraham. As we understand that circumcision was a sign, it's also important to understand what circumcision meant as a sign of the covenant between Abraham and the Lord.

The Sign of Circumcision

The word *circumcision* carries with it the idea of clipped, to be cut down, or to be cut off. Thus, right away we can clearly see how circumcision was meant to signify the Abrahamic Covenant. We see that the Lord was going to clip off or separate one man, Abraham, from all other people. He was going to clip off or separate a nation for Himself. Through this sign, we see that the Lord was going to clip off or separate a land where this people would dwell and clip off or separate a people who would be His people and He would be their God. Thus, we see that circumcision rightly characterized the Lord circumcising a man, a nation, a land, and a people for Himself. As we progress, the sign of circumcision will be expanded to include the Lord circumcising the hearts of men for Himself. In the book of Deuteronomy, we gain a better progressive revelation of what circumcision was intended to convey. Deuteronomy 10:12–16 (NASB) helps us gain a clearer picture of the sign of circumcision:

> "Now, Israel, what does the Lord your God require from you, but to fear the Lord your God, to walk in all His ways and love Him, and to serve the Lord your God with all your heart and with all your soul, and to keep the Lord's commandments and His statutes which I am commanding you today for your good? Behold, to the Lord your God belong heaven and the highest heavens,

*the earth and all that is in it. Yet on your fathers did the
Lord set His affection to love them, and He chose their
descendants after them, even you above all peoples, as it
is this day. **So circumcise your heart**, and stiffen your
neck no longer."* (emphasis added)

In this passage of Scripture, we start to see what circumcision is intended to signify. The book of Deuteronomy was written sometime around 1405 BC. In the last few weeks of Moses's life, his explanations of the law were to be passed down to the coming generations. The original recipients of Deuteronomy were the second generation of the nation of Israel. Joshua and Caleb were the only ones remaining from the first generation; the second generation was born and reared in the wilderness. Deuteronomy, also known as the "second law," recalled Israel's history and rebellion against the Lord; reminded her of the Lord's faithfulness; called for Israel to take the land that was promised; and then called for faithfulness, reverence, love, and obedience toward the Lord. This chapter will give two distinct definitions of what circumcision was meant to signify (Deuteronomy 10:12–16, 30:6).

In Deuteronomy 10:16 Israel is told, *"Circumcise therefore the foreskin of your heart, and be no longer stubborn,"* but in Deuteronomy 10:12, we're given a qualified statement of what a circumcised heart looks like where it says:

*And now, Israel, what does the Lord your God require
of you, but to **fear the Lord** your God, to **walk in all***

***His ways,* to *love Him,* to *serve the Lord* your God
*with all your heart and with all your soul.*** (emphasis added)

Here we see that the circumcised heart fears the Lord
God, is faithfully obedient, loves Him, and serves Him
wholeheartedly. Therefore, to understand what a circumcised
heart is, we'll start by understanding the fear of the Lord.

The Fear of the Lord

The fear of the Lord could be described as a heart or state of
mind that knows and understands the Lord as He is, responds
in reverence toward God, and exchanges one's own attitudes,
will, feelings, and deeds for God's. Proverbs 1:7 says, "*The
fear of the Lord is the beginning of knowledge; fools despise wisdom and instruction,*" and Proverbs 9:10 says, "*The fear of the
Lord is the beginning of wisdom, and the knowledge of the Holy
One is understanding.*" This definition helps us understand
how the Israelites would have understood reverence toward
the Lord based on how God had made Himself known to
them through divine revelation, physical manifestations, and
His actions. To better understand the fear of the Lord, we'll
look at the attributes and revealed knowledge of the Lord
that the Israelites would have known up through the book of
Deuteronomy. This perspective will help us see God's attributes through His divine revelation throughout history.

The Israelites had knowledge of the *aseity* of God; that
is, they would have known that God is independent of all

things. He is perfectly *self-sufficient*, not depending on anything outside Himself for anything; He is, therefore, the eternal, foundational being, the source of life, and sustenance for all other beings.[2]

This characteristic was made known to them when the Lord declared that His name was YHWH, which meant "I am the One who is and will be," alluding to His self-existence (Exodus 3:14). They also would have known of His aseity through the creation account, which demonstrated that all created order came from God (Genesis 1). Job speaks of this attribute when he acknowledges who gave him life when he says, "*The Spirit of God has made me, and the breath of the Almighty gives me life.*" (Job 33:4). The uncreated Lord who existed outside time, matter, and space was ultimately the source of all creation and life.

The Israelites would have known of the *goodness* of God, that is, they believed that God is the perfect sum, source, and standard (for Himself and His creatures) of that which is wholesome, virtuous, beneficial, and beautiful.[3] They would have seen His goodness to them in how He fed them, clothed them, cared for them, led them (as fire and a cloud), and how He blessed their work and watched over them as they traveled in the wilderness for forty years despite their stubbornness and rebellion (Deuteronomy 2:7).

The Israelites would have known of the *immutability* of God, which is His perfect unchangeability in His essence, character, purpose, and promises.[4] They knew of the covenant God made with Abraham, which was an everlasting covenant that He would never break (Deuteronomy 7:9). They knew that if He broke His promise to Abraham, He had vowed that He would be torn in two (Genesis 15:17). This would have led them to know that God doesn't change and that He keeps His promises.

This Israelites also would have known of the *infinity* and *eternality* of God, which describe His nature as perfectly transcending all limitation of time and space.[5] He is without beginning and without ending; God is not limited by moments of time. They also would have known the creation account, which detailed God's creation of time, space, and matter (Genesis 1) inevitably demonstrating that He is infinite and outside time, space, and matter.

The Israelites would have known of the *omnipresence* of God; that is, God is perfectly present with Himself, transcending all limitation of space and yet present in every point of space with all that He is.[6] He is greater than and independent of the creation. The Lord declared to the Israelites that the heavens, the highest heavens, and the earth all belonged to Him (Deuteronomy 10:14). There is nothing outside God's control because He is the Creator and Sustainer of everything He has made and is intricately involved and omnipresent in His creation.

The Israelites would have known of God's *omniscience*, which is His perfect knowing of Himself and all things outside Himself.[7] This omniscience includes full knowledge of all things from eternity past to eternity future. In the span between creation to the book of Deuteronomy, this may have been the most clearly demonstrated when the Lord predicted to Abraham that the Israelites would be enslaved for 400 years, which came to pass (Genesis 15:13). Only the all-knowing and sovereign God over creation would have this foreknowledge to know future events.

The Israelites would have known of God's *omnipotence*, which is His ability to do anything consistent with His nature.[8] They would have known of His creative power in creation (Genesis 1). They would have seen His power over their enemy when they saw the Lord deliver Sihon, king of Hesbon, to them (Deuteronomy 2:30–35). They would have seen His power when He delivered Og, king of Bashan, into their hands (Deuteronomy 3:1–11). They would have known of the signs and wonders that God performed in Egypt (Deuteronomy 7:18). They would have seen that the heavens, the highest heavens, and the earth all belonged to the Lord, and He sustained everything (Deuteronomy 10:14).

The Israelites would have known of God's *love*, which is His determination to give of Himself to Himself and to others and is His affection for Himself and His people.[9] The Lord explained that He loved Israel not because of her size or righteousness, but because He loved her outside of any self-redeeming virtue (Deuteronomy 7:7, 9:5–6). Israel did nothing to merit God's love. Rather, it was the divine and determined love of the Lord, which caused Him to love Israel.

The Israelites would have known of God's *grace*, which is God perfectly bestowing favor on those who cannot merit it because they have forsaken Him and are under the sentence of divine condemnation.[10] The Lord did not destroy the Israelites when they made the golden calf and worshipped it. Rather, He relented from destroying them (Deuteronomy 9:7–29), and he revealed Himself to Moses in a most magnificent passage of Scripture:

> *The Lord, the Lord, a God merciful and gracious, slow to anger, and abounding in steadfast love and faithfulness, keeping steadfast love for thousands, forgiving iniquity and transgression and sin, but who will by no means clear the guilty, visiting the iniquity of the fathers on the children and the children's children, to the third and the fourth generation.*

—Exodus 34:6–7

Rather than punish and destroy the Israelites for worshipping a golden calf, He displayed divine grace and spared them. He even spared Aaron who led all of Israel into this worship (Exodus 32).

The Israelites would have known of God's *mercy*, which is God having perfect deep compassion for creatures, such that He demonstrates benevolent goodness to those in a pitiable or miserable condition even though they do not deserve it.[11] The Lord knew that the Israelites would worship false gods, but He promised that He would be merciful and would not abandon or destroy His people and that He would not forget His covenant even when they rejected

Him for false gods (Deuteronomy 4:25–31). God's mercy was also demonstrated when He spared the Israelites after worshipping the golden calf (Deuteronomy 9:7–29). They had also seen the Lord's mercy when He declared that He would spare Sodom if only ten righteous people were found in the city even though the city abounded in wickedness and rebellion against Him (Genesis 18:22–33).

The Israelites would have known of God's *long-suffering*, which speaks of God being perfectly placid in Himself and toward sinners in spite of their continual disobedience and disregard for His warnings.[12] God's long-suffering would have been magnificently demonstrated in his waiting 120 years before sending the flood to destroy humanity when the heart of man was only wicked continually (Genesis 6–8). For all the iniquity and wickedness that filled the earth, the Lord gave time for people to repent when Noah, the preacher of righteousness, was preparing the ark (2 Peter 2:5).

The Israelites would have known of God's *faithfulness* and *truthfulness*, which are the perfect correspondence of God's nature with what God should be, with reliability of His words and deeds, and with the accuracy of His knowledge, thoughts, and words.[13] They would have known what Balaam said to Balak about the Lord: "God is not a man, that he would lie, or a son of man, that he should change his mind. Has he said, and will he not do it? Or has he spoken, and will he not fulfill it" (Numbers 23:19)? The Lord cannot lie. The Lord only speaks truth. When the Lord makes a promise, He will keep it. His words are faithful and true. He is the one and only God who keeps His covenant and steadfast love with those who love Him (Deuteronomy 7:9).

The Israelites would have known of God's *holiness*, which is His inherent and absolute greatness, in which He is perfectly distinct and separate above everything outside Himself and absolutely morally separate from sin.[14] The Israelites would have seen this when the Lord came to Mount Horeb and they were not allowed to approach the mountain (Deuteronomy 4:10–12, 5:22–27). They would have seen God's holiness when Nadab and Abihu lit unauthorized fire and were killed by the Lord because they did not worship the Lord as He commanded (Leviticus 10:1–3). They would have seen God's holiness and separateness because entering the Most Holy Place would lead to death except for the High Priest who could enter only on the Day of Atonement (Leviticus 16). God had revealed to them that He was holy and separate from sinners.

The Israelites would have known of God's *righteousness*, which is His perfect absolute justice in and toward Himself, His prevention of any violation of the justice of His character, and His revelation of Himself in acts of justice.[15] They would have known of Abraham's righteousness by faith (Genesis 15:6); they would have known that God punishes sin (Exodus 34:6–7). They would have known of God's righteous judgment on Sodom and Gomorrah for their immorality, but also His willingness to spare those cities if ten righteous people could be found (Genesis 18–19). The Israelites would have known the Ten Commandments and understood that breaking a command was a sin, which violated God's character and law (Deuteronomy 5:1–21). The Israelites were trained to see that because of the Lord's righteousness, He could not look upon sin with favor and that sin required death.

The Israelites would have known of God's *jealousy*, which is His protectiveness of all that belongs to Him.[16] That is, God is jealous for Himself, His name, His glory, His people, and His sole right to receive worship and obedience. They would have known that the Lord forbade idolatry (Deuteronomy 4:15–19) and commanded that He alone was to be worshipped as God (Deuteronomy 4:39–40). The Lord is a jealous God and will not share His glory with false gods.

The Israelites would have known of God's *wrath*, which is His righteous retribution against those who have offended Him.[17] They would have known of God's wrath against sin and disobedience when they were terrified of the Amorites, did not trust the Lord, and were not allowed to enter the land that was promised (Deuteronomy 1:26–46). They would have known of the Flood, which was God's righteous retribution against the sinfulness of mankind (Genesis 6–8). They would have known of God's wrath when the people committed immorality and worshipped Baal at Peor and 24,000 were killed (Numbers 25). They would have known of God's wrath when they grumbled against Him and a plague broke out (Numbers 16). They would have known that God is a God of vengeance and wrath as He says in Deuteronomy 7:10 that God *"repays to their face those who hate him, by destroying them. He will not be slack with one who hates him. He will repay him to his face."* The Lord is a God who will personally destroy those who hate Him and do not trust in Him because He is a righteous and wrathful God.

Therefore, we can see what fearing the Lord God meant to the Israelites. They were expected to know who God is, what He had done, and what He had promised; they were to revere Him alone. Let us remember that fear of the Lord is the beginning of wisdom, and the knowledge of the Holy One is understanding (Proverbs 9:10). There is no fear of the Lord without understanding who He is. We know that the fear of the Lord was to be taught to all generations as the Lord commanded in Deuteronomy 31:13: *"And . . . their children, who have not known it, will hear and learn to fear the Lord your God, as long as you live on the land that you are going over the Jordan to possess."*

Now that we have a basic understanding that the fear of the Lord comes by knowing Him and His will, we will look at what it means to have a circumcised or an uncircumcised heart. Since there are several characteristics of a circumcised and uncircumcised heart, let's start by exploring Deuteronomy 10:12–16 and the progressive revelation of what heart circumcision is.[18]

The Circumcised Heart versus the Uncircumcised Heart

A *circumcised heart* is one that fears the Lord. The Israelites knew who God was and what He had done. They were to reflect on this and revere Him in their hearts (Deuteronomy 12:12). Thus, we can see that a person who has a circumcised heart has knowledge of God and fears Him. A person with a *circumcised heart* knows of God's character and His works; they know what God loves and what God hates. They know of His hatred toward sin, but they also know of His willingness to show mercy and compassion and to forgive iniquity. A person with a *circumcised heart* responds in reverence toward God and exchanges their own attitudes, will, feelings, and deeds for God's.

In contrast, a person with an *uncircumcised heart* is someone with a heart that lacks knowledge of the Lord. The person who has an *uncircumcised heart* may know the facts about the character of the Lord, know His works, know what He loves and hates, but their heart is not moved toward reverence. Rather they are indifferent, apathetic, or in rebellion against Him. Where there is no knowledge of the Lord, there is a person with an uncircumcised heart that has no fear of the Lord. If there is no knowledge and reverence of the Lord, there remains an individual who has an uncircumcised heart.

Pharaoh of Egypt was an example of a man who had an uncircumcised heart and no fear of the Lord. Although Pharaoh heard Moses and Aaron speak the words the Lord gave them to speak and was given signs and wonders, his heart was consistently hardened. He did not fear the Lord and was ultimately destroyed (Deuteronomy 7:18). Pharaoh is an example of someone who knew of the Lord, but he did not fear the Lord. Thus, we can see that a circumcised heart is one that knows the Lord and fears the Lord wholeheartedly (Deuteronomy 10:12).

On the other hand, we also see that a person with a *circumcised heart* is one who walks in all His ways (Deuteronomy 10:12). A person with a heart that fears the Lord responds to the Lord by obeying Him; such a person walks in all His ways and trusts in the Lord, His words, and promises. This person is submissive to the Lord, not self-willed. They are meek, meaning that they exercise strength under control, but most importantly, under the Lord's will. This person learns to hate what the Lord hates and love what the Lord loves; they learn what pleases Him, and they seek to do that which pleases Him. They also learn what displeases and angers the Lord and seek to avoid such things. This person is also repentant because to walk in the Lord's ways, they must have a life that is characterized by turning from sin and turning to the Lord. This person hates sin and circumcises it out of their life; they see their own sin and the need for spiritual cleansing and cut away the sin. Just as the foreskin was cut from the male member, so sin is cut away and repented of. The male organ, which only proliferated sinfulness was the same male organ that the Lord chose to demonstrate the need for spiritual cleansing. Thus, we see that walking in the

Lord's ways describes a repentant, meek, trusting, and obedient person whose heart has been circumcised.

In contrast, the person with an *uncircumcised heart* does not walk in all the Lord's ways and has a stubborn, unsubmissive heart. Such a person does not walk in all His ways, does not fear the Lord, and does not cut away or repent of sin. This person walks after their own selfish desires, and has an idolatrous and unbelieving heart that does not trust the Lord, His promises, or His Word. This person has an unrepentant heart. Only a person with a circumcised heart will fear the Lord and walk in His ways with all their heart and soul while the person with an *uncircumcised heart* remains unsubmissive, unrepentant, and unbelieving.

Additionally, a person with a *circumcised heart* loves the Lord for who He is with all their heart and soul. This is not to say that the person loves the Lord perfectly, but it is to say that they love the Lord wholeheartedly. They know of God's attributes, such as His compassion, love, mercy, omnipotence, omniscience, eternality, goodness, kindness, righteousness, and holiness, and loves Him for who He is. They know what God has done such as His work in creation, His wrath poured out in the Flood, His kindness toward Noah, His faithfulness toward Abraham, His goodness toward Lot and his family, His long-suffering with Jacob, His anger and judgment toward Sodom and Gomorrah, and they love Him with all their heart and soul. This person is one who hears His Word and loves it because it is the Word of their Lord, Savior, and Master. They hear the Lord's promises and trust them because they know their Lord is faithful and true; they simply love God for who He is, what He's done, what He's said, what He has promised, and what He will do.

In contrast to the person with a *circumcised heart*, the person with an *uncircumcised heart* does not love the Lord for who He is, what He's done, what He's said, what He has promised, and what He will do. They are indifferent, apathetic, or hostile to the Lord, His Word, and His promises. Therefore, we see that only the person with a *circumcised* heart will love the Lord.

Additionally, the person with a *circumcised heart* is one who serves the Lord and obeys His commandments. They worship the Lord as He ought to be worshipped; they serve the Lord by learning His statutes, commands, and ordinances, and they carry them out wholeheartedly. They serve the Lord by obeying from the heart and soul, not just externally. The person with a *circumcised heart* who loves the Lord can succinctly be described in Deuteronomy 30:15–16 (NASB):

> *"See, I have placed before you today life and happiness, and death and adversity, in that I am commanding you today to **love the Lord your God**, to **walk in His ways** and **keep His commandments, His statutes, and His judgments**, so that you may live and become numerous, and that the Lord your God may bless you in the land where you are entering to take possession of it."* (emphasis added)

The person with a circumcised heart simply loves the Lord for who He is and what He's done; they love and trust Him and seek to serve and obey Him.

In contrast to the person with a *circumcised heart*, a person who has an *uncircumcised heart* does not serve the Lord as He ought to be served. Moses knew the Israelites' hearts would not serve or obey Him when He says this in Deuteronomy 31:27 (NASB): "*For I know your rebellion and your stubbornness; behold, as long as I have been alive with you until today, you have been rebellious against the Lord; how much more, then, after my death?*" The person with an *uncircumcised heart* is simply one who does not serve or obey the Lord from the heart.

A person who has an *uncircumcised heart* is stiff-necked. A stiff-necked animal is one that refuses to bow its head in submission to the yoke of its master, and they do not perform any real work. The animal refuses to obey or submit to its master; therefore, it is worthless. Because such an animal fights back against the master and only performs according to its own will, it cannot be instructed. The stiff-necked animal does not listen and does not fear its master. This is the picture of a person with an uncircumcised heart. They are self-willed, stubborn, disobedient, ignorant, apathetic, indifferent, unbelieving, unregenerate, unconverted, sinful, and rebellious toward the Lord (Leviticus 26:40–41).

We should note that in Deuteronomy 30:6, the Lord is the one who performs the heart circumcision: "*Moreover, the Lord your God will circumcise your heart and the hearts of your descendants, to love the Lord your God with all your heart and all your soul, so that you may live"* (NASB). Man cannot circumcise His own heart; he is completely dependent on the sovereign grace of God for this heart surgery. Man cannot circumcise another man's heart. No, the circumcision of the heart is a sovereign act of compassion, mercy, and salvation, which is performed by the Lord Almighty. Although the Lord commands that we circumcise our hearts, it becomes evident in Deuteronomy 30:6 that He is the one who must do it. Although man is responsible for the condition of his uncircumcised heart, he must look to the Lord to circumcise his heart. Though the man cannot circumcise his own heart, he is still responsible for repenting and trusting in the Lord. We should also note that just as man is only circumcised once outwardly by cutting away the flesh, so the circumcision of the heart is a one-time sovereign, salvific, gracious, merciful, and compassionate work of the Lord.

Once again, note that circumcision was strictly a sign, not salvific in and of itself. The Lord spoke this command through Jeremiah to the rebellious house of Judah and Jerusalem: *"Circumcise yourselves to the Lord; remove the foreskin of your hearts, O men of Judah and inhabitants of Jerusalem; lest my wrath go forth like fire, and burn with none to quench it, because of the evil of your deeds"* (Jeremiah 4:4). It wasn't the physical act of circumcision that saved but rather, the circumcision of the heart. We should also see that an uncircumcised heart is a heart that is outside God's kingdom; it remains under the wrath of God. An uncircumcised heart is a heart that is not reconciled to God and does not possess saving faith. Jeremiah 9:24–26 says this about the circumcised and uncircumcised heart:

> *" but let him who boasts boast in this, that he understands and knows me, that I am the Lord who practices steadfast love, justice, and righteousness in the earth. For in these things I delight, declares the Lord. Behold, the days are coming, declares the Lord, when **I will punish all those who are circumcised merely in the flesh**— Egypt, Judah, Edom, the sons of Ammon, Moab, and all who dwell in the desert who cut the corners of their hair, **for all these nations are uncircumcised, and all the house of Israel are uncircumcised in heart.**"*
> (emphasis added)

Once again, this emphasizes that the one who has a circumcised heart understands and knows the Lord. The circumcised heart knows of the Lord's mercy, justice, and righteousness. On the contrary, the uncircumcised heart has no such knowledge of the Lord or fear of the Lord. Additionally, we see that the Lord makes a distinction between a circumcision of the flesh and a circumcision of the heart when He says, "*'Behold, the days are coming,' declares the Lord, 'that I will punish all who are circumcised and yet uncircumcised.'*" How is it possible to be circumcised and yet uncircumcised? As we learned earlier, it is possible to be circumcised in the flesh of the male organ yet be uncircumcised in heart.

This distinction between physical circumcision and heart circumcision makes it clear that there is something wrong with man's heart. If man's heart was right with God, there would be no need for a heart circumcision. Therefore, the Lord's command to circumcise your heart indicates that the heart needs to be circumcised. If there is no heart circumcision, there is no salvation. The heart must be pierced by the Spirit of God through the Word of God. Apart from this, there is no heart circumcision and no salvation.

At this point, we can define the terms *circumcised heart* and *uncircumcised heart*. A *circumcised heart* can be described thus: It is a saved, redeemed heart that has been circumcised by the Lord and is now a heart that is regenerate and believes and trusts in the Lord. The regenerate and believing heart knows, understands, and fears the Lord for who He is, what He's done, what He's promised, and what He will do. The person whose heart has been circumcised is submissive and repentant—one who loves the LORD and seeks to serve and obey Him with all their heart and soul.

On the other hand, an *uncircumcised heart* can be described thus: It is an unredeemed heart that is unregenerate and unbelieving toward the Lord. An uncircumcised heart does not know or understand the Lord and does not fear Him for who He is, what He's done, what He's promised, and what He will do. The uncircumcised heart is stubborn, not submissive, unrepentant, disobedient, unconverted, rebellious, and idolatrous toward the Lord. The person whose heart has not been circumcised does not love Him or seek to serve and obey Him with all their heart and soul.

Finally, we can see how circumcision applied to Abraham and the Abrahamic Covenant. Abraham was a man who previously worshiped other gods as it says in Joshua 24:2:

And Joshua said to all the people, "Thus says the Lord, the God of Israel, 'Long ago, your fathers lived beyond the Euphrates, Terah, the father of Abraham and of Nahor; and they served other gods."

Abraham was a pagan and had an unredeemed and uncircumcised heart. However, the Lord led him out of his father's house and land and circumcised his heart so he would believe in Him and inherit the Lord's promises. To understand the Abrahamic Covenant sign is to also understand the spiritual circumcision and salvific work of the Lord in the heart of men. Abraham's heart was circumcised in Genesis 15:6, and the cutting away of the flesh from the male organ signified the many blessings of the Abrahamic Covenant, which include a spiritual circumcision of the heart.

Circumcision During the Life and Times of Paul and the Fulfillment of the Abrahamic Covenant Sign

In the New Testament, we see much discourse about circumcision, the Abrahamic Covenant sign. For example, in

Matthew 3:7–9 John the Baptist warned the Pharisees and Sadducees to repent and not rely on their Jewish heritage for salvation:

> *But when he saw many of the Pharisees and Sadducees coming to his baptism, he said to them, "You brood of vipers! Who warned you to flee from the wrath to come? Bear fruit in keeping with repentance. And do not presume to say to yourselves, 'We have Abraham as our father,' for I tell you, God is able from these stones to raise up children for Abraham.*

John the Baptist was preparing the nation of Israel and the hearts of the people for the Messiah (Luke 1:16–17). He was warning them that they needed to repent and accept the Messiah and not simply believe they possessed right standing with God because they were Israelites, because of the Abrahamic Covenant, or because they had been circumcised. John the Baptist was warning the people of Israel, Pharisees, and Sadducees of the disaster of not having a repentant heart that accepted the Messiah (Luke 3:3–17).

During Paul's ministry, he confronted the belief and teaching that circumcision had salvific merit. Many of Paul's epistles dealt with this very issue (Romans 2:28–29, 1 Corinthians 7:19, Galatians 1–6, Ephesians 2:11, Philippians 3:2–3, Colossians 2:11–12, Titus 1:10). In fact, Paul went up to the Jerusalem Council in Acts 15 to address the issue of whether circumcision had a role in salvation in the first-century church era.

To understand why Jews perceived circumcision as having salvific merit, we can briefly refer to some historical Jewish works. For example, the *Book of Jubilees* is a noncanonical book that was written toward the end of the era before Christ. The *Book of Jubilees* says the following:

> "And every one that is born, the flesh of whose foreskin is not circumcised on the eighth day, belongeth not to the children of the covenant which the Lord made with Abraham, but to the children of destruction; nor is there, moreover, any sign on him that he is the Lord's, but (he is destined) to be destroyed and slain from the earth, and to be rooted out of the earth, for he hath broken the covenant of the Lord our God."[19]

Furthermore, the *Book of Jubilees* states:

> And now I announce unto thee that the children of Israel will not keep true to this ordinance, and they will not circumcise their sons according to all this law; for in the flesh of their circumcision they will omit this circumcision of their sons, and all of them, sons of Beliar, will leave their sons uncircumcised as they were born. And there will be great wrath from the Lord against the children of Israel, because they have forsaken His covenant and turned aside from His Word, and provoked and blasphemed, inasmuch as they do not observe the ordinance of this law; for

they have treated their members like the Gentiles, so that they may be removed and rooted out of the land. And there will no more be pardon or forgiveness unto them [so that there should be forgiveness and pardon] for all the sin of this eternal error.[20]

This is essentially saying that circumcision put them in the Lord's covenant; whereas uncircumcision put them outside God's covenant. While there is certainly precedence concerning God's anger and wrath for not giving the sign of circumcision to the male members of Israel (Exodus 4:24–26), these statements certainly tied circumcision to forgiveness of sins and being in the Abrahamic Covenant. They also tied uncircumcision to breaking God's covenant; that is, the uncircumcised were considered to be outside God's covenant people, sons of Beliar/Belial and not forgiven. Therefore, we can see that some rabbinic writing and teaching supported the idea that circumcision carried salvific merit.

In the *Midrashim*, which are ancient commentaries of the Old Testament, Rabbi Levi said this regarding circumcision:

In the age to come Abraham will sit at the gate of Gehenna [hell], and he will not permit a circumcised Israelite to go down there. Then what will he do for those who sinned too much? He will remove the foreskin from infants who died before they were circumcised and will place it over [Israelite sinners] and then lower them into Gehenna.[21]

Here, we see a statement that Abraham guards hell so that those who have undergone circumcision will not receive eternal punishment. Rabbi Menachem wrote in his commentary on the *Book of Moses*, "Our Rabbins [rabbis] have said that no circumcised man will ever see hell."[22] The Jalkut Rubem stated that "Circumcision saves from hell" (num 1). In the Midrash it was written, "God swore to Abraham that no one who was circumcised should be sent to hell."[23] The book of Akedath Jizehak taught that "Abraham sits before the gate of hell, and does not allow that any circumcised Israelite should enter there."[24] Thus, we can clearly see why Paul fought with such might against circumcision, the sign of the Abrahamic Covenant, as a means of salvation.

Paul addressed this issue with the Romans in his epistle to them. He emphasized that the most significant ritual in the Jewish religion, the Abrahamic Covenant sign, is not what gave right standing with God. Rather, Paul taught that only a circumcision of the heart performed by the Spirit was salvific as he explains in Romans 2:28–29:

> *For he is not a Jew who is one outwardly, nor is circumcision that which is outward in the flesh. But he is a Jew who is one inwardly; and circumcision is that which is of the heart, by the Spirit, not by the letter; and his praise is not from men, but from God* (NASB).

In this verse, Paul makes the distinction between a spiritual circumcision and the physical circumcision. The spiritual circumcision is performed by the Holy Spirit on the heart and is salvific, while the physical circumcision is done by man on the flesh and is not salvific.

In Romans 4:9–12 Paul explains that it was because of Abraham's faith in God that God credited His righteousness to Abraham before he was circumcised:

> *"Is this blessing then only for the circumcised, or also for the uncircumcised? For we say that faith was counted to Abraham as righteousness. How then was it counted to him? Was it before or after he had been circumcised? It was not after, but before he was circumcised. He received the sign of circumcision as a seal of the righteousness that he had by faith while he was still uncircumcised. The purpose was to make him the father of all who believe without being circumcised, so that righteousness would be counted to them as well, and to make him the father of the circumcised who are not merely circumcised but who also walk in the footsteps of the faith that our father Abraham had before he was circumcised."*

Therefore, Paul demolishes any argument that a covenant sign, ritual, or sacrament would have any salvific merit. He also affirms that the covenant sign was strictly a sign of the righteousness that Abraham possessed, which was by faith and not by circumcision of the male organ. In fact, the sign was given to Abraham after he had faith in the Lord. So, Abraham was justified by faith in God, and all who trust in the Lord, as Abraham did, will be blessed and justified by faith.

Paul also addressed this issue with the Philippians in his epistle to them. He emphasized that the true circumcision was comprised of those who put their faith in Christ as opposed to the false circumcision who put confidence in the flesh and works. He states this plainly in Philippians 3:3: *"For we are the circumcision, who worship by the Spirit of God and glory in Christ Jesus and put no confidence in the flesh."* According to Paul, those who put confidence in the flesh and outward circumcision are dogs, evildoers, and mutilators of the flesh (Philippians 3:2). However, those who are the true circumcision are those who have a righteousness that comes through faith in Christ and not the law or ceremonial rites (Philippians 3:9). Clearly Paul wanted the Philippians to know that no works and no covenant sign had any value in salvation; only faith in Christ was salvific.

Paul also addressed this issue with the Colossians in his epistle to them. In Colossians 2:11, he explains that Christ is the one who performed the circumcision, which is without hands: *"In him also you were circumcised with a circumcision made without hands, by putting off the body of the flesh, by the circumcision of Christ."* Therefore, we can understand that Christ is the one who performed the spiritual and salvific circumcision, which is distinct from physical circumcision. Physical circumcision is done outwardly using hands, but spiritual circumcision is done by Christ on man's heart.

Additionally, we know that saving faith comes from hearing and hearing through the word of Christ (Romans 10:17). Thus, when we combine Romans 2:28–29, 10:17, Philippians 3:3, and Colossians 2:11, we have a definition and a diagram of spiritual circumcision which is this:

> Spiritual circumcision is the monergistic work of salvation performed by Christ on the heart of men through the work of the Holy Spirit. All those who have been spiritually circumcised are those who have put their faith in Christ.

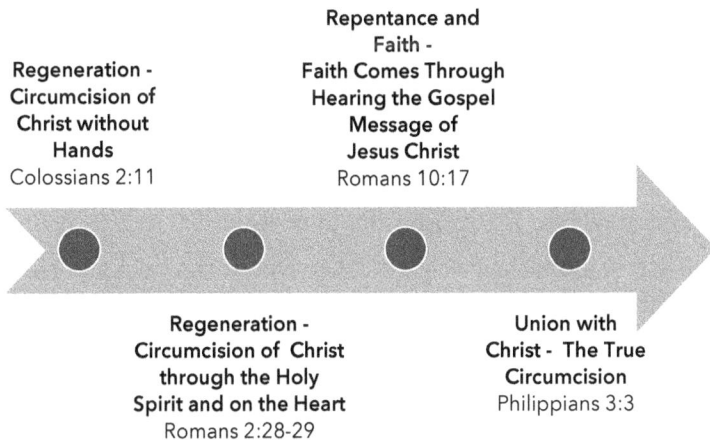

Regeneration - Circumcision of Christ without Hands
Colossians 2:11

Repentance and Faith - Faith Comes Through Hearing the Gospel Message of Jesus Christ
Romans 10:17

Regeneration - Circumcision of Christ through the Holy Spirit and on the Heart
Romans 2:28-29

Union with Christ - The True Circumcision
Philippians 3:3

Clearly, Paul knew the difference between a spiritual circumcision and a physical circumcision. To go even further, Paul knew the difference between Spirit baptism (Colossians 2:11–12, 1 Corinthians 12:13) and water baptism (1 Corinthians 1:14–17). He wanted the Colossian church to know that the Abrahamic Covenant sign had no merit toward salvation, and Paul emphasized to the Colossians that they were saved by believing the gospel (Colossians 1:5–8).

Paul addresses this in a different way to the Corinthians in 1 Corinthians 7:19: "*For neither circumcision counts for anything nor uncircumcision, but keeping the commandments of God.*" Paul is not teaching or proclaiming a works-based salvation by keeping commandments, but rather, he's explaining that keeping the commandments is an outflow of a redeemed life as a result of faith in Christ. Paul is also telling the Corinthians that the most significant ritual and Abrahamic Covenant sign in the Jewish religion is nothing and means nothing as it pertains to having right standing with God.

Paul addresses circumcision to the Galatian churches as well. In Paul's letter to the Galatian churches, he proclaims that any salvific reliance on the most significant ritual in the Jewish religion, the Abrahamic Covenant sign, was damning and that such a reliance on circumcision for salvation would damn them and sever them from Christ. where he says in Galatians 5:2–4:

> *Look: I, Paul, say to you that if you accept circumcision,* **Christ will be of no advantage to you.** *I testify again to* **every man who accepts circumcision that he is obligated to keep the whole law. You are severed from Christ**, *you who would be justified by the law; you have fallen away from grace.* (emphasis added)

To put one toe in the water and place one's hope of salvation in physical circumcision is to take one giant leap into alienation and damnation from Christ. To put hope in physical circumcision for one's salvation is to be severed, cut off, and circumcised away from Christ, not to Christ.

Paul emphasizes again that the Abrahamic Covenant sign meant nothing in terms of salvation, but what meant everything was an active faith that loved Christ. He says this in Galatians 5:6: *"For in Christ Jesus neither circumcision nor uncircumcision means anything, but faith working through love."* He goes on to explain that any reliance on circumcision for salvation would render them full-blown pagans much like the worshippers of Cybele who castrated themselves to worship their pagan god where he says this in Galatians 5:11–12: *"But if I, brothers, still preach circumcision, why am I still being persecuted? In that case the offense of the cross has been removed. I wish those who unsettle you would emasculate themselves!"* Finally, Paul tells the Galatian churches that neither being circumcised or uncircumcised in the flesh means anything for salvation. However, being a new creature in Christ, regeneration, or the new birth is what matters according to Paul in Galatians 6:15: *"For neither is circumcision anything, nor uncircumcision, but a new creation"* (NASB2020). Therefore, we can clearly see that Paul was adamant that the Abrahamic Covenant sign of circumcision merited no salvation, and reliance on this sign for salvation only severed one from Christ. Paul fiercely denounced those who taught ceremonial, ritualistic, works-based, and rites-based salvation.

Paul addresses circumcision in his letter to the Ephesian church as well. He states that the circumcision the Jews emphasized as a means of salvation was only performed in the flesh and by hands; it was not the true circumcision. In Ephesians 2:11 Paul says, "*Therefore remember that previously you, the Gentiles in the flesh, who are called 'Uncircumcision' by the so-called 'Circumcision,' which is performed in the flesh by human hands*" (NASB2020). Here, Paul states that although the Ephesians were called the uncircumcision by the Jews, the Ephesians had been reconciled to God through Christ by faith and had become fellow citizens with the saints and members of God's household (Ephesians 2:8–3:19). The Ephesians' right standing with God was not based on circumcision as propagated by the false teaching Judaizers. Paul clearly wanted to emphasize to the Ephesians that being saved was not of works and not of ritual, sacramental covenant signs.

Additionally, Paul warned Titus of the circumcision group, the Jews, who were propagating a salvation that depended on the physical circumcision of the Abrahamic Covenant sign. He says, "*For there are many rebellious people, empty talkers, and deceivers, especially those of the circumcision*" (Titus 1:10 NASB2020). As you see, Paul categorized Judaizers as rebellious people, empty talkers, and deceivers because they taught circumcision as a means of salvation. Paul was clearly concerned about teaching that salvation could come through the Abrahamic Covenant sign of circumcision.

Ultimately, Paul saw the fulfillment of the Abrahamic

Covenant in Jesus Christ. In Galatians 3:16, Paul says this about God's promise to Abraham: "*Now the promises were spoken to Abraham and to his seed. He does not say, 'And to seeds,' as one would in referring to many, but rather as in referring to one, 'And to your seed,' that is, Christ*" (NASB2020). Paul is referencing back to the Abrahamic Covenant in Genesis 12:7 where the Lord promised to bless Abraham's descendants. However, in Galatians 3:16, Paul narrows down "*seeds*" to "*seed.*" He deliberately notes that all promises and blessings would come through the one seed, Jesus Christ. All nations would be blessed through Jesus Christ. Paul understood that we received all the blessings of the covenant through Jesus Christ. Not only this, but Paul also saw that "*the seed*" that would come from Abraham was ultimately the same "*seed*" promised in Genesis 3:15 when He said, "*I will put enmity between you and the woman, and between your offspring and her offspring; he shall bruise your head, and you shall bruise his heel.*" Paul saw that "*the seed*" that brought blessing to all nations was a realization of the promise of Genesis 3:15 and Genesis 12:7. Paul again talks about all people being blessed through faith in Christ and being Abraham's offspring in Galatians 3:25–29:

> "*But now that faith has come, we are no longer under a guardian, for in Christ Jesus you are all sons of God, **through faith**. For as many of you as were baptized into Christ have put on Christ. There is neither Jew nor Greek, there is neither slave nor free, there is no male*

*and female, for you are all one in Christ Jesus. **And if you are Christ's, then you are Abraham's offspring,** heirs according to promise.*" (emphasis added)

Thus, the Abrahamic Covenant was fulfilled in Christ where the Lord circumcised Abraham to Himself, circumcised Israel to Himself, circumcised the land of Israel to Himself, and promised that all nations would be blessed through Christ who would circumcise the heart. We saw earlier that the circumcision of the heart is performed by Christ and not by human hands (Colossians 2:11). We saw that a true Jew was one whose heart had been circumcised by the Holy Spirit and who has put their faith in Christ because Jesus Christ is the True Israel (Romans 2:28–29; Philippians 3:3, 9; Isaiah 49:3). Therefore, we see that circumcision of the heart is performed by Christ and with the Holy Spirit, not with human hands and that all who have had a heart circumcision have put their faith in Christ and are Abraham's offspring and heirs according to the promise. Romans 4:16 says, "*Therefore, **the promise comes by faith**, so that it may be by grace and may be guaranteed to all Abraham's offspring—not only to those who are of the law but also to those who have the faith of Abraham*" (NIV). (emphasis added)

As we close this chapter, we can see that circumcision was meant only to be a sign of the covenant between the Lord and Abraham, which signified that God had cut away Abraham for Himself, cut away a people for Himself, cut away a nation for Himself, cut away a land for His people, and most importantly, cut away the foreskin of the heart to have a people for Himself through Christ. In this chapter, we learned the characteristics of a circumcised heart and an uncircumcised heart. We examined how the covenant sign was viewed by Jews during the life and times of Paul and how Paul came to understand spiritual circumcision and the Abrahamic Covenant sign after his conversion. This chapter concludes by emphasizing that the Abrahamic Covenant sign was never a means of salvation, but solely a sign to point to the meaning of God's promise to Abraham and the need for a spiritual heart circumcision performed by the Lord. Paul clearly grasped that this most significant covenant sign was not a means for conversion, salvation, or right standing with God. Paul contended fiercely against those who taught that a sign, sacrament, ceremony, or ritual carried any salvific merit in the Old Testament or New Testament.

Chapter 2

Ceremonial Defilement and Washings

Now when the Pharisees gathered to him, with some of the scribes who had come from Jerusalem, they saw that some of his disciples ate with hands that were defiled, that is, unwashed.

—Mark 7:1–2

I thank God that I baptized none of you except Crispus and Gaius, so that no one may say that you were baptized in my name. . . . For Christ did not send me to baptize but to preach the gospel, and not with words of eloquent wisdom, lest the cross of Christ be emptied of its power. For the word of the cross is folly to those who are perishing, but to us who are being saved it is the power of God.

—1 Corinthians 1:14–15, 17–18

This chapter will address ceremonial uncleanness or ceremonial defilement, look at the ceremonial washings that were biblically required, understand how ceremonial washings were practiced during the life of Paul, and finally, how Paul viewed ceremonial washings, most specifically baptism, as pointing to the internal and salvific spiritual washing that would be performed in the heart by God through the gospel of Jesus Christ. This chapter also explores how the people should have understood ceremonial uncleanness and what it would have been like living under those laws. As we approach this chapter, it's important to consider how easy it was to become ceremonially unclean or defiled according to Levitical law. It is important that we understand how prevalent ceremonial washing was during the life of Paul. This chapter is significant because in some parts of modern Christianity, water baptism is considered efficacious to bring about regeneration, conversion, the indwelling of the Holy Spirit, forgiveness of sins, and eternal life. By the end of this chapter, it should be abundantly clear why the apostle Paul would never have thought of an external ceremonial washing as a means of being converted to Christ, especially water baptism.

Let's begin this chapter with a basic definition of what it meant to be *ceremonially unclean*. To be ceremonially unclean or ceremonially defiled meant that an individual had defiled themselves or become unclean by some act such as eating unclean food, childbirth, infectious diseases, bodily discharges, touching a corpse, touching anyone or anything that was unclean or defiled, and more. The individual who became ceremonially unclean was unable to worship at the Lord's temple or tabernacle.

Ceremonial Defilements

In Leviticus 11, the Lord spoke to Moses and Aaron and told them to tell the Israelites what they could eat and what they could not eat. Some of the restrictions might have been to ensure health and avoid food sickness, but the primary reason the Lord gave for strictures on food can be found in Leviticus 11:43–45 (NASB2020):

> *Do not make yourselves detestable through any of the swarming things that swarm; and you shall not make yourselves unclean with them so that you become unclean. For I am the* Lord *your God. Consecrate yourselves therefore, and* **be holy, because I am holy**. *And you shall not make yourselves unclean with any of the swarming things that swarm on the earth. For I am the* Lord *who brought you up from the land of Egypt, to be your God; so you shall* **be holy, because I am holy**. (emphasis added)

From this text, it is clear that the Lord wanted His people to be holy and different from all the other nations. Therefore, the Lord made distinctions between all types of animals on land, sea, and air. Using the list in Leviticus 11:1–47, the Israelites needed to distinguish between clean and unclean food and learn and practice making these distinctions of what could not be eaten (Leviticus 11:47). The Lord's people were to be continually making distinctions of what was clean and unclean. If a person violated these laws, they would become ceremonially unclean until evening, potentially needing to wash their clothes, but most importantly, they could not worship at the temple. This was a sign to the people that they needed to be vigilant and holy so they would always be ready to worship the Lord in His sanctuary or temple. God was teaching His people through food strictures that they were to be separate from the surrounding idolatrous nations, which had no such restrictions. The Lord was showing His people that they must learn to live His way. This was a vivid way of teaching His people that they needed to live their life in obedience to Him in everything, even in the mundane areas of life. How and what they ate was important to God. As Leviticus 11:45 puts it so succinctly, "*So you shall be holy, because I am holy.*"

Animals that were considered unclean included camels (Leviticus 11:4), the hyrax (Leviticus 11:5), rabbits (Leviticus 11:6), pigs (Leviticus 11:7), whatever is in the seas and rivers but does not have fins and scales (Leviticus 11:10), certain birds (Leviticus 11:13–19), certain insects (Leviticus 11:20–23), and many other animals and animal carcasses (Leviticus 11:29– 40). Scripture indicates that touching or eating anything unclean would make one ceremonially unclean until evening. Additionally, there were specific instances in which a person would need to wash their clothes when they touched a dead animal (Leviticus 11:25, 28, 40).

You can see how this would have brought special meaning to Paul when he wrote this in 1 Corinthians 10:31: "*So, whether you eat or drink, or whatever you do, do all to the glory of God.*" Because the Lord was their God, they were to manifest outward holiness and obedience even in the most minute aspects of life that would express a circumcised and separated heart unto God.

Another way one could become unclean was through childbirth. Leviticus 12 describes how women became ceremonially unclean by childbirth. A woman who had given birth to a boy would be unclean for seven days; she would present the boy to be circumcised on the eighth day and would then be unclean for thirty-three more days before she could offer a burnt offering. If a woman had a girl, she would be unclean for two weeks and then she would need to wait sixty-six days before she could offer a burnt offering to become ceremonially clean. Interestingly, women were ceremonially unclean twice as long if they had a girl rather than a boy (Leviticus 12:4–5). The sacrifices required after the birth of a child were to remind the parents of the reality of sin that the child had inherited. Additionally, circumcision for boys was symbolic to remind the parents that the child needed a circumcision of the heart and spiritual cleansing. The ceremonial defilement that came from childbearing was a somber reminder to the mother that, although she was joyful over her child, she became painfully aware that her child had a heart that needed to be circumcised. The mother was unable to worship in the tabernacle for thirty-three or sixty-six days, which would also serve as another reminder of the reality of sin and not being able to worship at the temple.

Another way someone could become ceremonially defiled was through skin disease. Leviticus 13:1–46 gives instructions on determining defilement for different types of skin diseases. This included the examinations for leprosy (Leviticus 13:1–8), of infectious skin (Leviticus 13:9–11), for the outbreak of an infection (Leviticus 13:12–17), of boils on the skin (Leviticus 13:18–23), of burns on the skin (Leviticus 13:24–28), of sores on a person's head (Leviticus 13:29–37), of white spots on the skin (Leviticus 13:38– 39), of the loss of hair (Leviticus 13:40–44), and the result of leprosy (Leviticus 13:45–46). Leviticus 13:47–59 gave instructions on dealing with defiling molds in clothing materials; this too was to protect God's people from disease and keep them holy and pure. Defiling molds in clothing material, much like skin diseases, required examination by priests. In some instances, clothes could be washed and, in other instances, the water of purification could be applied to purify a house.

These laws were given to protect people from diseases, but they also showed God's desire for His people to be pure, holy, and separated. Of all the skin diseases, leprosy was considered the worst by far. Leprosy was compared to sin in that it spread to the whole body; it caused decay and death, and it made people deformed. Ultimately, leprosy required those who had it to live outside the camp. They were considered unclean and could not worship in the temple or tabernacle. Leviticus 14 covers the requirements for becoming ceremonially clean after a defiling skin disease. The people had to satisfy many regulations to become ceremonially clean after a skin disease, including washing their clothes, bathing in water, bringing offerings, sacrificing guilt offerings, sacrificing sin offerings, and more.

Another way one could become ceremonially defiled was through bodily discharges. Leviticus 15 deals with defilement that comes from bodily discharges for both men (Leviticus 15:1–18) and women (Leviticus 15:19–30). The discharges covered in Leviticus 15:1–15 deal with abnormal discharges, which were most likely from the male organ. Men who had abnormal bodily discharges from the male organ were considered unclean and would need to wash their clothes and body with running water and offer sacrifices. The discharges in Leviticus 15:16–18 were for the seminal emissions, which caused one to be ceremonially unclean. The man was required to wash his body and was considered unclean until evening. This type of ceremonial defilement served as a reminder that all sexual activity was to be pleasing to God and according to His ways and purposes. Likewise, women were considered ceremonially unclean during menstruation (Leviticus 15:19–24). Although the woman wasn't required to bathe, anyone who touched anything she sat on was also considered unclean and required them to wash their clothes and bathe in water. Such a law also taught men to say no to sexual urges during the woman's menstruation. There were also laws for women who had abnormal discharges, which rendered them ceremonially unclean and required a sin offering and a burnt offering. All these laws about discharges were meant to show the Israelites that there was brokenness in sexuality in both blood and semen, and there was a need for purity and holiness in this area of life. Such ceremonial defilements were to serve as reminders that the sexuality of one's life could render them ceremonially unclean and not able to worship at God's temple.

There was also a water cleansing that was to be performed when someone touched a human corpse or entered a tent where someone had died (Numbers 19). We won't go into detail on this cleansing, but all this is to show that there were laws in the Old Testament to help the Israelites discern between clean and unclean things. These were all given to set the Israelite nation apart and to serve as constant reminders that they were to live a separated and holy life. Not only this, but these regulations showed how easy it was to become ceremonially defiled and unable to worship the Lord in His temple. These would ultimately show the need to be internally cleansed of sin. Some commentaries and books go into much greater detail on ceremonial defilement, but this high-level overview allows us to gain a running start as we examine ceremonial washings during the life and times of Paul. Even when the High Priest entered the most Holy Place on the Day of Atonement, it wasn't the washing of his body that allowed him to go into the Most Holy Place, but rather, following the prescribed and detailed instructions laid out in Leviticus 16. In this short overview of washings, we find that ceremonial washings were never a means to be right with

God in the Old Testament. There was no ceremonial washing that allowed someone access into the Most Holy Place and right standing with the Lord.

Ceremonial Washings During the Life and Times of Paul

As we look into the New Testament, we will move immediately to Mark 7 where Jesus confronts the Pharisees and attacked their man-made traditions of washing their hands, which they believed made them ceremonially clean. Jesus was very concerned with true worship (John 4:23–24), and He confronted the Pharisees and scribes regarding ceremonial washings and their false worship and dead religion. Prior to this confrontation, the Lord had several other interactions with the Pharisees, so it would be helpful to understand how much revealed truth the Pharisees had rejected prior to the confrontation on ceremonial handwashing.

To assemble this timeline of events, I used a harmony of the Gospels to illustrate the false teachers' constant, intentional, deliberate, and personal rejection of the person and work of Jesus as well as their refusal to repent and believe.[25] In the list that follows, the solid bullet points are instances where the false teachers openly rejected either the person or work of Jesus or the subjective response of repentance and faith. The open circle bullet points are instances where the false teachers likely were aware of what Jesus had said and done because news about Him was spreading everywhere, but they didn't directly interact with Him. Below is a time-line that brings us right up to the time when Jesus confronted the Pharisees about ceremonial washings:

- The Subjective Response – Pharisees rejected John the Baptist's message for repentance (Matthew 3:1–9, John 7:30).

- The Person and Work of Jesus – Pharisees rejected and began persecuting Jesus for healing the invalid at the Pool of Bethesda on the Sabbath. They also rejected His claim to be equal with God and sought to kill Him (John 5:1–45):

  ◌ The Work of Jesus – Pharisees would have had knowledge of Jesus's miracle of turning water to wine, which manifested Jesus's deity and divine power and authority to create matter out of nothing (John 2:1–11).

  ◌ The Work of Jesus – Pharisees would have had knowledge of Jesus's miracle of healing of the official's son, which manifested Jesus's divine power and Messiahship to save Gentiles and heal disease regardless of distance (John 4:46–54).

  ◌ The Work of Jesus – Pharisees would have had knowledge of Jesus's miracle of healing the demoniac on the Sabbath, which manifested Jesus's authority over demons and demonstrated that His kingdom was superior to the kingdom of darkness (Luke 4:31–37).

◻ The Work of Jesus – Pharisees would have had knowledge of Jesus's miracle of healing Peter's mother-in-law as well as many others. This manifested His divine power and substantiated the prophecy that He was the Anointed One of God, the Messiah, and Deliverer according to Isaiah (Luke 4:38–41).

◻ The Work of Jesus – Pharisees would have had knowledge of Jesus's miracle of healing the leper, which manifested that Jesus's deity was holy, innocent, undefiled, and separate from sinners in that He could touch and heal the worst of diseases in a defiled and ceremonially unclean leper, make the leper ceremonially clean, and yet He remained undefiled (Luke 5:12–16).

◻ The Work of Jesus – Pharisees would have had knowledge of Jesus's miracle of healing the paralytic, which manifested Jesus's deity in that He had authority to forgive sins (Luke 5:17–26).

• The Person and Work of Jesus – Pharisees rejected Jesus's claim to be Lord of the Sabbath.

This claim as well as Jesus's healing on the Sabbath manifested the compassion of Jesus as well as His divine power to heal deformities. It also manifested that Jesus was Lord over the entire Levitical system, which was a claim to deity (Matthew 12:1–14):

▫ The Work of Jesus – Pharisees would have had knowledge of Jesus's healing of the multitudes, which was a fulfillment of Isaiah 42. This manifested Jesus as the servant of Yahweh and exhibited Christ's compassion and mercy (Matthew 12:15–21).

▫ The Work of Jesus – Pharisees would have had knowledge of Jesus's healing of the centurion's servant, which proved Jesus was willing to reach out and save Gentiles, but not just any Gentile, but a Gentile of the Roman army, which oppressed Israel. This also demonstrated Jesus could heal disease regardless of distance and was evidence of His deity (Matthew 8:5–13).

▫ The Work of Jesus – Pharisees would have had knowledge of Jesus raising a widow's son from the dead, which demonstrated Jesus's authority to give life and resurrect the dead and also showed forth His compassion for widows and the helpless (Luke 7:11–17).

- The Work of Jesus – Pharisees rejected Jesus's work of casting out a demon of a blind and mute man, which demonstrated that Jesus's kingdom was separate, distinct, different, more powerful, and greater than Satan's kingdom. He also manifested His deity and omniscience by reading the Pharisee's thoughts (Matthew 12:22–28).

- The Person of Jesus – Pharisees rejected Jesus's title of Son of David and called Him Beelzebul (Matthew 12:22–28).

- The Person and Work of Jesus – Pharisees rejected Jesus's claims, teachings, and miracles and demanded a sign (Matthew 12:38–42):

  - The Work of Jesus – Pharisees may have had knowledge of Jesus's miracle of calming the storm, which manifested Jesus's control over nature as evidence of His deity (Matthew 8:23–27).

  - The Work of Jesus – Pharisees would have had knowledge of Jesus's miracle of restoring two demon-possessed men in the Gadarenes. This was a sign that Jesus had authority over demons and to spiritually heal and save a defiled and demon-possessed Gentile (Matthew 8:28–34).

- ▫ The Work of Jesus – Pharisees would have had knowledge of Jesus's miracle of raising Jairus's daughter from the dead and healing the woman with the hemorrhage. This manifested Jesus's authority to give life and resurrect the dead. It also showed Jesus as the compassionate Savior by healing and saving a woman who was continually ceremonially unclean and ostracized from the Jewish community because of her continual unclean and defiled state (Matthew 9:18–26).

- The Work of Jesus – Pharisees rejected Jesus's works of healing the blind man and the mute, which demonstrated the Messiah's power over demons as well as His authority to restore sight and sound (Matthew 9:27–34):

  - ▫ The Work of Jesus – Pharisees would have had knowledge of Jesus's miracle of feeding of the five thousand, which manifested Jesus's compassion as well as His creative power and authority (Matthew 14:13–21).

  - ▫ The Work of Jesus – Pharisees would have had knowledge of Jesus's miracle of healing the sick of Gennesaret (Matthew 14:34–36).

- The Person of Jesus – Pharisees would have had knowledge of Jesus's claim to be the Bread of Life, which was a claim to deity (John 6:25–69).

When we review this timeline, we see there had been conflicts between the Pharisees and Jesus over His teaching, controversy over Him performing miracles on the Sabbath, and outrage over His claims to deity. When we get to Paul's conversion in a later chapter, we will see that Paul was raised as a Jew, became a Pharisee, and studied under one of the most revered Pharisees, Gamaliel (Acts 22:3). Therefore, we can reasonably conclude that Paul would have been familiar with many of the altercations and conflicts with the Pharisees that had taken place up to this point as news was spreading about Him (Luke 5:15), and Paul noted to King Agrippa that Jesus's ministry was public and was not "done in a corner" (Acts 26:26). This is important because we are to remember that Paul was a zealous Pharisee who was advancing in Pharisaic teachings beyond many of his own age (Galatians 1:14). We are to remember that Paul was extremely knowledgeable in Pharisaic teachings. Let us not forget Paul's extensive knowledge of ritual washings and ceremonial cleansings with mikvahs as we begin the exposition of Mark 7:

> *Now when the Pharisees gathered to him, with some of the scribes who had come from Jerusalem, they saw that some of his disciples ate with hands that were defiled, that is, unwashed. (For the Pharisees and all the Jews do not eat unless they wash their hands properly, holding to the tradition of the elders, and when they come from the marketplace, they do not eat unless they wash. And there are many other traditions that they observe, such as the washing of cups and pots and copper vessels and*

dining couches.) And the Pharisees and the scribes asked
him, "Why do your disciples not walk according to the
tradition of the elders, but eat with defiled hands?"

— Mark 7:1–5

This confrontation about ceremonial washings opens
when the Pharisees came to Jesus and saw that His disciples ate with unwashed hands. It's important to note that
the conflict between the Pharisees and Jesus over handwashing doesn't arise out of a concern that they were eating with
unsanitary hands or a concern over foodborne illnesses. The
Pharisees were pronouncing Jesus's disciples ceremonially
unclean because they ate without ceremonially washing their
hands. As we learned from the book of Leviticus, sometimes
a person would become ceremonially unclean and need to
either wash their clothes or their body. However, we do not
see any regulation or warning from the Lord that a person
could become ceremonially unclean because they did not
ceremonially wash their hands before eating. It is true that
the Israelites were commanded to distinguish between eating
unclean and clean foods; however, there was no Old Testament regulation that required hands to be washed to remain
ceremonially clean.

The Pharisees had not only developed a ritualistic ceremony that involved washing their hands, but they had also
created a system of ceremonial washings that included washing cups, pots, vessels, utensils, and dining couches or porta-
ble mats. They created all these extra-biblical ceremonial and

external washings with the illusion that this would keep them ceremonially clean. As we noted earlier, there were numerous ways one could become ceremonially unclean; however, becoming ceremonially unclean did not always mean that one needed to be ceremonially washed. As we see in Mark 7:2, the Pharisees were claiming that Jesus's disciples were ceremonially defiling themselves by not washing their hands according to the tradition of their elders, which implied that this was extra-biblical instruction. Therefore, we can be sure that the Pharisees' concern was not just about washing cups, pots, vessels, and utensils for sanitary conditions. No, this was washing cups, pots, vessels, and utensils for the purposes of remaining ceremonially clean. The Pharisees had created laws around washing hands, the body, and inanimate objects as a means of remaining ceremonially clean. So, where would these extra-biblical traditions have come from? To get a better understanding of this, we will review some of the oral tradition that is captured in Jewish literature.

The Mishnah is a written collection of Jewish oral tradition that is reflective of how the Jews interpreted the Old Testament. It includes chapters about ceremonial ritual cleansing of pots and pans, instructions for washing hands, and the Gemara, which is commentary on the Mishnah. All these combined make up the Talmud; there is a Babylon Talmud and a Jerusalem Talmud. After this came the Midrash, which is a collection of interpretations on the books of the Bible. So, there was oral tradition upon oral tradition, which gave instructions on ceremonial washings. Not only did the extra-biblical ceremonial washings come from this oral tradition, but the Pharisees' teachings were also given powerful authority.

We see the power and authority that was given to rabbinic teaching in various places. For example, Rabbi Tarphon said, "Know then, that 'the words of the Scribes are more lovely than the words of the law."[26] Rabbi Tarphon also said:

> "If a man does not read, he only transgresses an affirmative; but if he transgresses the words of the school of Hillell, he is guilty of death, because he hath broke down a hedge, and a serpent shall bite him. It is a tradition of Rabbi Ishmael, the words of the law have in them both prohibition and permission; some of them are light, and some heavy, but 'the words of the Scribes' are all of them heavy." He would go on to say, "Weightier are the words of the elders, than the words of the prophets."[27]

Thus, we can see how much weight the teaching of the Pharisees was given. In some instances, the rabbis' and Pharisees' interpretation of the law superseded the Word of God. This was exactly why Jesus said in Mark 7:8, *"You leave the commandment of God and hold to the tradition of men."* The Pharisees were treating their oral tradition as more authoritative than the Word of God. They had created a system of man-made laws that let them nullify God's Word and disobey it.

The hand washing instructions are taken directly from the Mishnah. As you'll see, the instructions are frivolous and difficult to understand. I've chosen not to alter the instructions to help you understand the many rules and instructions as well as the absurd nature of ceremonial handwashing that was prevalent. Let's look at some of the regulations on washing hands that were captured in the Mishnah to get an understanding of the numerous external washing rituals the Jewish leaders created as well as the scrupulous and ubiquitous nature of these man-made laws:[28]

How Much Water Can Be Used:

- A minimum of a quarter of a log of water must be poured over the hands for one person and even for two (Mishnah Yadayim 1:1).

  □ A log was about a half liter of water.

- A minimum of half a log must be poured over the hands for three or four persons (Mishnah Yadayim 1:1).

- A minimum of one log [is sufficient] for five, ten, or 100 persons (Mishnah Yadayim 1:1).

- Rabbi Yose says: "As long as there is not less than a quarter of a log left for the last person among them" (Mishnah Yadayim 1:1).

- More water may be added to the second water,
  but more may not be added to the first water
  (Mishnah Yadayim 1:1).

What Kind of Vessel Could Be Used to Pour Water Over
One's Hands:

- Water may be poured over the hands out of any
  kind of vessel, even out of vessels made of animal
  dung, out of vessels made of stone, or out of vessels made of clay (Mishnah Yadayim 1:2).

- Water may not be poured from the sides of [bro-
  ken] vessels or from the bottom of a lade or from
  the stopper of a jar (Mishnah Yadayim 1:2).

- Nor may one pour [water] over the hands of
  his fellow out of his cupped hands (Mishnah
  Yadayim 1:2)

- Because one may not draw, nor sanctify, nor
  sprinkle the water of purification, nor pour
  water over the hands except in a vessel (Mishnah
  Yadayim 1:2).

- And only vessels closely covered with a lid protect [their contents from uncleanness] (Mishnah
  Yadayim 1:2).

- And only vessels protect [their contents from
  uncleanness] inside earthenware vessels (Mishnah
  Yadayim 1:2).

Water Used for Netilat Yadayim:

- Water which had become unfit that it could not be drunk by a beast: If it was in a vessel it is invalid, but if it was in the ground it is valid (Mishnah Yadayim 1:3).

- Shimon of Teman says: "Even if he intended to soak his bread in one water and it fell into another water the water is invalid" (Mishnah Yadayim 1:3).

- Water in which the baker dips his loaves is invalid; but if he moistened his hands in the water it is valid (Mishnah Yadayim 1:5).

- A person may place the jug between his knees and pour out the water or he may turn the jug on its side and pour it out (Mishnah Yadayim 1:5).

- If he poured water over one of his hands with a single rinsing his hands become clean (Mishnah Yadayim 2:1).

- If over both his hands with a single rinsing: Rabbi Meir declares them to be unclean until he pours a minimum of a quarter of a log of water over them (Mishnah Yadayim 2:1).

- Hands become unclean and are made clean as far as the joint (Mishnah Yadayim 2:3).

- If he poured the first and the second water over the hands beyond the joint and they flowed back to the hands, the hands remain unclean (Mishnah Yadayim 2:3).

- If he poured the first water over one of his hands and then changed his mind and poured the second water over both his hands, they are unclean (Mishnah Yadayim 2:3).

- If he poured water over one of his hands and rubbed it on the other hand it remains unclean (Mishnah Yadayim 2:3).

- If he rubbed it on his head or on the wall it is clean (Mishnah Yadayim 2:3).

Cases of Doubtful Impurity Involving Hands:

- If there was a doubt whether any work has been done with the water or not, a doubt whether the water contains the requisite quantity or not, a doubt whether it is unclean or clean, In these cases the doubt is considered to be clean because they have said in a case of doubt concerning hands as to whether they have become unclean or have conveyed uncleanness or have become clean, they are considered to be clean. Rabbi Yose says: In a case [of doubt as to] whether they have become clean they are considered to be unclean (Mishnah Yadayim 2:4).

Dispute between Rabbi and Sages

- Anything which disqualifies terumah defiles hands with a second degree of uncleanness (Mishnah Yadayim 3:2).

- One [unwashed] hand defiles the other hand, the words of Rabbi Joshua. But the sages say: That which has second degree of uncleanness cannot convey second degree of uncleanness (Mishnah Yadayim 3:2).

- He said to them: But do not the Holy Scriptures which have second degree of uncleanness defile the hands? They said to him: The laws of the Torah may not be argued from the laws of the scribes, nor may the laws of the scribes be argued from the laws of the Torah, not may the laws of the scribes be argued from [other] laws of the scribes (Mishnah Yadayim 3:2).

- The straps of the tefillin [when connected] with the tefillin [boxes] defile the hands (Mishnah Yadayim 3:3).

- The margin on a scroll which is above or below or at the beginning or at the end defiles the hands (Mishnah Yadayim 3:4).

As you can see, many rules were developed concerning handwashing. These man-made laws dictated the amount of water to be used, how the water was to be poured, the importance on the source of the water, the importance of the container holding the water, and much more. Not only were there instructions on handwashing, but there are even more instructions on *mikvahs*, which were ritual pools filled with water from a natural source. Mikvahs were also used to purify and ceremonially cleanse people who became ceremonially unclean. Thus, there were many teachings on how much water made a mikvah, what type of water made a mikvah, what happened if objects fell into the mikvah, and more. These pools were also used as part of the process for converting Gentiles to Judaism. For the reader's information, this section on Mikvah purification rituals is inserted to help the reader understand the widespread water immersions and baptisms that took place during the life and times of Jesus and Paul. I've also chosen to keep the unaltered instructions in this book. As you'll see, the Oral Law instruction on water baptisms for ceremonial cleanliness was trivial and hard to understand. Below are some of the teachings from the Mishnah on mikvahs and ritual washings.

Mikvah Cleansing Instructions

The Mishnah also includes various purification rituals for the Mikvah, which was similar to water baptism:

- Superior to such [water] is [the water of] the mikveh containing forty seahs, for in it people may immerse themselves and immerse other [things]. Superior to such [water] is [the water of] a spring whose own water is little but has been increased by a greater quantity of drawn water. It is equivalent to the mikveh in as much as it may render clean by standing water, and to an [ordinary] spring in as much as one may immerse in it whatever the quantity of its contents (Mishnah Mikvaot 1:7).

- An unclean man who went down to immerse himself: If it is doubtful whether he did immerse himself or not; and even if he did immerse himself, it is doubtful whether the mikveh contained forty seahs or not; and if there were two mikvehs, one containing forty seahs but the other not containing forty seahs, and he immersed himself in one of them but he does not know in which he immersed himself, in such a doubt he is unclean (Mishnah Mikvaot 2:1).

- If there were three cavities in a mikveh each holding a log of drawn water, if it is known that forty seahs of valid water fell in before reaching the third cavity, [such a mikveh is] valid; otherwise it is invalid. Rabbi Shimon declares it valid, since it resembles a mikveh adjoining another mikveh (Mishnah Mikvaot 2:6).

- All seas are equivalent to a mikveh, for it is said, "and the gathering (ulemikveh) of the waters He called the seas" (Genesis 1:10), the words of Rabbi Meir. Rabbi Judah says: Only the Great Sea is equivalent to a mikveh, for it says "seas" only because there are in it many kinds of seas. Rabbi Yose says: All seas afford cleanness when running, and yet they are unfit for zavim, and metzoraim and for the preparation of the hatat waters. (Mishnah Mikvaot 5:4).

- These are the men who had a seminal emission who require immersion: If he noticed that his urine issued in drops or was murky: At the beginning he is clean; in the middle and at the end, he is unclean; from the beginning to the end, he is clean. If it was white and viscous, he is unclean. Rabbi Yose says: What is white counts like what is murky (Mishnah Mikvaot 8:2).

- Any handles of vessels which are too long and which will be cut short, need only be immersed up to the point of their proper measure. Rabbi Judah says: [They are unclean] until the whole of them is immersed. The chain of a large bucket, to the length of four handbreadths, and a small bucket, to the length of ten handbreadths, and they need only be immersed up to the point of their proper measure. Rabbi Tarfon says: It is not clean unless the whole of the chain-ring is immersed. The rope bound to a basket is not counted as a connection unless it has been sewn on (Mishnah Mikvaot 10:5).

This is but a sample of the oral tradition that Jesus was rebuking. This is the environment in which Paul lived, where the rabbis' oral tradition superseded the Bible and where ceremonial handwashing and ritual washings determined whether one was clean or defiled. There were rules upon rules for ceremonial handwashing and for ceremonial mikvah washings, baptisms, and immersions. Thus, there was widespread belief that external washing with water kept a person ceremonially clean.

> *"'This people honors me with their lips, but their heart is far from me; in vain do they worship me, teaching as doctrines the commandments of men.'"*
>
> —Mark 7:6

Rather than commend the Pharisees for their attempt to remain ceremonially clean by their man-made traditions, the Lord gives a blistering rebuke, citing Isaiah 29:13 and calling the Pharisees hypocrites (Mark 7:6) and announcing to them that they were idolators with dead religion. Jesus was saying that the Pharisees were the fulfillment of Isaiah's prophecy in Isaiah 29:13; that was a devastating indictment. If the Pharisees were paying attention to what Jesus was saying, they should have understood that they were responsible for Israel's unbelief in the Messiah and that they were blind spiritual leaders.

In Isaiah 29:1, the Lord denounces Israel and mocks her for her false worship where He says, *"Woe, Ariel, Ariel the city where David once camped! Add year to year, keep your feasts on schedule"* (NASB2020). Though Jerusalem (Ariel) had been diligent to keep the appointed festivals, this had the pretense of being religions but there was not true worship. We can know this because Jerusalem had been warned that they were full of evil, oppression, and spiritual adultery (Isaiah 1:16–23). They were still performing religious activities even though they were full of evil and spiritual adultery. Jerusalem was still sacrificing burnt offerings, offering incense, holding New moon and Sabbath convocations, and offering prayers (Isaiah 1:11–15). However, Jerusalem was full of dead religious activities, empty of true spiritual worship, and full of wickedness and spiritual adultery. This was the reason for the Lord's warning of woe and judgment that would fall upon Jerusalem. In Isaiah 29:2–8, the Lord details the judgment that would come to Jerusalem for her disobedience, but in Isaiah 29:9–10, He declares this judgment upon the prophets and seers:

> *"Astonish yourselves and be astonished;* **blind yourselves and be blind!** **Be drunk,** *not with the wine; stagger, but not with strong drink! For the* Lord *has poured out upon you a spirit of deep sleep, and* **has**

closed your eyes (the prophets), **and covered your**
heads *(the seers)."* (emphasis added)

Note the judicial punishment given to the spiritual leaders of Jerusalem. They were to be blinded and made blind.
They were to be drunk, unstable, and staggered. The false
prophets and seers had ignored the warnings of the true
prophets and become insensitive, indifferent, and apathetic
to the warnings of judgment and doom (Isaiah 5). They had
not yielded and had not repented of their wickedness. The
people and leaders would hear but not understand, see but
not perceive (Isaiah 6:9–10). Thus, we see that the spiritual
leaders blinded themselves by their apathy and indifference
to the Lord's warnings, and the Lord poured out judgment
and closed their eyes and blinded them. But how blind were
the prophets and seers when the Lord said He would close
their eyes and cover their heads? What would this blindness
look like? In Isaiah 29:11–12, the Lord describes this blindness when He says:

And the vision of all this has become to you like the
words of a book that is sealed. When men give it to one
who can read, saying, "Read this," he says, **"I cannot,**
for it is sealed." *And when they give the book to one*
who cannot read, saying, "Read this," he says, **"I cannot**
read." (emphasis added)

Here we see exactly what this blindness would look like;
it would be akin to giving someone a sealed book and telling

them to read it. It would be impossible to read a book that is closed and sealed. Though a book has words and meanings, it does one no good if the person can't open it, read it, and correctly interpret it. This was the judgment that was to come on the spiritual leaders; the Word of God that would be spoken to them would do them no good because they would not be able to understand it. There would be no divine illumination or interpretation for them. They had rejected the divine warnings, and they had blinded themselves, and so the Lord blinded them so they would not be able to understand divine truth. This is the terrifying reality of spiritual leaders who ignored the call to repent and rejected the true message of judgment: The Lord poured out blindness on them because they had blinded themselves. There was no point of return. Ultimately, Jerusalem was sieged by the Babylonians because of her unrepentant ways.

This is what we are to keep in mind when Jesus calls the Pharisees hypocrites and announces that they are the fulfillment of Isaiah 29:13. The Pharisees professed to honor God with their lips, but their hearts were far from Him. Yes, the Pharisees had much religious activity; they gave offerings and prayers, observed the Sabbath, performed extra-biblical external washings, and fasted. Yet the Pharisees gave offerings to practice their righteousness before others; they offered lengthy prayers to be seen by others; they fasted so they could be seen by others; and they desecrated the Sabbath with their man-made rules even as they desired to kill Jesus for doing good and healing on the Sabbath. They practiced religion but had hearts that were far from God. They looked righteous on the outside, but on the inside they were full of dead men's bones. They literally cleaned the outside of the cup, but on the inside, they were full greed and self-indulgence. Their handwashing rituals appeared righteous to others, but on the inside, they were full of hypocrisy and lawlessness. Their worship was in vain. Their prayers were useless. Their fasting was pointless. Their offerings and almsgiving were futile. Their handwashing rituals and external baptisms were purposeless. They taught man-made traditions and abrogated the Word of God.

Jesus strongly and fiercely denounced the Pharisees for their man-made traditions and for nullifying the Word of God. They neglected the Word of God for the tradition of men. Just like the false prophets during Isaiah's time who ignored the Word of God and established their own self-willed apostate religion, the Pharisees did the very same thing. They found ways to hold fast to their money, rather than helping their fathers or mothers, so, in effect, they dishonored their fathers and mothers (Mark 7:9–12). Additionally, Jesus said that they were *"making void the word of God"* (Mark 7:13). The word for *making void* comes from *akuroó*, which means "disannulling," "invalidating," or "making of no effect." This word gives the idea of making something powerless or legally void. The Pharisees had elevated their teachings above the Word of God. It is obvious that they scorned the Word of God and loved their extra-biblical teachings, such as their many washings and other practices (Mark 7:13). Jesus's denunciation was strong and confrontational and included the following points regarding the Pharisees:

- Christ called the Pharisees and scribes hypocrites or rather false teachers and false worshippers of God (Mark 7:6).

- Christ told the Pharisees and scribes they only had external worship while their hearts remained far from God, or rather, their hearts were not right with God (Mark 7:6).

- Christ told the Pharisees they had dead religion (Mark 7:7).

- Christ told the Pharisees they elevated the tradition of men over God's Word (Mark 7:7–9).

- Christ told the Pharisees that they voided the Word of God by their traditions, or rather, their tradition conflicted with God's Word (Mark 7:13).

In Matthew's account of this event, Jesus clarified that it was not what went into a person's mouth that defiled them because what comes out of the mouth proceeds from the heart, which produced all types of sin and wickedness (Matthew 15:17–20). Instead of being concerned with external washings, the Pharisees needed to be concerned that the inside was full of dead men's bones, lawlessness and hypocrisy, and greed and self-indulgence (Matthew 23:25–28).

The Pharisees didn't need another external washing of hands, another Mikvah baptism, or another ceremonial water immersion ritual. No, the Pharisees needed an internal cleansing of the heart. It was their hearts that were not right with God. It was their hearts that were far from God. It was their hearts that were defiled. It was their hearts that were unclean. The Pharisees should not have been worried about ceremonial washings of their hands, bodies, pots, utensils, bed mats, and more. Rather, they were supposed to be concerned with their hearts. As we learned earlier, becoming ceremonially unclean was God's way of showing His people that all areas of their life needed to be consecrated and holy. They were to see the need for a heart circumcision and internal cleansing of the heart. This is what the Pharisees were blind to.

Recall that in Isaiah 29:10, we noted that the false prophets and seers in Isaiah's day were blind and had led the nation of Israel into further spiritual blindness and judgment. So, just like the false prophets and seers, the Pharisees did exactly what their fathers did. Their false religion, self-willed interpretations, and man-made traditions led the nation of Israel away from God. As we learned earlier in this chapter, they continually, deliberately, and unrepentantly opposed the person and work of Christ and rejected John the Baptist's message. They had an abundance of divine revelation through Jesus's teaching, life, ministry, and miracles. Yet, they preferred their apostate Judaism. Jesus told His disciples this regarding the Pharisees in Matthew 15:14: "*Let them alone; they are blind guides. And if the blind lead the blind, both will fall into a pit."* Just like the false prophets during Isaiah's time, the Pharisees were left in their hardened and spiritually blind state. This was a judicial act by the Lord to leave them in their hardened, impenitent, and self-condemned state. They were blind, they would remain blind, and they would lead the blind into destruction. They were not planted by the heavenly Father, and they would be rooted up and thrown in the eternal fire (Matthew 15:13).

The Pharisees had oral laws regarding washing hands, cups, dishes, and other household items. However, Christ rebuked them for their inability to see the defilement in their own hearts. Not only, this, but Christ also denounced them in Matthew 23:24 where He says, *"You blind guides, straining out a gnat and swallowing a camel!"* Here Jesus is bringing them back to Leviticus 11. The gnat was the smallest of unclean animals and the camel was the largest of unclean animals. Jesus was telling them that they were ceremonially defiling themselves to the greatest extent that was possible by rejecting Him. Although they had laws on how to wash their hands, dishes, cups, and utensils, and thought they were ceremonially clean, they were ceremonially defiled to the greatest extent possible by rejecting Him as the Christ. They had all sorts of washings with water and ceremonial baptisms, but there is no baptism with water that can save the unclean sinner who rejects Christ.

Because Paul was a Pharisee, he had a strong understanding and knowledge of what the Pharisees were teaching in terms of ceremonial washings, and he would likely have known of this encounter with Jesus and the Pharisees regarding ceremonial washings. We can say this with confidence because Paul was advancing in Judaism past many of his own peers and was extremely zealous for the traditions of his fathers (Galatians 1:14).

The Salvific Baptism – the Baptism of the Holy Spirit

We learned earlier that after Paul's conversion, he understood the difference between a physical circumcision and a spiritual circumcision. We also learned that Paul would never have given salvific merit to the physical circumcision, which was the sign of the Abrahamic Covenant. We now learn that after Paul's conversion, he would never put any salvific merit in a ceremonial or ritualistic washing, including baptism. He knew that it was not the external washing with water that made someone clean; the work of cleansing the heart needed to be done on the inside. There was nothing in the Levitical law that gave a promise of salvation for a ceremonial washing. Additionally, ceremonial washings only increased during Paul's life, and Paul would have been schooled in the oral tradition of the Mishnah and would have been familiar with these teachings. After his conversion, Paul would have known that no ceremonial washing would give right standing before God. In fact, one of Paul's strongest affirmations that water baptism gave no merit towards salvation is in 1 Corinthians 1:14–18.

I thank God that I baptized none of you except Crispus and Gaius, so that no one may say that you were baptized in my name. (I did baptize also the household of Stephanas. Beyond that, I do not know whether I baptized anyone else.) *For Christ did not send me to baptize but to preach the gospel,* and not with words of eloquent wisdom, lest the cross of Christ be emptied of its power. *For the word of the cross is folly to those who are perishing, but to us who are being saved it is the power of God.* (emphasis added)

In these verses we see the power and position of the gospel and water baptism as Paul reasoned that preaching the gospel took priority over water baptism. Additionally, Paul reasoned that preaching the gospel had the power to save, but he gave no such salvific power to water baptism. The priority and power of salvation is found in the gospel, not water baptism.

Additionally, we can see from Paul's epistles and teachings that he was fully aware of the difference between a water baptism and a Spirit baptism. In fact, he declared the baptism of the Holy Spirit as a salvific work performed by God (1 Corinthians 12:13):

For in one Spirit we were all baptized into one body—Jews or Greeks, slaves or free—and all were made to drink of one Spirit. (emphasis added)

Here we clearly see that in the same letter to the Corinthians, Paul distinguished between water baptism and Spirit baptism (1 Corinthians 1:14–18, 12:13). Once again, Paul declared that water baptism did not save, but the gospel was powerful to save (1 Corinthians 1:14–18). Here we see that a Spirit baptism is different from a water baptism in that the Spirit baptism is salvific and puts one into union with Christ and into the body of believers (1 Corinthians 12:13). Just as Paul distinguished between a physical circumcision and a spiritual circumcision in his letter to the Philippians, he clearly distinguishes between a water baptism and a Spirit baptism in his letter to the Corinthians. Paul took his knowledge of ceremonial washings and the need for spiritual cleansing and applied that in the New Testament. As a Pharisee, Paul had learned what ceremonial handwashing, ceremonial dish washing, ceremonial utensil washing, ceremonial mat washing, and ceremonial mikvah purification washings were able to do for his salvation: absolutely nothing. Paul had learned what physical circumcision and external washing accomplished: absolutely nothing. After his conversion, Paul learned that a spiritual circumcision of the heart is what mattered. Paul also learned that a washing by the Holy Spirit is what mattered in terms of salvation. Paul wasn't the only one who was aware of the difference between a water baptism and the baptism of the Holy Spirit. Below are others who knew the difference between a water baptism and the baptism of the Holy Spirit:

- Matthew understood that John and all other men could only baptize with water, but Christ could baptize with the Holy Spirit (Matthew 3:11–12).

- Mark understood that John and all other men could only baptize with water, but Christ could baptize with the Holy Spirit (Mark 1:8).

- Luke understood that John and all other men could only baptize with water, but Christ could baptize with the Holy Spirit (Luke 3:16).

- The Apostle John understood that John and all other men could only baptize with water, but Christ could baptize with the Holy Spirit (John 1:31–33).

- John the Baptist understood that he and all other men could only baptize with water, but Christ could baptize with the Holy Spirit (Matthew 3:11–12; Mark 1:8; Luke 3:16; John 1:31–33).

- Peter understood that he and all other men could only baptize with water, but Christ could baptize with the Holy Spirit (Acts 1:5, 2:17–18, 10:44–48, 11:16).

- Jesus understood that only He could baptize with the Holy Spirit and that men could only baptize with water (Matthew 3:11–12; Mark 1:8; Luke 3:16, 24:49; John 1:31– 33, 7:38–39, 14:15–17, 14:26, 15:26, 16:7; Acts 1:4–5, 2:17–18, 10:44–48, 11:16).

- God the Father and God the Holy Spirit understood who baptized with the Holy Spirit

(Matthew 3:11–12; Mark 1:8; Luke 3:16, 24:49; John 1:31–33, 7:38–39, 14:15–17, 14:26, 15:26, 16:7; Acts 1:4–5, 2:17–18, 10:44–48, 11:16).

- Jesus understood water baptism as a work, which was part of His perfect obedience (Matthew 3:13–15).

The Baptism of the Holy Spirit – Regeneration

Paul would go on to speak of a washing of regeneration that was performed by the Holy Spirit (Titus 3:4–6). We see the baptism of the Holy Spirit in Titus 3:4–6, which includes the Triune God regenerating and saving man where it says:

> But when the goodness and loving kindness of God our Savior appeared, he [the **Father**] saved us, not because of works done by us in righteousness, but according to his [the **Father**] own mercy, by the washing of regeneration and renewal of the Holy Spirit, whom he [the **Father**] poured out on us richly through Jesus Christ our Savior." (emphasis added)

In Titus 3:4–6, we see that God the Father poured out the Holy Spirit through Jesus Christ. All three members of the Godhead are involved in the salvific work of salvation. Another way to say this is that the Son pours out or baptizes man with the Holy Spirit whom the Son received from the Father. Thus, Titus 3:4–6 captures the regenerating work of the Holy Spirit who is poured out by the Father and through the Son.

But how does the Holy Spirit regenerate a man? Does the Holy Spirit just randomly regenerate sinners when they're sitting through a college lecture, watching a movie, cooking supper, taking a walk in the park, or any of the like? Not at all. We learn that God gives new birth or regeneration through the Word of Truth as it says, "*Of His own will He **brought us forth by the word of truth**, that we should be a kind of firstfruits of His creatures*" (James 1:18 NKJV emphasis added). The word *apokueó* means to "bring forth" or "give birth." *Apo* means "away from," and *kueó* means "to be pregnant." *Apokueó* conveys the idea of giving birth. But how do we know what the "*word of truth*" is? Paul helps us understand this in Ephesians 1:13 where he says, "*In him you also, **when you heard the word of truth**, **the gospel of your salvation**, and believed in him, were sealed with the promised Holy Spirit*" (emphasis added). Here, we clearly see that the "*word of truth*" is the gospel. When someone hears the gospel, the Holy Spirit works through the message of the gospel, regenerates the person, and the person immediately responds to the Lord Jesus Christ in repentance and faith.

Peter helps us understand that a person is regenerated by the Holy Spirit who works through the gospel message. We see this in 1 Peter 1:23–25 where Peter says:

> *Since you have been **born again**, not of perishable seed but of imperishable, **through the living and abiding***

word of God; for 'All flesh is like grass and all its glory like the flower of grass. The grass withers, and the flower falls, but the word of the Lord remains forever.' **And this word is the good news that was preached to you.** (emphasis added)

Here, Peter clearly helps us understand that one is born again by the Word of God, the gospel. From the previous passages, we learn that it is the Holy Spirit who regenerates a person. Thus, we understand that the baptism of the Holy Spirit includes the Father pouring out the Holy Spirit through the Son and the Holy Spirit causing someone to be born again or regenerated through hearing the gospel message.

The Baptism of the Holy Spirit – Granted Repentance and Faith

As mentioned earlier, immediately after a person is regenerated by the Holy Spirit, they are granted repentance and faith. We learn this when we read Acts 11:15–18 where Peter describes the first conversion of Gentiles:

As I [Peter] *began to speak,* **the Holy Spirit fell on them just as on us at the beginning.** *And I remembered the word of the Lord, how he said,* **"John baptized with water, but you will be baptized with the Holy Spirit."** *If then* **God gave the same gift to them as he gave to us when we believed in the Lord Jesus**

Christ, who was I that I could stand in God's way? When they heard these things they fell silent. And they glorified God, saying, "Then to the Gentiles also God has **granted repentance that leads to life.** *"* (emphasis added)

When Peter gave the gospel to Cornelius and his household (Acts 10:34–48), Cornelius and his household were baptized with the Holy Spirit. In this section of Scripture, we see that the Holy Spirit is given as a gift. Not only this, but we see that when one is baptized with the Holy Spirit, the person is granted repentance and faith in the Lord Jesus Christ.

The Baptism of the Holy Spirit – Receive the Holy Spirit, Indwelt by the Holy Spirit, Justified by Faith

So what happens the moment that someone savingly believes in the Lord Jesus Christ? In Galatians 3:2, Paul challenges the Galatians with this question: *"Let me ask you only this:* **Did you receive the Spirit** *by works of the law* **or by hearing with faith**" (emphasis added)? When someone believes in the Lord Jesus Christ, they receive the Holy Spirit. Again, in Galatians 3:14, Paul emphasizes the point about receiving the Holy Spirit when someone comes to faith where he says: *"So that in Christ Jesus the blessing of Abraham might come to the Gentiles, so that* **we might receive the promised Spirit through faith**" (emphasis added). Again, in his letter to the Ephesians, Paul explains that at the moment of salvation when someone believes the gospel and comes to saving faith, they receive and are sealed by the Holy Spirit: *"In him you also, when **you heard the word of truth, the gospel of your salvation, and believed in him, were sealed with the promised Holy Spirit**"* (Ephesians 1:13 emphasis added). In 2 Corinthians 1:21–22, Paul says this regarding God the Father giving the Holy Spirit to us: *"And it is God who establishes us with you in Christ, and has anointed us, and **who has also put his** [the **Father's**] **seal on us and given us his Spirit in our hearts** as a guarantee"* (emphasis added). In this verse, we see that the Holy Spirit is given to the believer by the Father. Additionally, we learn that every believer who receives the Holy Spirit is indwelt by the Holy Spirit and is a temple of the Holy Spirit (1 Corinthians 6:19). Thus, it's clear from Paul that when a person savingly believes in the Lord Jesus Christ and puts their faith in Him, they receive and are indwelt by the Holy Spirit.

Let's ask another question. What else happens the moment someone savingly believes in the Lord Jesus Christ? We read throughout Scripture that when one savingly believes in the Lord Jesus Christ, they are justified by His grace, meaning that they are positionally declared righteous before the throne of God because Christ's perfect righteousness has been reckoned and imputed to the one who believes (Titus 3:7; Romans 4:3, 5). All of one's sins are forgiven, and all of Christ's righteous merit is credited and imputed to the believer; they are reckoned and imputed with the perfect righteousness of Christ and declared righteous before the

throne of God. Thus, they are justified by faith in the Lord
Jesus Christ.

Baptism of the Holy Spirit – Spiritually Baptized into Christ and Baptized into the Body of Believers by Faith in Christ

The baptism of the Holy Spirit also includes the believer
being put into spiritual union with Christ and being put into
the body of believers. We can understand this from reading
Romans 6:3–4:

> *Do you not know that all of us who have **been baptized
> into Christ Jesus were baptized into his death?** **We
> were buried therefore with him by baptism into
> death**, in order that, just as Christ was raised from the
> dead by the glory of the Father, we too might walk in
> newness of life.* (emphasis added)

These verses are used by many denominations and
churches to support the teaching that water baptism unites
people with Christ. In fact, many Bible-believing scholars
have interpreted this passage to mean that water baptism
brings about unity with Christ. However, it is important
to remember other passages of Scripture that have been
explained in this chapter as well as the Apostle Paul's life as
a Pharisee when interpreting these verses. There are two possible explanations. Either this verse is speaking of water baptism, or it is speaking of baptism with the Holy Spirit. Jesus,

the apostles, and many others were able to draw distinctions between water baptism and the baptism with the Holy Spirit, and this verse demands that level of attention. Paul would undoubtedly be speaking of baptism with the Holy Spirit, for if water baptism could save, he would have baptized as many people as he could (1 Corinthians 1:14–30). However, Paul reasoned that preaching the gospel took priority because it had the power to save. He gave no such priority and power to water baptism. Additionally, he understood baptism with the Holy Spirit to include the operation whereby man was made to drink of the Spirit and be put into the body of Christ (1 Corinthians 12:13).

Paul also makes an argument in Romans that justification comes by faith in Christ. He even states that we are not saved by works (Romans 4:1–8), not saved through rituals or sacraments (Romans 4:9–12), and not saved through observance of the law (Romans 4:13–24). To claim Romans 6:3–4 as being water baptism is a serious misinterpretation of Scripture, which does not align with the rest of the book of Romans, the distinction Scripture makes between water baptism and the baptism of the Holy Spirit, or Paul's life as a ritualistic Pharisee. In fact, interpreting Romans 6:3–4 to mean that water baptism gives union with Christ contradicts many other passages of Scripture and demolishes the argument Paul made in Romans 4. To say that water baptism brings about spiritual union with Christ is the wrong interpretation.

The baptism that Paul describes in Romans 6:3–4 is

salvific because it brings a person into union with Christ. Therefore, we know that this is a part of the baptism of the Holy Spirit. Paul helps clarify this in Galatians 3:25–27:

> *But now that **faith has come**, we are no longer under a guardian, for **in Christ Jesus you are all sons of God, through faith**. For as many of **you as were baptized into Christ have put on Christ**.* (emphasis added)

Here, we see that faith in Christ, not water baptism, is what unites us to Christ. When someone puts their faith in Christ, they are justified by faith, become a child of God, are brought into spiritual union with Christ, and clothed with Christ's perfect righteousness. Galatians 3:25–27 is not saying that water baptism accomplishes this. Rather, Paul is arguing that when one puts their faith in Christ, they receive the Holy Spirit (Galatians 3:2, 14, 25), become a child of God (Galatians 3:26), are brought into union with Christ (Galatians 3:27), and are clothed with Christ's perfect righteousness (Galatians 3:27). Therefore, we see that both Romans 6:3–4 and Galatians 3:25–27 speak of being spiritually united with Christ by faith, which is an aspect of the baptism of the Holy Spirit.

Jesus made a similar statement about receiving the Holy Spirit when one came to faith in Him. In John 7:37–39 He said:

> *On the last day of the feast, the great day, Jesus stood up and cried out, "If anyone thirsts, let him come to me*

*and drink. **Whoever believes in me**, as the Scripture
has said, **'Out of his heart will flow rivers of living
water.'" Now this he said about the Spirit, whom
those who believed in him were to receive**, for as yet
the Spirit had not been given, because Jesus was not yet
glorified.* (emphasis added)

Here, Jesus connected coming to saving faith in Him
with drinking and receiving the Holy Spirit. Paul certainly
understood what Jesus was saying in John 7:37–39. In
fact, Paul states this same reality in 1 Corinthians 12:13
where he says, *"For **in one Spirit we were all baptized
into one body**—Jews or Greeks, slaves or free—and all were
made to drink of one Spirit"* (emphasis added). Therefore,
Paul understood that drinking of the Holy Spirit is syn-
onymous with coming to faith in Christ and receiving the
Holy Spirit. We also see that Paul understood that when
someone is baptized by the Holy Spirit, they are put into
the body of believers. Thus, Paul understood that the baptism of the Holy Spirit included drinking of the Spirit (1
Corinthians 12:13), receiving the Holy Spirit (Galatians
3:2, 14), being sealed by the Holy Spirit (Ephesians 1:13),
being spiritually baptized and united with Christ (Romans
6:3–4), being justified and clothed with Christ's righteousness (Galatians 3:26–27), and being indwelt by the Holy
Spirit (1 Corinthians 6:19).

Baptism of the Holy Spirit – Sanctified (Positional)

Paul would also speak of being washed, sanctified, and justified by the Spirit of God, or rather, washed, sanctified, and justified by the Holy Spirit (1 Corinthians 6:11). This verse speaks of being washed, which is in reference to the internal spiritual washing and regeneration of the Holy Spirit and also being justified by the Holy Spirit, which we have already addressed. Additionally, Paul speaks of being sanctified by the Holy Spirit (1 Corinthians 6:11). Theologians speak of sanctification in four ways, which include pre-conversion sanctification (Election), positional sanctification (Justification), progressive sanctification (Christlikeness), and perfect sanctification (Glorification). In 1 Corinthians 6:11, Paul is speaking of the positional sanctification work of the Holy Spirit where he says, *"And such were some of you. But you were washed, **you were sanctified**, you were justified **in the name of the Lord Jesus Christ and by the Spirit of our God**"* (emphasis added). When a person comes to faith in the Lord Jesus Christ, they are positionally sanctified in that they are justified by faith and set apart for God. Additionally, at justification, the believer immediately begins their walk of sanctification to be conformed to the image of Christ, which is progressive sanctification (Romans 8:29–30). Therefore, we can know that the baptism of the Holy Spirit includes positional sanctification in which the believer is justified by faith and set apart as God's child.

Paul's Distinction Between Water Baptism and Baptism of the Holy Spirit

Paul had seen a lot of external washing with water, and he knew that the Pharisees had been denounced for all their external ceremonial washing. He understood that the heart was defiled and that it needed to be washed. Paul was present at the Jerusalem Council with Peter and fully agreed with Peter's assertion that when the Holy Spirit was given by God and one came to faith in Christ, the heart would be cleansed by faith:

> *And God, who knows the heart, bore witness to them,* ***by giving them the Holy Spirit*** *just as he did to us, and he made no distinction between us and them,* ***having cleansed their hearts by faith***.
>
> —Acts 15:8–9 (emphasis added)

The internal cleansing of the Holy Spirit was needed—not another ceremonial handwashing, ceremonial body washing, or ceremonial mikvah purification washing. Paul realized that the Holy Spirit of God needed to bring about an internal washing, renewal, and regeneration to man's heart through the Word of God or the gospel. Paul understood that baptism with the Holy Spirit or Spirit baptism, which caused one's heart to be cleansed by putting their faith in Christ, was what really mattered.

The author of Hebrews also understood that the heart

could not be made right with God through ceremonial, ritualistic, and sacramental washings:

> By this the Holy Spirit indicates that **the way into the holy places is not yet opened** as long as the first section is still standing (which is symbolic for the present age). According to this arrangement, gifts and sacrifices are offered that **cannot perfect the conscience of the worshiper**, but deal only with food and drink and **various washings**, regulations for the body imposed until the time of reformation.
>
> —Hebrews 9:8–10 (emphasis added)

Here, the author of Hebrews notes that the Old Testament Levitical system could not perfect the conscience of the worshiper. This simply means that the Levitical system could not give or enable a right standing with God. Additionally, the author of Hebrews says that various washings could not perfect the conscience either. The word for washings comes from *baptismos*, which refers to ceremonial washings, including immersion. To rely on ceremonial washings, ritual baptisms, or any of the like for salvation is to enter back into the Old Covenant, which could never perfect the conscience of the worshiper and give right standing with God. In fact, the Holy Spirit used these ceremonial washings as a symbol to show that the way to God had not yet been opened. The word for symbol comes from *parabole*, which means a "figure" or "parable", meaning that it is an illustration and a symbol that veils spiritual truth. Ceremonial washings and baptism, though commanded in both the New Testament and Old Testament, were not the means to a right standing with God. Rather, a right standing with God comes through faith in the Lord Jesus Christ (Hebrews 10:22, 11:6, 12:2).

Likewise, Luke is intentional to record that Simon the sorcerer believed and was baptized, but Simon was not saved (Acts 8:13–24). We see much evidence that Simon the sorcerer was not saved in that Simon did not possess the Holy Spirit (Acts 8:18); he thought the Holy Spirit could be received by giving money (Acts 8:18–19); Peter told him he was perishing (Acts 8:20); Simon had no part in the ministry of the Word (Acts 8:21); Simon's heart was not right before God (Acts 8:21); Simon needed to repent and be forgiven (Acts 8:22); Simon was full of gall, bitterness, and a slave to iniquity (Acts 8:23); and Simon did not personally repent and ask God for forgiveness but rather, asked Peter to pray for him (Acts 8:24). Does Acts 8:13 contradict Mark 16:15–16 which says, *"And he said to them, 'Go into all the world and proclaim the gospel to the whole creation. **Whoever believes and is baptized will be saved**, but whoever does not believe will be condemned"* (emphasis added)? Not at all. Simon the Sorcerer simply possessed a non-saving or non-justifying faith. The Bible warns against false conversion (Matthew 7:21– 28), false repentance (Luke 3:3–17), and non-saving faith (John 12:42) with continuous repetition and fervency. Those who come to true faith in the Lord Jesus Christ will be saved. In this account between Simon the sorcerer and Peter, Luke is intentional to point out that water baptism does not save anyone.

We've demonstrated that there is a distinction between water baptism and baptism with the Holy Spirit. The following is a definition and diagram of the baptism of the Holy Spirit which was described in this chapter:

- The baptism of the Holy Spirit is the sovereign monergistic work of salvation performed by God the Father, God the Son, and God the Holy Spirit (Titus 3:4-6).

- The Son asks the Father to send the Holy Spirit (John 14:16) [**Diagram Step 1**].

- The Holy Spirit is given from the Father to the Son (John 14:16, 15:26; Luke 11:13) [**Diagram Steps 2 and 3**].

- The Son pours out or gives the Holy Spirit in the Father's name (Matthew 3:11–12; Mark 1:8; Luke 3:16, 24:49; John 1:31–33, 14:16, 26; 15:26; 16:7; Acts 1:4–5, 2:17–18, 10:44–48, 11:16; Titus 3:6) [**Diagram Step 4**] through hearing the Word of God, the Gospel (James 1:18; Ephesians 1:13; Romans 1:15–17, 10:17; 1 Corinthians 1:21) [**Diagram Step 5**].

- The Holy Spirit then regenerates or causes man to be born again (John 3:3–10, Titus 3:5, Ezekiel

36:25–27), which gives spiritual life to the previously spiritually dead man (Ephesians 2:1–3, Colossians 2:13) [**Diagram Step 6**].

- Man, then repents, which is a gift granted by God (Acts 11:18, 2 Timothy 2:25), and man puts saving faith in Jesus Christ, which is also gifted and granted by God (Ephesians 2:8–9, Philippians 1:29, John 7:38–39) [**Diagram Step 7**].

- Man is then justified by grace through faith in Christ (Titus 3:7); he receives and is indwelt by the Holy Spirit (Galatians 3:2, 3:14; Ephesians 1:13; 1 Corinthians 6:19), and the Holy Spirit spiritually unites or immerses man with Jesus Christ and puts the man into the body of Christ and gives gifts to the man for the benefit of the church (1 Corinthians 12:7, 12:13; Romans 6:3–4) [**Diagram Step 7**].

The baptism with the Holy Spirit is not water baptism, and water baptism is not the baptism with the Holy Spirit, for only Christ can baptize with the Holy Spirit; man can only baptize with water (Matthew 3:11–12; Mark 1:8; Luke 3:16; John 1:31–33, 3:8, 7:38–39, 14:15–17, 26; 15:26, 16:7; Acts 1:4–5, 2:17–18, 10:44–48, 11:16; 1 Corinthians 1:17). The baptism of the Holy Spirit is a one-time, instantaneous, and salvific work of God (1 Corinthians 12:13).

Diagram of Baptism of the Holy Spirit

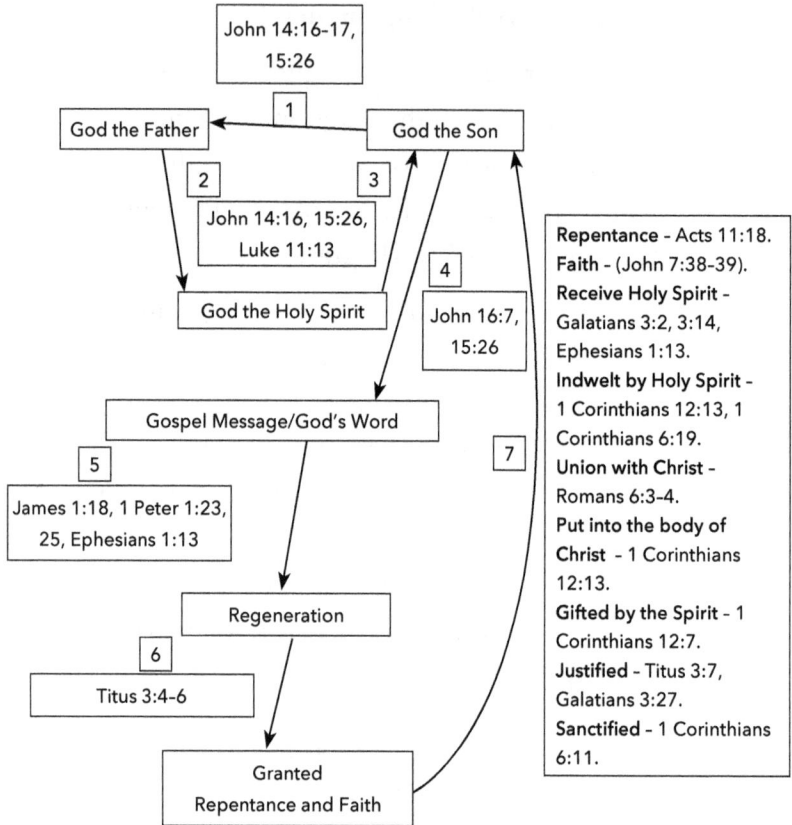

John 14:16-17, 15:26

God the Father ← 1 → God the Son

2   3

John 14:16, 15:26, Luke 11:13

God the Holy Spirit

4

John 16:7, 15:26

Gospel Message/God's Word

5   7

James 1:18, 1 Peter 1:23, 25, Ephesians 1:13

Regeneration

6

Titus 3:4-6

Granted Repentance and Faith

Repentance - Acts 11:18.
Faith - (John 7:38-39).
Receive Holy Spirit - Galatians 3:2, 3:14, Ephesians 1:13.
Indwelt by Holy Spirit - 1 Corinthians 12:13, 1 Corinthians 6:19.
Union with Christ - Romans 6:3-4.
Put into the body of Christ - 1 Corinthians 12:13.
Gifted by the Spirit - 1 Corinthians 12:7.
Justified - Titus 3:7, Galatians 3:27.
Sanctified - 1 Corinthians 6:11.

In this chapter, we've learned that the Abrahamic sign of circumcision had no salvific merit. Physical circumcision was the sign; spiritual circumcision was salvific. We have also learned that ceremonial washings with water had no salvific merit; ceremonial washings and baptisms were the symbol, but Spirit baptism was salvific. Would the apostle Paul place any hope of salvation in a ceremonial, ritualistic, sacramental washing with water? The clear answer is "May it never be!" Is water baptism a command to be obeyed in the New Testament? The answer is yes. Does water baptism save in the New Testament? The answer is no. Paul, the former Pharisee, made clear distinctions between water baptism and Spirit baptism. He made clear distinction between ceremonies and faith in Christ. As we move forward, we will continue to see the religious environment in which Paul lived. Understanding this biblical and historical background will help us comprehend why Paul would have given no salvific merit to covenant signs, ceremonial washings, or Sabbath observances as we will learn in the next chapter. Paul believed that none of these things gave right standing with the Lord.

Chapter 3
Sabbath Day Observance

"You are to speak to the people of Israel and say, 'Above all you shall keep my Sabbaths, for this is a sign between me and you throughout your generations, that you may know that I, the Lord, sanctify you. . . . It is a sign forever between me and the people of Israel that in six days the Lord made heaven and earth, and on the seventh day he rested and was refreshed.'"

—Exodus 31:13, 17

Therefore let no one pass judgment on you in questions of food and drink, or with regard to a festival or a new moon or a Sabbath. These are a shadow of the things to come, but the substance belongs to Christ.

—Colossians 2:16–17

Much has been written about the fourth commandment, and I don't intend that this chapter will provide the fullest and most detailed explanation of the Lord's commandment to remember the Sabbath Day and keep it holy. However, I will attempt to explain the purpose of the fourth commandment, describe how the Sabbath was observed during the life and times of Paul, and how Paul saw the Sabbath fulfilled in Christ.

As we begin, it will be most beneficial to understand why the Sabbath was to function as a sign between the Lord and Israel, but notice how burdensome the Sabbath had become during Paul's life. Just as we've explained why Paul would put no hope in the Abrahamic Covenant sign of circumcision or ceremonial washings, this chapter will hopefully provide greater insight into why Paul would put no salvific hope in Sabbath observances or works as a means for a right standing with God.

To trace the purposes of the Sabbath, let's start where the Sabbath is first mentioned, the creation account.[29] The Sabbath is first mentioned in Genesis 2:1–3 (NASB2020), where it says:

> *"And so the heavens and the earth were completed, and all their heavenly lights. By the seventh day God completed His work which He had done, and He rested on the seventh day from all His work which He had done. Then* **God blessed the seventh day and sanctified it**, *because on it He rested from all His work which God had created and made."* (emphasis added)

In the creation account, we are told that all creation was made by God in six days and that all God created was good. God blessed the living creatures (Genesis 1:22), and He blessed man (Genesis 1:28). God blessed the Sabbath, and He made it holy as it says in Genesis 2:3: *"Then God blessed the seventh day and sanctified it, because on it He rested from all His work which God had created and made."* The root word for *sanctified* essentially means that it was "holy," "set apart," or "consecrated" unto the Lord. Though it was not immediately made known how the Sabbath would be set apart for the Lord, through progressive revelation, we will see the many reasons why this day would be made holy.

A primary purpose for making the Sabbath Day holy is seen in Genesis 2:2 where it says, *"By the seventh day God completed His work which He had done, and He rested on the seventh day from all His work which He had done."* The reason the Sabbath was made holy was for mankind to stand in awe and fear the Lord for His work in creation and to observe that it was complete and good. Creation was a finished and perfect work. All God's creation of light and darkness, water, land, sea, vegetation, days, galaxies, stars, all living creatures, and mankind was fully finished, and it was good. There was nothing that needed further evolution. All things that were created were finished and complete, and so God ceased from working. This rest was not a rest of becoming tired or weary for we see in Isaiah 40:28 that *"he does not faint or grow weary."* The Sabbath was to be a holy day to observe God's work in creation.

As we learned earlier, the Sabbath was a day to learn to fear the Lord. It was a day to stand in awe of His omnipotence and mighty power in creating all things (Isaiah 45:18). It was a day to stand in awe of His omniscience and unfathomable understanding (Proverbs 3:19–20). It was a day to stand in awe of His goodness and see that all He did was good (Genesis 1:31). It was a day to stand in awe of His aseity and observe that He is the source of all that has been created and has life, and that all life originates from Him (Nehemiah 9:6). It was a day to observe his holiness in that there is no other god except the Lord that made creation (Deuteronomy 32:39). It was a day to observe that man was created in the image of God, which means that man is relational; man is creative; and rational by evidence of his reason, will, emotion, and intellect. Thus, the Sabbath was set apart as a day to fear the Lord.

It's important to note that the Sabbath was originally not a command for man to abstain from work or a command to keep the Sabbath Day holy. How could there be such a command? In the beginning, man enjoyed perfect communion with the Lord. Man was not at enmity with Lord and had not rebelled. Although man was put in the Garden of Eden to tend and watch over it, he still enjoyed perfect communion with the Lord. It wasn't until Adam and Eve sinned that there was broken communion with God (Genesis 3:1–14). Man was promised that the day he ate of the fruit of the knowledge of good and evil, he would surely die (Genesis 2:17). The repercussions of one sin were astronomical, which included woman being cursed (Genesis 3:16), man being cursed (Genesis 3:17–19), the earth being cursed (Genesis 3:17), death came into the world (Romans 5:12, 1 Corinthians 15:22), sin was imputed to all mankind (Romans 5:12), man's relationship with God was broken and man died spiritually (Genesis 3:22–24), and man earned the wages of both physical and spiritual death (Romans 6:23). However, there was originally no Sabbath restriction on working or keeping the Sabbath holy because there was perfect communion between man and God.

The Sabbath Day is not mentioned again until we come to Exodus 16 where the Lord gives the Israelites instructions on gathering food on the sixth day and resting on the Sabbath as it says in Exodus 16:23:

> *"He said to them, 'This is what the Lord has commanded: "Tomorrow is a day of solemn rest, a holy Sabbath to the Lord; bake what you will bake and boil what you will boil, and all that is left over lay aside to be kept till the morning.'"*

Here is the first command to set aside the Sabbath Day as a day of rest, but up until this point, there was no such command to set aside the Sabbath as a day to cease from work and an imperative to rest.

The next time we see a command regarding the Sabbath is in Exodus 20. Here we see again that the Lord wants the Sabbath to be a day of no work or labor, a day to remember

God's creation account, and a day that would be holy unto the Lord:

> "*Remember the Sabbath day, to keep it holy. Six days you shall labor, and do all your work, but the seventh day is a Sabbath to the Lord your God. On it you shall not do any work, you, or your son, or your daughter, your male servant, or your female servant, or your livestock, or the sojourner who is within your gates. For in six days the Lord made heaven and earth, the sea, and all that is in them, and rested on the seventh day. Therefore the Lord blessed the Sabbath day and made it holy.*"

—Exodus 20:8–12

The next time we see a command regarding the Sabbath is in Exodus 31 where the Sabbath Day is to be a sign between the Lord and all generations. It is also to be a day of rest and no work, and it is to be a day to remember the Creation account where it says:

> "*You are to speak to the people of Israel and say, 'Above all you shall keep my Sabbaths, for this is a **sign** between me and you throughout your generations, that you may know that I, the Lord, sanctify you. You shall keep the Sabbath, because it is holy for you. Everyone who profanes it shall be put to death. Whoever does any work on it, that soul shall be cut off from among his people. Six days shall work be done, but the seventh day*

*is a Sabbath of solemn rest, holy to the Lord. Whoever does any work on the Sabbath day shall be put to death. Therefore the people of Israel shall keep the Sabbath, observing the Sabbath throughout their generations, as a covenant forever. It is a **sign** forever between me and the people of Israel that in six days the Lord made heaven and earth, and on the seventh day he rested and was refreshed."*

—Exodus 31:13–17 (emphasis added)

From Exodus 31, we learn that the Sabbath was to function as a sign (v. 12, 17); the Sabbath was to serve as a sign that the Lord had sanctified a people for Himself (v. 13). This passage contains the following restrictions: profaning the Sabbath was worthy of death (v. 14); no work was to take place on the Sabbath (v. 14); anyone who worked on the Sabbath was to be put to death (v. 15), and the Sabbath was to serve as a sign of the Lord's work of creation (v. 17).

Later in Exodus, we see that another restriction on the Sabbath, which includes not kindling a fire in one's dwelling place. We see this in Exodus 35:2–3:

*Six days work shall be done, but on the seventh day you shall have a Sabbath of solemn rest, holy to the Lord. Whoever does any work on it shall be put to death. **You shall kindle no fire in all your dwelling places on the Sabbath day.** (emphasis added)*

We learn additional information when the Sabbath is mentioned in Leviticus 23:3. Here, the Lord gives another command regarding the Sabbath, which includes having a gathering or convocation for the Israelites:

*"Six days shall work be done, but on the seventh day is a Sabbath of solemn rest, **a holy convocation**. You shall do no work. It is a Sabbath to the Lord in all your dwelling places."* (emphasis added).

The Sabbath is mentioned again in Deuteronomy 5:12–15. Here, we encounter more progressive revelation in that the Sabbath is be a day to remind Israel of her deliverance from Egypt as it says:

*"Observe the Sabbath day, to keep it holy, as the Lord your God commanded you. Six days you shall labor and do all your work, but the seventh day is a Sabbath to the Lord your God. On it you shall not do any work, you or your son or your daughter or your male servant or your female servant, or your ox or your donkey or any of your livestock, or the sojourner who is within your gates, that your male servant and your female servant may rest as well as you. **You shall remember that you were a slave in the land of Egypt, and the Lord your God brought you out from there with a mighty hand and an outstretched arm**. Therefore the Lord your God commanded you to keep the Sabbath day."* (emphasis added).

As we move through the rest of the Old Testament, we begin to see some more restrictions being given on the Sabbath, including a restriction on buying/selling or performing normal work/commerce on the Sabbath. We see these restrictions in Nehemiah and Jeremiah:

> **And if the peoples of the land bring in goods or any grain on the Sabbath day to sell, we will not buy from them on the Sabbath or on a holy day.** *And we will forego the crops of the seventh year and the exactation of every debt.*
>
> —Nehemiah 10:31 (emphasis added)

> *In those days I saw in Judah people* **treading winepresses on the Sabbath,** *and* **bringing in heaps of grain and loading them on donkeys, and also wine, grapes, figs, and all kinds of loads, which they brought into Jerusalem on the Sabbath day. And I warned them on the day when they sold food. Tyrians also, who lived in the city, brought in fish and all kinds of goods and sold them on the Sabbath to the people of Judah, in Jerusalem itself.** *Then I confronted the nobles of Judah and said to them,* **"What is this evil thing that you are doing, profaning the Sabbath day?** *Did not your fathers act in this way, and did not our God bring all this disaster on us and on this city? Now you are bringing more wrath on Israel by profaning the Sabbath."*
>
> —Nehemiah 13:15–18 (emphasis added)

*This is what the Lord said to me: "Go and stand at the Gate of the People, through which the kings of Judah go in and out; stand also at all the other gates of Jerusalem. Say to them, 'Hear the word of the Lord, you kings of Judah and all people of Judah and everyone living in Jerusalem who come through these gates. This is what the Lord says: **Be careful not to carry a load on the Sabbath day or bring it through the gates of Jerusalem. Do not bring a load out of your houses or do any work on the Sabbath, but keep the Sabbath day holy, as I commanded your ancestors.** Yet they did not listen or pay attention; they were stiff-necked and would not listen or respond to discipline. But if you are careful to obey me, declares the Lord, and bring no load through the gates of this city on the Sabbath, but keep the Sabbath day holy by not doing any work on it, then kings who sit on David's throne will come through the gates of this city with their officials. They and their officials will come riding in chariots and on horses, accompanied by the men of Judah and those living in Jerusalem, and this city will be inhabited forever.*
(emphasis added).

—Jeremiah 17:19–25 (emphasis added)

These passages give us a good understanding of how the Sabbath was to be kept—commands of things to be done and things not to be done. When we view the Sabbath commands in totality along with how the Lord wanted the Sabbath to be remembered, we can see that the Sabbath was to be a sign to both the Israelites and Gentiles.

The Sign of the Sabbath

As we mentioned at the beginning of this chapter, the Sabbath initially served as a sign for the Israelites to stand in awe and fear the Lord for His work in creation and to observe that it was complete and good. The Sabbath was a time to remember God's attributes and meditate on who He is and what He did in creation. Nehemiah 9:6 captures this wonderfully where it says:

> *You are the Lord, you alone. You have made heaven, the heaven of heavens, with all their host, the earth and all that is on it, the seas and all that is in them; and you preserve all of them; and the host of heaven worships you.*

The Sabbath was a day to learn to reverence the Creator of heaven and earth.

A second way the Sabbath served as a sign was to show Israel that the Lord was faithful to keep the Abrahamic Covenant. The Lord had reminded the Israelites of this purpose for the Sabbath in Deuteronomy 5:12–15 when He detailed their delivery out of Egypt. The Lord cut away Abraham for Himself, cut away a people for Himself, cut away a nation for Himself, cut away a land for Himself where His people could dwell. Ultimately, He circumcised or to cut away men's hearts for Himself. The Lord single-handedly demonstrated His power to deliver His people from Egypt. He showed signs, wonders, and miracles to Pharaoh and proved that He was the Savior and Redeemer of His people. Deuteronomy 7:8 states it this way:

> *But it is because the Lord loves you and is keeping the oath that he swore to your fathers, that the Lord has brought you out with a mighty hand and redeemed you from the house of slavery, from the hand of Pharaoh king of Egypt.*

Nehemiah 9:7 also conveys the same message: "*You are the Lord, the God who chose Abram and brought him out of Ur of the Chaldeans and gave him the name Abraham.*" Therefore, the Sabbath was a sign to the Israelites of the Abrahamic Covenant and how the Lord had kept His promise to Abraham by delivering the Israelites out of Egypt and from Pharaoh. It was to show that the Lord was a faithful covenant-keeping God.

A third way the Sabbath served as a sign was to show all other nations that only the Lord was to be worshipped. No other nation would set aside a day to fear the Lord and remember Him for His work in Creation (Genesis 1–2) and remember Him for being faithful to His promises and cutting away or separating the nation for Himself (Deuteronomy 5:12–15). Setting aside one day as the Sabbath served as a sign to other nations that the Lord is the one who created the world, and not the false gods of the pagan nations. Other nations would learn why the Sabbath was holy to the Lord. The other nations would know that the Lord rested on the Sabbath Day and saw that His creation was good. The other nations would learn that there was once fellowship between the Lord and man, but that this fellowship was broken because of sin. The other nations would know that the Israelites kept the Sabbath Day to remember how they had been delivered from Egypt. This would serve as a sign to all other nations in that the Lord's people lived and worshipped differently than the rest of the world. Deuteronomy 33:29 captures this where it says, *"Who is like you, a people saved by the Lord, the shield of your help, and the sword of your triumph! Your enemies shall come fawning to you, and you shall tread upon their backs."* Therefore, we can see that the Sabbath was to serve as a sign to all other nations of the goodness, faithfulness, mercy, and holiness of the Lord and that only the Lord was to be worshipped.

A fourth way the Sabbath served as a sign was to show that God was merciful and compassionate and that He desired fellowship with His people. The Lord gave His people rest and protected them from enemies. Deuteronomy 12:9–10 conveys this idea:

> *For you have not as yet come to the rest and to the inheritance that the Lord your God is giving you. But when you go over the Jordan and live in the land that the Lord your God is giving you to inherit, and when **he gives***

you rest from all your enemies around, so that you live in safety, then to the place that the Lord your God will choose, to make his name dwell there, there you shall bring all that I command you: your burnt offerings and your sacrifices, your tithes and the contribution that you present, and all your finest vow offerings that you vow to the Lord. (emphasis added)

The Lord desired to give His people rest, safety, and to fellowship with Him. The Lord is a good and compassionate God, and the Sabbath was a day to remember His mercy, goodness, and compassion toward His people and to give them rest and allow them to worship and have fellowship with Him.

A fifth way the Sabbath served as a sign was to show how the Lord was to be worshipped. Keeping the Sabbath Day allowed for a holy convocation or gathering to take place on the Sabbath. The Sabbath was to be a day when God's chosen people could gather and worship and praise the Lord (Leviticus 23:3). This served as a sign that the Lord's people worshipped together and according to His prescribed instruction. As we'll see later in this chapter, the Sabbath Day was highly organized and included reading from the Torah, reading from the Prophets, singing psalms, and expositing the Word of God. This was to be a day that the Lord's people would gather and worship Him for who He is and what He had done. The Lord was not to be worshipped on the whims and opinions devised by man. No, the Lord had a prescribed way of how He was to be worshipped because He is a holy God.

A sixth way the Sabbath served as a sign was to bring Israel and the nations to repentance; I believe this may have been the most important reason for the Sabbath. It was to serve as a sign that on the seventh day God rested from His work, a reminder that man and God had once shared perfect fellowship and communion together. The Sabbath was a sign of what man had forfeited by his disobedience in the Garden of Eden. It was a sign to remind man of the curse of sin, the curse of death, the curse of pain in childbearing, the curse of toiling on the earth, and the curse of strife between man and woman. This sign was to bring man to repentance and a yearning for a right relationship and fellowship with God. This sign was to serve as a sign of God's goodness and man's brokenness and sinfulness. This is why a punishment of death was to be given to the Sabbath law breaker (Exodus 31:14). This is why there was such a strong punishment of death for the man who gathered wood on the Sabbath (Numbers 15:32–36). Man was not to go about working on this day. No, he was to rest and be reminded of the rest that had been forfeited by sin. I believe that this was and is one of the most important purposes of the sign of the Sabbath. Just as we learned that physical circumcision pointed to the need for heart circumcision, so the Sabbath would stand as a sign of the communion and fellowship with the Lord that was forfeited in the Garden of Eden. The sign of the Sabbath was meant to bring man to repentance and a desire for a circumcised heart and right relationship with the Lord.

Therefore, the purpose for keeping the Sabbath was to learn to fear the Lord for His work in creation, to remind the Israelites of the Abrahamic Covenant, to serve as a sign to all other nations that the Lord was the only God to be worshipped, to show forth the compassion and mercy of the Lord, to allow God's people to gather together to worship Him, and to bring His people and all other nations to repentance and the desire for a heart circumcision and a right relationship with Him. There is no doubt that other authors have plumbed and excavated this commandment far more thoroughly than what I have done here, but for the time being, this serves as a good overview of how God intended the Sabbath to be kept and how it served as a sign.

Sabbath Observance During the Life and Times of Paul

The Sabbath Day observance was very important in Jewish life during the life and times of the Apostle Paul. There was good reason for this. The nation had been punished for its idolatry by being overtaken by the Assyrian and Babylonian armies. The Lord had warned the Israelites that they had committed spiritual adultery. The Israelites had worshipped Baal (Jeremiah 2:23), run after other gods (Jeremiah 2:25), worshipped carved images (Jeremiah 2:27), and killed their own prophets (Jeremiah 2:30). Their idolatry was compared to that of a prostitute with many lovers (Jeremiah 2:33), and they were unrepentant over their sins (Jeremiah 2:35). Judah was similar in that her idolatry was compared to adultery (Jeremiah 3:6), and she was not repentant toward God (Jeremiah 3:10).

The Israelites were not only being punished for their idolatry and for forsaking the Lord, but they were also being taught not to worship other gods. In fact, the Lord tells the people that their Sabbaths were completely worthless as He says this to them in Isaiah 1:13:

> Bring no more vain offerings; incense is an abomination to me. New moon and Sabbath and the calling of convocations—I cannot endure iniquity and solemn assembly. Your new moons and your appointed feast my soul hates; they have become a burden to me; I am weary of bearing them.

Therefore, as we come to the New Testament, we see a heightened focus by the Pharisees and religious leaders to observe the Sabbath and to worship the one true God, Yahweh.

With that being said, I am going to attempt to describe what life was like as a child in Jewish culture, what a Sabbath Day would have looked like from a synagogue perspective, and the regulations the Pharisees had put on the Sabbath. We'll start first with what life would have been like as a child in Jewish culture. This will hopefully draw a detailed picture of the religious life of a child who was reared in Judaism. This will also help us understand what life looked like during the life of the Apostle Paul.

Life as a Child in Jewish Culture During the Life and Times of Paul

Much of the content in this section reflects accounts from Alfred Edersheim's book, *The Life and Times of Jesus the Messiah*.[30] Edersheim was a Jewish convert to Christianity, and his work will help fill in the cultural and historical background during Jesus's life. Edersheim wrote his book through studying the Talmud and consulting rabbinic law because he believed that understanding the historical and cultural background was important to understanding the New Testament. We'll first review what life was like as a Jewish child and then transition to what it was like worshipping in a synagogue on the Sabbath.

Jewish women were very important in the life of the child. If Jewish women were faithful to their religion, they would know of many of the noble Hebrew mothers and would seek to follow their example. The children would be trained from infancy to recognize God as their Father, and as Maker of the world. They were trained to have knowledge of the laws from earliest youth and to have these impressed in their souls or, rather, engraven on their souls as commanded in Deuteronomy 6:6–7 and Deuteronomy 11:18–19:

> *And these words that I command you today shall be on your heart. **You shall teach them diligently to your children**, and shall talk of them when you sit in your house, and when you walk by the way, and when you lie down, and when you rise.* (emphasis added)

*You shall therefore lay up these words of mine in your heart and in your soul, and you shall bind them as a sign on your hand, and they shall be as frontlets between your eyes. **You shall teach them to your children,** talking of them when you are sitting in your house, and when you are walking by the way, and when you lie down, and when you rise.* (emphasis added)

Jewish children were brought up learning and exercising in the laws; they learned about the acts of their predecessors in order to imitate them.

However, while the earliest religious teaching would, of necessity, come from the mother, it was the father who was "bound to teach his son." He was to impart to his child the knowledge of the Torah with great spiritual clarity as if he had been the one to receive the law from Mount Horeb. Every engagement was to be a time where he could teach his child, even at the necessary mealtime. The men were to see this as serious labor that would not prove fruitless. In fact, men who had sons and had failed to bring them up in the knowledge of the law were considered profane and vulgar. Therefore, the man had a high duty and calling to instruct his child.

When the child learned to speak, his religious instruction was to begin. Such instruction would begin with verses from Scripture which could include Jewish liturgy, such as the Shema, which would have certainly included Deuteronomy 6:4–5: *"Hear, O Israel: The Lord our God, the Lord is one.*

You shall love the Lord your God with all your heart and with all your soul and with all your might." Special attention was given to memorization since forgetfulness might prove fatal in its consequences as this might lead to ignorance or neglect of the law.

Very early, the child would be taught what might be called his birthday text, which was some verse of Scripture beginning, ending with, or at least containing the same letters as his Hebrew name. This verse would be inserted in the child's daily prayers. They were also taught hymns that would be the psalms for the days of the week, or festive psalms, such as the *Hallel* (Psalms 113–118).

Regular instruction would begin when the child reached the age of five or six years (according to strength) when the child would be sent to school. There are several references to schools existing throughout the land during this time period. The existence of higher schools and academies would not have been possible without a primary education. Tradition ascribes to Joshua the son of Gamla the introduction of schools in every town, and the compulsory education in them of all children above the age of six. In fact, it was deemed unlawful to live in a place where there was no school, and it was thought that such a city deserved to be destroyed.

The education that took place was marked by extreme care, wisdom, accuracy, and a moral and religious purpose as the end goal. The children could be gathered in synagogues or schoolhouses where they stood or sat in a semicircle, facing the teacher. The teacher was generally the *hazan*, the leader of the synagogue or an officer of the synagogue. The teacher was to impart to the children the precious knowledge of the law with constant adaptation to their capacity, with unwearied patience, intense earnestness, strictness tempered by kindness, but above all, with the highest object of their training in view. He was to keep the children away from contact with vice; to train them to gentleness, even when the bitterest wrong had been received; to show sin in its repulsiveness, rather than to terrify by its consequences; to train to strict truthfulness; to avoid all that might lead to disagreeable or indelicate thoughts; and to do all this without showing partiality, without undue severity or laxity of discipline. He was to teach with judicious study and work and with careful attention to thoroughness in conveying knowledge. This was the ideal set before the teacher and made his office one of high esteem in Israel.

It was believed that the Bible should be the exclusive textbook up to ten years of age. From ten to fifteen years of age, the child was to learn the Mishnah, or traditional law. After this, the child would enter theological discussions, which occupied time and attention in the higher academies of the rabbis. However, it's not that this progression always occurred. If a child entered Mishnic studies and did not show the necessary aptitude, there was little hope for his future.

A child would start his learning with the book of Leviticus to teach the child of their guilt and the need of justification. After this, they would study other parts of the Pentateuch, then the Prophets, and finally, the Hagiographa, which included Ruth, Psalms, Job, Proverbs, Canticles, Lamentations, Ecclesiastes, Daniel, Esther, Ezra, and Chronicles. Then they would learn the Gemara, which was the commentary on the Mishnah, and would be taught the Talmud if they progressed to the academies. Care was taken not to send a child to school too early and, thus, overwork them. Therefore, school hours were fixed, and attendance shortened during the summer months.

The teaching in school would be aided by the services of the synagogue as well as the influences in the homelife. Not every home would have copies of the whole Old Testament in Hebrew, but if there were portions of the Word of God in the home, it would be the most cherished treasure of a pious household. The academies had copies of Holy Scripture, and great care was taken to preserve the integrity of the text; it was deemed unlawful to make copies of small portions of a book of Scripture. This was to prevent misquotes and misinterpretations in Scripture.

In *The Life and Times of Jesus the Messiah*, Edersheim restrains from going any further in terms of detail regarding the teaching of Jesus. He notes that historians are not sure whether there was a school system in Nazareth or whether the order and method that were described would have been universal throughout Israel. However, he does note that, in all probability, there was likely a school in Nazareth. In our connection to the Apostle Paul, it would be fair to say that since Paul grew up during the same time as Jesus, he would have had a very similar upbringing as to what was described above. Especially since Paul became a Pharisee, and he would have likely needed primary school before going on to higher education.

Synagogue Life During the Life and Times of Paul

In the synoptic Gospels, we learn that Jesus's ministry was one of teaching and preaching as it says in Matthew 4:23: "*And he went throughout all Galilee,* **teaching in their synagogues** *and proclaiming the gospel of the kingdom and healing every disease and every affliction among the people*" (emphasis added). As we saw in the previous section, synagogue life was a very important part of Jewish life. Therefore, we will dedicate this section to understanding what synagogue life would have looked like during the life and times of Paul.[31]

As we noted earlier, synagogues were an extremely important part of the Jewish life. In fact, it may be argued that the synagogue was the most important institution in the Jewish life, which was centered around the synagogue. As we learned earlier, the teacher who taught the children would most likely have been the synagogue leader or an officer of the synagogue. In fact, not having a part in synagogue life would be the worst outcome imaginable. In John 12:42, we see that many people were fearful of following Jesus because they might be put out of their synagogues: "*Nevertheless, many even of the authorities believed in him, but for fear of the Pharisees they did not confess it, so that they would not be* **put** *out of the synagogue*." (emphasis added). The word for "*put out of the synagogue*" is *aposunagógos*, which means "expelled from the synagogue," "excommunicated," or "away from the synagogue," which mean being put out of the assemblies of the Israelites. To be put out of a synagogue was tantamount to being declared a pagan Gentile. Thus, synagogue life was very important.

In most cases, the synagogue would be built on a hill using the most prominent hump in the city of a little town. The synagogue would be the highest place in the city and would have a distinguished tall pole so everyone could focus on it. If you went into a Jewish town, you would typically see a synagogue spire; they were just as common to seeing a church steeple with a cross.

Worship took place in a synagogue every Sabbath (i.e., every Saturday). The Sabbath was from Friday at sundown to Saturday at sundown. The format of the service would include a reading of the Law (Torah), a reading of the Prophets, and then prayers were offered by the leader along with responses by the people. The people would respond with amens or various praises to God. After this, there would be an exposition of some text of the Scripture. If there was a visiting dignitary or rabbi, he would be given the right to speak the exposition of the text. As we see in the book of Acts, this is exactly what Paul did; as he traveled, he would preach in a synagogue or place of worship.

The affairs of the synagogue were administered by ten men who were basically elders. Of the ten men, three were called the "rulers of the synagogue," and they acted as judges. They would admit proselytes or not admit them, and they would settle issues or disputes among the people. There was a fourth ruler called "the angel of the church" who was a type of chairman of the board. There were others called "servers" who would carry out the direction of the rulers. There was also a Hebrew interpreter who took the ancient Hebrew and translated it into the vernacular. Every synagogue had a theological school in it as we learned earlier.

Thus, the synagogue became the court of law for the Jews as well as the place of worship. The rulers of the synagogue would settle disputes, court problems, or civil issues. The synagogue was also the place for the children to go and learn the Bible and the Mishnah or oral law; it was the place for teaching and preaching. It was essentially the life of the town. The structure and organization of the modern-day church has been modeled after the synagogue. Therefore, we can see how important synagogue life was and how it functioned on the Sabbath.

Sabbath Restrictions During the Life and Times of Paul

The Sabbath Day observance was a major source of conflict between Jesus and the Pharisees. We see that Jesus purposefully performed miracles on the Sabbath, which included healing the demoniac in the synagogue at Capernaum (Mark 1:21–28), healing Peter's mother-in-law (Mark 1:29–31), healing the man with the withered hand (Mark 3:1–6), healing the paralytic at the Pool of Bethesda (John 5:1–16), healing the blind man at the Pool of Siloam (John 9:1–7), healing the woman who was infirmed or bent over (Luke 13:10–17), and healing the man with dropsy (Luke 14:1–6). Not only was there controversy when He performed miracles on the Sabbath, but there was controversy when He and His disciples walked through a field of grain and His disciples picked heads of the grain and ate them on a Sabbath (Matthew 12:1–8).

The rabbis and Pharisees had become zealous about protecting the Sabbath because they had learned that disobedience and idolatry led Israel into the Babylonian Exile. In their attempt to keep the Sabbath, however, they created many burdensome laws and restrictions.

The Sabbath Day restrictions captured in the Talmud include the following: carrying, burning, extinguishing, finishing, writing, erasing, cooking, washing, sewing, tearing, knotting, untying, shaping, plowing, planting, reaping, harvesting, threshing, winnowing, selecting, sifting, grinding, kneading, combing, spinning, dyeing, chain-stitching, warping, weaving, unraveling, building, demolishing, trapping, shearing, slaughtering, skinning, tanning, smoothing, and marking. The minuteness, trivial nature, and heavy burden of these laws can be understood from the examples below:[32]

- And one may not search his garments [for lice or fleas], nor read by the light of a lamp (Mishnah Shabbat 1:3).

- In truth it was said, the hazzan may see where the children are reading from, but he himself must not read (Mishnah Shabbat 1:3).

- Similarly, a zav (man) must not eat together with a zavah (woman), because it may lead to sin (Mishnah Shabbat 1:3).

- Beth Shammai says: Ink, dyes, and vetch may not be soaked [on Friday afternoon] unless they can be fully soaked while it is yet day; and Bet Hillel permits it (Mishnah Shabbat 1:3).

- Meat, onion[s], and egg[s] may not be roasted unless they can be [fully] roasted while it is still day. Bread may not be put into an oven just before nightfall, nor a cake upon coals, unless its surface can form a crust while it is still day. Rabbi Elazar says: There must be time for the bottom to form a crust (Mishnah Shabbat 1:10).

- A donkey may not go out with a saddlecloth, when it is not tied to it (Mishnah Shabbat 5:4).

- With what may a woman go out and with what may she not go out? A woman may not go out with wool ribbons, linen ribbons, or straps around her head (Mishnah Shabbat 6:1).

- A woman may not go out with a hairnet into the public domain (Mishnah Shabbat 6:1).

- A man may not go out with a nail-studded sandal, nor with a single [sandal] if he has no wound on his foot; nor with tefillin, nor with an amulet, if it is not from an expert; nor with a breastplate, nor with a helmet; nor with iron boots (Mishnah Shabbat 6:2).

- He who carries out a cow's mouthful of straw, a camel's mouthful of bean stalks, a lamb's mouthful of clover, a goat's mouthful of grasses, moist leaves of garlic or moist leaves of onion the size of a dried fig, [or] a goat's mouthful of dry [leaves], [is liable]. And they do not combine with each other, because they are not alike in their standards. (Mishnah Shabbat 7:4).

- He who carries out [human] food the size of a dried fig is liable, and they combine with each other, because they are equal in their standards, except their shells, kernels, stalks, husks, and coarse bran. Rabbi Judah said: Excluding the shells of lentils, because they are boiled together with them (Mishnah Shabbat 7:4).

- Paper, in order to write a tax collector's receipt on it. And one who carries out a tax-collector's receipt is liable (Mishnah Shabbat 8:3).

- One is liable for carrying enough ink for writing two letters (Mishnah Shabbat 8:3).

- [If one carries out] a basket which is full of produce and places it on the outer threshold, though most of the produce is outside of the threshold, he is not liable unless he carries out the whole basket (Mishnah Shabbat 10:2).

- If one carries out less than the standard quantity of food in a utensil, he is not liable for the utensil, because the utensil is secondary to the [food] (Mishnah Shabbat 10:5).

- If one throws from the private domain into the public domain [or] from the public domain into the private domain, he is liable (Mishnah Shabbat 11:1).

- He who writes two letters, whether with his right hand or with his left hand, whether the same letter or two different letters or in two pigments, in any language, is liable (Mishnah Shabbat 12:3).

- He who feels pain in his teeth may not sip vinegar through them, but he may dip [his bread in vinegar] in the usual manner, and if he is cured, he is cured (Mishnah Shabbat 14:4).

These are just a few examples of the restrictions that were enacted by the rabbis and Pharisees to prevent work from occurring and the restrictions that were imposed on the Sabbath. The Mishnah goes on and on about things that are allowed and things that are prohibited on the Sabbath. As we learned earlier, work was not allowed, but we also see the man-made traditions and laws the Pharisees put on the people for the Sabbath.

As we noted earlier, Jesus healed several times on the Sabbath, which brought confrontation with the Pharisees. On one account in Mark 3, Jesus heals a man with a withered hand on the Sabbath, in the synagogue, and in front of the Pharisees and the people in the synagogue to demonstrate that doing God on the Sabbath was lawful; thus, he confronted the Pharisees for their misunderstanding of what it meant to truly keep the Sabbath day holy.

Jesus proclaimed that He was Lord of the Sabbath, which was a claim to deity as God was the sovereign Lord over the whole Levitical system. Jesus had just addressed the Pharisees when they criticized His disciples for plucking heads of grain on the Sabbath, and He had used the story of Abiathar and David to illustrate to the Pharisees that no ceremony or ritual should take precedence over someone's life. His point was that mercy and grace triumph over ceremony. Jesus was pointing out that human life is far greater than ceremony. He was demonstrating that ceremony, ritual, and tradition should never stand in the way of mercy, kindness, goodness, and necessity. In fact, Jesus made this unequivocal statement regarding Sabbath keeping in Mark 2:27: "*And he said to them, 'The Sabbath was made for man, not man for the Sabbath.'*"

In essence, He was telling them that the Sabbath had

a purpose. The Sabbath was important. Keeping the Sabbath Day was not a trivial matter. As we learned earlier, the Sabbath was given as a sign (Exodus 31:13, 17). This sign was given to teach all people to fear the Lord for His work in creation, to remind the Israelites of the Abrahamic Covenant, to serve as a sign to all other nations, to show forth the compassion and mercy of the Lord, to allow His people to gather to worship Him, and to bring His people to repentance and the desire for a heart circumcision and a right relationship with Him. Rather than understanding the meaning of the Sabbath, the Pharisees had made it into a burdensome, legalistic, and ritualistic day and did not understand that the Sabbath was made for man and not man for the Sabbath.

Therefore, Jesus used the man with the withered hand to emphasize this point for the Pharisees. The man with the withered hand was in no life-threatening situation; he was not in danger of losing his life. However, this was the perfect demonstration, which would display Christ's point in Mark 2:27–28. Jesus had the man stand up in the middle of the whole synagogue; He wanted the man front and center. He didn't want to perform some secret miracle. No, Christ Jesus brought the man in front of the synagogue and asked this question to the Pharisees in Mark 3:4: "'*Is it lawful on the Sabbath to do good or to do harm, to save life or to kill?' But they were silent.*" The implications were that it is lawful to do good to others, but it is unlawful to harm others or take a life. The answer to Jesus's question is obvious. The Pharisees should have known that it was good and lawful to do good and save a life on the Sabbath. No law is broken when someone does good to someone or saves their life. However, the Pharisees would not acknowledge the answer because this would have unmasked their utter hypocrisy. It would have shown that their minute and meticulous rules were worthless when it came to answering Jesus's fundamental question. They could not answer the question because it would have exposed their hypocrisy and lack of understanding of the Sabbath. They could not even admit that one could keep the Sabbath by doing good to others. The Pharisees had completely missed the point of the Sabbath.

Jesus looked into their hearts, and what He saw filled Him with white-hot righteous anger. This is the only place in the Bible where it says that Jesus was angry. Jesus wasn't nonchalant. He wasn't apathetic. He wasn't indifferent. He wasn't passive. No, Jesus looked at the Pharisees as all eyes were on Him in the synagogue, and He saw the uncircumcised and hypocritical hearts of the Pharisees and was wrathful. Jesus looked at their uncircumcised, stubborn, stiff, and calcitrant hearts and this made His blood boil as it says in Mark 3:5: "*And he looked around at them with **anger**, **grieved** at their hardness of heart*" (emphasis added). The word used for *anger* is *orgé*, which means "wrath" or "passion." It is the swelling up and ongoing and settled anger against opposition. It is not a sudden outburst of anger, but rather a fixed, controlled passionate feeling against sin; it is a holy indignation. Jesus saw the religious leaders' false Jewish system, their stiff-necked pride, and their hard and unrepentant hearts, and he was moved with both anger and grief.

Jesus, the Lord of the Sabbath, was going to answer His own question definitively. He was going to put to shame the Pharisees who shut their mouths, remained silent, and could not give the correct answer lest they acknowledge their own hypocrisy by answering Jesus's question correctly (Mark 3:4). Jesus healed the man's withered hand and clearly showed that it was lawful to do good to others and to save a life on the Sabbath (Mark 3:5). The Pharisees clearly saw Jesus do what only God could do. This was a clear demonstration of how God had mercy and acted to do good versus the Pharisees who would not even lift a single finger to help the man with the withered hand. Here we see the answer to Jesus's question. This act so enraged the Pharisees that they planned to kill Jesus (Mark 3:6), which shows how far the Pharisees were from God and that they loved their man-made rules rather than God's commands. This is why Jesus denounced and condemned the Pharisees in Matthew 23:4 when He said, "*They tie up heavy burdens, hard to bear, and lay them on people's shoulders, but they themselves are not willing to move them with their finger.*" They created heavy, burdensome laws regarding the Sabbath that no one could keep; they thought their Sabbath observance laws were righteous, but they completely missed the point of the Sabbath. The Sabbath was made for man and not man for the Sabbath. They forgot that the Sabbath was a sign, which was supposed to point them toward the need of a greater salvific rest (Hebrews 4:9–10).

They forgot that the Sabbath was to remind them of the fellowship with God that all mankind had forfeited by their disobedience. They forgot that the Sabbath was meant to bring Israel and the nations to repentance and cause them to desire and yearn for a right relationship with the Lord.

Paul's Understanding of the Sabbath: Sabbath Is the Sign and Shadow; Christ Is the Substance

As we now know, Paul would have been aware of these Sabbath regulations and man-made laws because Paul was a Pharisee who was extremely zealous for the traditions of his fathers (Galatians 1:14). So what did Paul think of the Sabbath after his conversion? Did Paul believe that keeping the Sabbath would merit salvation? Did Paul think that keeping the Sabbath would give him right standing before the throne of God? We see Paul answer this in his letter to the Colossians when he addressed whether observing the Sabbath and days or festivals had any salvific merit:

> *Therefore let no one pass judgment on you in questions of food and drink, or **with regard to a festival or a new moon or a Sabbath. These are a shadow of the things to come, but the substance belongs to Christ.** Let no one disqualify you, insisting on asceticism and worship of angels, going on in detail about visions, puffed up without reason by his sensuous mind, and **not holding fast to the Head,** from whom the whole body,*

nourished and knit together through its joints and ligaments, grows with a growth that is from God. If with Christ you died to the elemental spirits of the world, why, as if you were still alive in the world, do you submit to regulations— "Do not handle, Do not taste, Do not touch" (referring to things that all perish as they are used)—according to human precepts and teachings? These have indeed an appearance of wisdom in promoting self-made religion and asceticism and severity to the body, but they are of no value in stopping the indulgence of the flesh.

—Colossians 2:16–22 (emphasis added)

Paul wanted his readers to know that the Sabbath and religious festivals were only a shadow of things that pointed to Christ. The Sabbath is just a shadow, not the substance. Just as when a person is standing in the daylight and the sun casts a shadow, the shadow is not the substance; rather, the person is the substance. Christ is the sum and substance that the Sabbath and all the Sabbath festivals pointed to. The Sabbath was to be a sign that pointed to the reality of Christ.

So how was Christ to be the substance and reality of the Sabbath and Sabbath festivals? Christ is the substance of the Year of Jubilee, which was to be celebrated on the fiftieth year after seven sabbath years. On the Year of Jubilee, the trumpet would sound on the tenth day of the seventh month on the Day of Atonement of the fiftieth year and liberty would be proclaimed throughout the land (Leviticus 25:8–10). All debts and bondages were released, and all prisoners and captives were set free. This was to be a picture of Christ who was the substance of the year of Jubilee. Christ was the one who paid the debt for sin, freed the captives from the punishment and power of sin, and gave liberty to those who were under the wrath of God. Thus, the Year of Jubilee was the shadow, and Christ is the substance.

Christ is the substance of the Day of Atonement, which was to be celebrated on the tenth day of the seventh month. On the Day of Atonement, the high priest would make atonement for the nation of Israel. This day was full of symbolism: The high priest would wash himself, offer a bull as a sin offering for himself and his family, enter the Most Holy Place with the bull's blood, incense, and burning coals from the altar of burnt offering. He would sprinkle the bull's blood on the atonement cover seven times. He would sacrifice one goat as a sin offering for the people and sprinkle the blood on the atonement cover and the Holy Place. He would dispatch a scapegoat to the wilderness, remove his special Day of Atonement clothing, wash again, and put on regular high priest clothing, offer two rams as burn offerings for himself and the people, burn the fat of the sin offering, and have the bull and goat sin offerings carried outside the camp to be burned (Leviticus 16). This was a picture of Christ as the Great High Priest who intercedes and provides a better sacrifice for His people (Hebrews 7:23–25, 10:11–14). This was to be a picture of Christ who is the better sacrifice and who is the Lamb of God who takes away the sin of the world (John 1:29). Christ was the substance of the Day of Atonement; He is the Great High Priest and acts as the Mediator between God and man (1 Timothy 2:5). Christ is the substitutionary propitiation for the sins of His people (1 Corinthians 5:21). Thus, the Day of Atonement was the shadow, and Christ is the substance.

Christ is the substance of the Sabbath. The Sabbath was a day that provided physical rest; yet, it pointed to a better rest. The author of Hebrews shows us this in Hebrews 4:9–11, which says:

> *So then,* ***there remains a Sabbath rest for the people of God****, for whoever has entered God's rest has also rested from his works as God did from his. Let us therefore strive to enter that rest, so that no one may fall by the same sort of disobedience.* (emphasis added)

So who is it that enters this Sabbath rest? Who is it that enters this better rest? The author of Hebrews clarifies this this in Hebrews 4:3:

> ***For we who have believed enter that rest,*** *as he has said, "As I swore in my wrath, 'They shall not enter my rest,'" although his works were finished from the foundation of the world.* (emphasis added)

The better Sabbath rest is for all those who have put their faith in the Lord Jesus Christ. Those who have savingly put their faith in Christ have attained the Sabbath rest. Thus, the Sabbath day was the shadow, and Christ is the substance.

Paul knew of the Pharisees' harsh Sabbath laws, and he knew that these laws had no merit for salvation and justification with God. Paul knew that the Sabbath day and Sabbath festivals were just shadows, but the substance belonged to Christ. No amount of Sabbath observance would give man a right standing with God. Paul knew of the salvific Sabbath rest in Christ that the author of Hebrews spoke of. Paul saw the Sabbath as just a shadow of Christ, but the reality of the meaning and the substance of the Sabbath belonged to Christ. Christ was the true Sabbath rest—the rest from works and the rest for the soul (Matthew 11:28–30). Christ provided the restored relationship between man and God; he provided the means to fellowship, communion, and right standing with the Father; whereas Sabbath law observance could not provide a right relationship with God.

Although Paul would assign no salvific merit to observing the Sabbath, he did note how difficult it would be for new Christians coming out of Judaism not to obey or observe the Sabbath. In Romans 14, Paul admonished the weak and strong believers to bear with one another as they came out of Judaism or a Gentile pagan religion. He commanded them to not pass judgment on one another if their conscience was persuaded to worship God in how they ate or observed special days. In Romans 14, Paul noted that believers' faith would range from weak to strong, so he exhorted them to love one another and not cause each other to sin and to bear with one another in love. He certainly did not advocate the need to abstain from foods or observe days as a means of salvation, but rather, out of a heart devotion and clear conscience before God.

As we close this chapter, note that Paul was reared and steeped in Pharisaic Judaism practiced during the life of Jesus. The Apostle Paul was a Pharisee (Philippians 3:4–6) and studied under one of the most revered rabbis, Gamaliel (Acts 22:3). Paul was zealous for the traditions of his fathers as a Pharisee (Galatians 1:14). Paul would have been familiar with the accounts of Christ healing on the Sabbath; he would have been familiar with Sabbath traditions and the Mishnah. As we examined the Scriptures in this chapter, we learned why Paul put no hope in circumcision or ceremonial washings for salvation. And we saw clearly why the Apostle Paul put no hope in keeping the Sabbath as a means of salvation and why he also put no hope in works for salvation. The Sabbath was and is a sign and shadow. Christ is the substance of the Sabbath.

Chapter 4

The Burnt Offering

He shall lay his hand on the head of the burnt offering, and it shall be accepted for him to make atonement for him.

—Leviticus 1:4

Through . . . Christ Jesus, whom God put forward as a propitiation by his blood, to be received by faith. This was to show God's righteousness, because in his divine forbearance he had passed over former sins.

—Romans 3:25

Thus far we have explored how the Lord used the Abrahamic Covenant sign of circumcision, ceremonial defilement, and the Sabbath to show the Israelites how to worship Him and to express that they needed circumcised hearts, internal spiritual cleansing, and a restored relationship with Him. In this chapter, we will review the burnt offering, which was a foreshadowing of the sacrificial death of Christ.

As we learned earlier, the book of Leviticus was to teach the people that they were sinful and that God was holy. We saw this in Leviticus 11:45 where the Lord told the Israelites, "*I am the Lord, who brought you up out of Egypt to be your God; therefore be holy, because I am holy.*" The Lord was teaching His people that He was separate from everything created and that He was certainly separate from sinful man. The Lord was to be worshipped differently than all the gods of the pagan nations. He was teaching the Israelites that they were sinful and could not approach Him or worship Him on their own terms because He is a holy God. Chapters one through seven of Leviticus help us understand how the offerings were to typologically represent Christ:

- The burnt offering was to represent Christ's atonement and sinless nature (Leviticus 1:3–17, 6:8–13).

- The grain offering was to represent Christ's dedication/consecration and His complete dedication and devotion to the Father's will and purposes (Leviticus 2:1–16, 6:14–23).

- The fellowship offering was to represent Christ's reconciliation/fellowship and the peace He had with God.

- The sin offering was to represent Christ's propitiation for sin and His substitutionary death for sinners (Leviticus 4:1–5:13, 6:24–30).

- The guilt offering was to represent Christ paying the ransom and redemption for sin (Leviticus 5:14–6:7; 7:1–10).

As we examine the burnt offering, it is important to note several aspects of worship that the Lord was teaching His people through this offering. In the New Testament, the Apostle Paul was able to look back at the sacrificial system and make the connections to show how Christ fulfilled the sacrificial system.[33, 34, 35]

The Lord called Moses and spoke to him from the tent of meeting, saying, "Speak to the people of Israel and say to them, When any one of you brings an offering to the Lord, you shall bring your offering of livestock from the herd or from the flock. If his offering is a burnt offering from the herd, he shall offer a male without blemish. He shall bring it to the entrance of the tent of meeting, that he may be accepted before the Lord.

—Leviticus 1:1–3

The *tent of meeting*, tabernacle, was where God would meet with His people and receive worship. That was where the glory of the Lord would rest and dwell or reside among the Israelites (Exodus 25:22). It was the place where the Israelites would come and hear God's commands.

First, we learn that the burnt offering was an offering to the Lord. This was not an offering to Satan, Molech, Dagon, the priests, man, the nation of Israel, or any other false god. This was an offering given directly to the Lord, and this offering needed to please the Lord. It needed to be brought on His terms alone, not on man's terms, for God is a consuming fire (Deuteronomy 9:3). We see in Leviticus 1:13 that when offered on the Lord's terms, *"It is a burnt offering, a food offering, an aroma pleasing to the Lord."* In fact, we see in Amos 5:21–22 that when the worshipper did not bring the burnt offering to God according to His prescribed instruction, He was not pleased with them where He says:

> *"I hate, I despise your feasts, and I take no delight in your solemn assemblies. **Even though you offer me your burnt offerings and grain offerings, I will not accept them**. And the peace offerings of your fattened animals, I will not look upon them."* (emphasis added)

Additionally, we see that when the one offering the gift lived in opposition to God's will and ways, He was not pleased with the offering as He says in Jeremiah 6:20: *"What use to me is frankincense that comes from Sheba, or sweet cane from a distant land? **Your burnt offerings are not acceptable, nor your sacrifices pleasing to me**"* (emphasis added). Here, we can see that offering the burnt offering but living in opposition to God was not what the Lord desired. However, if there was no sacrifice, there was no access to fellowship with God. In fact, the root word for offering is *qarab*, which can also mean "to come near." Thus, to draw near to the

Lord required a sacrifice or offering that was given to the Lord on His terms or prescribed instruction.

Second, we learn that the burnt offering was to be a submissive or domesticated animal from one's own herd. The regulation excluded horses, dogs, pigs, camels, donkeys, lions, and birds of prey, which were used in pagan sacrifices. The burnt offering was to be a sacrifice from one's own cattle, sheep, goats, or non-predatory bird. Only domestic animals could be sacrificed. Only defenseless animals that needed to be defended were brought. Ultimately, this was to be a picture of the humble, submissive sacrifice of the Lord Jesus Christ who did not go to Calvary as a roaring lion, the Lion of the tribe of Judah. Rather this pictured a defenseless animal as in Isaiah 53:7, which describes the Lord's submissive attitude toward unjustly suffering: *"He was oppressed, and he was afflicted, yet he opened not his mouth; like a lamb that is led to the slaughter, and like a sheep that before its shearers is silent, so he opened not his mouth."* Leviticus 1:3 provides this instruction for those presenting burnt offerings: *"If his offering is a burnt offering from the herd, he shall offer a male without blemish. He shall bring it to the entrance of the tent of meeting, that he may be accepted before the* Lord.*"*

Third, note that the burnt offering had to be without blemish or defect. That is, the animal must be of a certain age, and it was not to be blind; injured; maimed; have warts; have festering sores; have running sores; be deformed; be stunted; or have bruised testicles that were crushed, torn, or cut (Leviticus 22:17–33). Worshipers were to pick a sacrifice that was their best as they were taught to give the best and most valuable livestock to the Lord. In fact, Israel would be reminded that offering a blemished animal was an affront and a sin. In the book of Malachi, the Lord confronted the priests and the people for presenting blemished offerings; He denounced this act as dishonoring, despising, and profaning His name (Malachi 1:6–14).

The burnt offering with no blemish foreshadowed Christ. Peter alludes to the spotless lamb in in 1 Peter 1:19 as does Paul in 1 Corinthians 5:7 where he says, *"For Christ, our Passover lamb, has been sacrificed."* Paul saw that Christ was the lamb without blemish who *"knew no sin"* and that the perfect lamb was to be sacrificed for sin. Therefore, the Lord was teaching Israel that the burnt offering was to be spotless and without blemish as it foreshadowed the sinless and perfect nature of the Lord Jesus Christ.

> *He shall lay his hand on the head of the burnt offering, and it shall be accepted for him to make atonement for him.*
>
> —Leviticus 1:4

Fourth, we learn that the burnt offering was to be an acknowledgment of sin. The symbolic gesture of placing one's hand on the head of the animal was to show the transfer of sins from the one sacrificing the animal to the sacrificial animal as cited in Leviticus 1:4: *"He shall lay his hand on the head of the burnt offering, and it shall be accepted for him to make atonement for him."* This symbolic gesture was also meant to bring about repentance. The transferring of sin to the sacrificial animal was to bring about sorrow for sin against the Lord and teach His people that death was the penalty for sin.

Fifth, through the burnt offering, the Lord was teaching that there was to be a substitutionary atonement. This substitutionary sacrifice would prefigure Christ. Isaiah 53:11–12 captures this substitutionary atonement:

> *Out of the anguish of his soul he shall see and be satisfied; by his knowledge shall the righteous one, my servant, make many to be accounted righteous, and he shall bear their iniquities. Therefore, I will divide him a portion with the many, and he shall divide the spoil with the strong, because **he poured out his soul to death and was numbered with the transgressors; yet he bore the sin of many and makes intercession for the transgressors**.* (emphasis added)

The Lord was teaching that sin would be dealt with through a substitutionary atonement that took the punishment for sin. The Lord Jesus Christ, who never committed sin, was to be the substitutionary atonement, an offering for the sin of His people so they could have right standing with God (1 Corinthians 5:21).

Sixth, we learn that the burnt offering was to be an atonement. We learn this in Leviticus 1:4, which says, "*It shall be accepted for him to make atonement for him.*" The word *atonement* comes from *kaphar* and means "to cover over" or "propitiate." This prefigured Christ in that He would ultimately be the once-for-all atonement for sin (Hebrews 7:26–27, 9:24–28). This was to show God's people that there would be a substitutionary atonement that would cover the sacrificer's sin, so God could no longer see it. Isaiah 43:25 expresses this idea of atonement where it says, "*I, **I am he who blots out your transgressions** for my own sake, and I will not remember your sins*" (emphasis added). Isaiah 44:22 also conveys this idea of covering sins where it says, "***I have blotted out your transgressions like a cloud and your sins like mist**; return to me, for I have redeemed you*" (emphasis added). Micah 7:19 captures this as well, mentioning how a substitutionary atonement would cover sin: "*He will again have compassion on us; **he will tread our iniquities underfoot. You will cast all our sins into the depths of the sea***" (emphasis added). David notes the blessedness of one whose sin the Lord does not count against him when he makes this statement in Psalm 32:1–2: "*Blessed is the one **whose transgression is forgiven, whose sin is covered. Blessed is the man against whom the Lord counts no iniquity**, and in whose spirit there is no deceit*" (emphasis added). Paul saw this atonement and the covering of sins, and he identifies Christ as the only propitiation for sinners when he says this in Romans 3:24–25:

> For all have sinned. . . . and are justified by his grace
> as a gift, through the redemption that is in Christ Jesus,
> whom God put forward as a propitiation by his blood,

to be received by faith. This was to show God's right-
eousness, because in his divine forbearance he had passed
over former sins.

Paul saw that the Father had punished His only Son with
the wrath that sinners deserve, and Christ was to be an atonement or propitiation for sin (Romans 8:2-3, Galatians 3:13).

Then he shall kill the bull before the Lord, *and Aaron's*
sons the priests shall bring the blood and throw the blood
against the sides of the altar that is at the entrance of
the tent of meeting. Then he shall flay the burnt offering
and cut it into pieces, and the sons of Aaron the priest
shall put fire on the altar and arrange wood on the fire.
And Aaron's sons the priests shall arrange the pieces, the
head, and the fat, on the wood that is on the fire on the
altar.

—Leviticus 1:5–8

Seventh, we learn that the death of the animal was a vivid
picture of the ugliness of sin. Everything about the sacrifice
was to show how grotesque sin was. The person offering the
sacrifice was to put his hands on the head of the animal and
then slaughter it. He would immediately see the effects of his
sin passed on to the animal. Then he would slit the throat
of the bull and see the ugliness of sin and death; he would
hear the horrific noise of the animal as it would scream in
pain and see blood gush out of the animal and he watched

the animal's life ebb away. The person sacrificing the animal would smell the horrible smell of blood. This was all meant to shock the senses of the person offering the sacrifice; it was a brutal picture of the horrendous nature of sin. The one sacrificing was to picture himself as deserving the animal's fate. This ritual should have left the one sacrificing the offering aghast at his sin; it should have driven a sword straight to the heart of the one sacrificing. It would not be out of line of the one sacrificing to say something like this, "Lord, I see my sin. I see that you cannot look at me or accept me based on any merit. I see that you are angry and abhor my sin. I see that I should be the one slaughtered. I see that I am the one who should have my throat slit. I see that if I were to enter your temple, you would need to strike me dead because I am loathsome, and you are holy." This sacrifice was to be the most graphic picture of the ugliness of sin.

The priest was then to sprinkle the blood against the altar. The one sacrificing the burnt offering would be bloody, and the priest would be bloody. The Lord was showing Israel and the Gentile nations that He was the God that could not tolerate sin. Again, this hearkens us back to Leviticus 11:45, which says, "*So you shall be holy, because I am holy.*" The Lord was showing the sinfulness of man and the holiness of God. In the New Testament, Paul saw the ugliness and devastation of sin. Paul understood that God the Father had but one Son and that He punished His Son with the divine wrath that sinners deserved (Romans 3:25). Paul saw Jesus as the sacrificial Lamb "*whom God put forward as a propitiation by his blood, to be received by faith."*

Eighth, we understand that in the burnt offering the Lord wanted to show that the internal motives, intentions, and will needed to be pure and clean. In Leviticus 1:9, the Lord commanded that the entrails and legs be washed with water: *"but its entrails and its legs he shall wash with water. And the priest shall burn all of it on the altar, as a burnt offering, a food offering with a pleasing aroma to the Lord."* Commentators will vary on the meaning of this; some believe that the entrails and legs needed to be washed with water to ensure there was no excrement that would be put on the altar. However, we have learned that the Lord desires a circumcised heart and a heart that loved Him totally as He says in Deuteronomy 10:12, 16:

> And now, Israel, what does the Lord your God require of you, but to fear the Lord your God, to walk in all his ways, to love him, to serve the Lord your God with all your heart and with all your soul . . . Circumcise therefore the foreskin of your heart, and be no longer stubborn."

The Lord not only wanted a sacrifice that was without blemish, but He was also wanted one that was fully devoted to Him. Of course, this points to Christ. Christ did nothing of His own will and fully submitted to the will of His Father. Jesus's pure devotion to the Father is captured in John 5:19, where it says, *"So Jesus said to them, 'Truly, truly, I say to you, the Son can do nothing of his own accord, but only what he sees the Father doing. For whatever the Father does, that the Son does likewise.'"* The Lord Jesus Christ lived His perfect and sinless life in full and total submission to His Father. Paul talks about this humble submission and pure devotion of Christ when he describes how Christ humbled himself by taking the form of a servant in the likeness of man and becoming obedient to death on a cross (Philippians 2:3–10).

Thus, we see that the Lord desired purity from the inside, and Christ Jesus did this perfectly. He looked not to His own needs, but fully submitted Himself to the will of His Father.

Ninth, we see that the burnt offering was to undergo divine judgment. The fire that burned up the sacrifice represented divine judgment on behalf of the sinner. The person who sacrificed the offering was to see himself as deserving divine judgment. As the perfect, blameless, and spotless sacrifice for sinners, Christ satisfied this requirement. Isaiah 53:10 captures this divine judgment of the suffering servant when it says:

> **Yet it was the will of the Lord to crush him;** *he has put him to grief; when his soul makes an offering for guilt, he shall see his offspring; he shall prolong his days; the will of the Lord shall prosper in his hands.* (emphasis added)

Yes, the Romans beat Jesus, but it wasn't the Romans who crushed Jesus. Yes, the Jewish leaders had Christ crucified, but it wasn't the Jewish leaders who crushed Jesus.

No, God the Father crushed His own Son like the burnt offering and delivered divine judgment on His Son in place of sinners. The Lord was teaching His people and the Gentile nations that a substitutionary sacrifice needed be slaughtered and undergo divine judgment in the place for sinners. Paul talks about this divine judgment in Galatians 3:13 where he says, *"Christ redeemed us from the curse of the law by becoming a curse for us—for it is written, 'Cursed is everyone who is hanged on a tree.'"*

Therefore, we know that Paul understood that when Christ suffered on the cross, He was being cursed as if He was the sinner, though He had done no wrong. Christ was cursed with every curse that had been promised to sinners (Deuteronomy 28:15–68). Every curse pronounced in the Bible was to fall on Jesus upon the cross. The divine curse and punishment that is due to sinners in hell, fell upon the beloved Son of God when the Father showed up in judgment and darkness to take His omnipotent, fiery, and vengeful wrath out on His Son (Matthew 27:45–6).

So how did God the Father treat Christ as a cursed sinner? We get a picture of this if we simply look at what it means to be cursed rather than blessed by examining the Beatitudes in Matthew 5:

- Because Christ became a curse, He was punished as one who is refused entrance into the Kingdom of heaven rather than inheriting the kingdom (Matthew 5:3).

- Because Christ became a curse, He was punished and suffered divine wrath rather than comfort (Matthew 5:4).

- Because Christ became a curse, all the goodness of God was taken away, and He suffered and died under the wrath of God as miserable and wretched rather than being satisfied (Matthew 5:6).

- Because Christ became a curse, He received divine justice and punishment rather than divine mercy (Matthew 5:7). Because Christ became a curse, He was cut off from God as one bearing disgrace rather than being called a Son of God (Matthew 5:9, Psalm 22:1).

Jesus offered himself up as a sinless offering to God the Father so that God the Father could place all the sins of God's people on Jesus and curse Jesus as if He was a vile sinner. Upon that cross, Jesus suffered the wrath of God for His elect (John 10:11). All those in hell are the only ones who have an idea of what Jesus suffered on the cross and know what it is to be cursed by God. It wasn't the nails, the flogging, the crown of thorns, the punching, and beatings that Jesus dreaded. Even in the first century, there were Christians who were killed by being hung on a tree and lit on fire, and they went to their deaths singing hymns of praise to God. Jesus didn't dread the physical beatings. No, it was the full cup of wrath and the righteous anger of God toward sin that Jesus was dreaded (Matthew 26:39). God didn't unload a rifle firing squad on His Son. God didn't unload a nuclear bomb on His Son. God didn't unload the full heat of the sun on His Son. No, God unloaded something far more terrifying than all those combined. God unloaded His full unbridled wrath on His only begotten Son; only the eternal Son of God could take the omnipotent wrath from His Father. Only the Son of God could be presented as a sinless propitiation. Only the eternal Son of God could suffer the eternal punishment we deserve.

The wrath of God that was taken out on Christ was the propitiation and satisfaction that paid for man's sin. Christ, the sacrificial Lamb bore the sins and punishment of His elect on the cross (Isaiah 53). Therefore, we should never forget and always seek to fathom the incomprehensible worth of Jesus Christ's substitutionary work on the cross for sinners. Not only did He suffer the wrath of God for one man, but He has also suffered the wrath of God for the sins of a great multitude of humanity (Revelation 7:9). Paul says in Romans 8:1, "*There is therefore now no condemnation for those who are in Christ Jesus.*" Why is there no condemnation for those in Christ? Because for those in Christ, the Lord Jesus took the condemnation and punishment for sinners. Every drop of wrath for those whom the Son of God died was satisfied and placated at Calvary. There is not one drop of wrath left for those in Christ Jesus. The wrathful cannon of God has been unloaded and emptied on the Son of God who loved us and gave Himself up for us (Galatians 2:20).

Finally, we see that when the burnt offering is offered up to the Lord on His terms, it is an aroma pleasing to Him. As we noted earlier, atonement was used to talk about the Lord making a covering for sin. In the Septuagint, the word *atonement* is translated as *propitiation*, which is an offering by which the wrath of a deity had been appeased.

Therefore, the burnt offering allowed the Lord to be satisfied because the worshipper had selected an animal without defect to be sacrificed to Him, and the worshiper had acknowledged that their sin was so vile and loathsome that it deserved to be punished by death and divine judgment. Therefore, the Lord's wrath was propitiated, and the offering that was a food offering was a pleasing aroma to the Lord.

Therefore, we can be certain that Paul knew of Christ's substitutionary atonement for sinners by taking the wrath of God in the place of sinners. Paul saw that Christ was the fulfillment of the Levitical sacrificial system as he says in 1 Corinthians 5:7: "*For Christ, our Passover lamb, has been sacrificed.*" Paul saw that animals were sacrificed in the morning and evening every day. Paul had most likely seen the mass sacrifice of animals in Jerusalem during Passover, which could range in the tens of thousands to hundreds of thousands. But Paul saw Christ as the sacrificial, once for all, Passover Lamb.

As we close this chapter, let's remember how the burnt offering foreshadowed Christ's substitutionary work for sinners. The burnt offering, the grain offering, the fellowship offering, the sin offering, and the guilt offering were meant to symbolize the person and work of Christ's sacrificial work on the behalf of sinners. While the Levitical sacrificial system was meant to foreshadow Christ, the sacrifices themselves never made one right with the Lord. The sacrificial system was meant to foreshadow Christ and help the one sacrificing understand the nature of their sin, and the need for a circumcised heart and right relationship with the Lord. Would Paul ever put hope in a burnt offering? Did Paul see the Levitical sacrificial system as a means to attain merit and right standing with God? Or rather, did Paul see Christ as the sacrificial substitutionary propitiation, which satisfied the wrath of God? The answer is clear: The blood of bulls and goats never gave right standing with God (Hebrews 10:4). However, we see that Christ's sacrifice gives sinners access to the holy place by His own blood (Hebrews 10:19). As we studied the burnt offering, we clearly saw that Paul understood how Christ fulfilled the sacrificial system. He saw Christ as the perfect Passover Lamb who knew no sin but became sin for His elect. The burnt offering was the shadow, and Christ is the substance.

Part 2

The Apostle Paul's Conversion

Chapter 5

Paul's Conversion

In this chapter, we'll cover the Apostle Paul's conversion. The point in writing about Paul's conversion is not to give the most exhaustive and detailed account of his conversion, but to highlight his conversion and response to the gospel. Jesus would often give gospel invitations or gospel calls to come to Him and follow Him. The emphasis that I'll highlight in this chapter is that Paul responded to the gospel call or invitation that Jesus had so often given. As we'll see in subsequent chapters, Paul gave the same gospel invitations to his audience that the Lord Jesus Christ gave. The call, of course, was for repentance toward God and faith in the Lord Jesus Christ (Acts 20:21).

Paul was an apostle of the Lord Jesus Christ, and the Lord used him mightily to spread the gospel in the early church. He penned thirteen books in the New Testament, including the book of Romans, which contains what some believe is the most thorough systematic theology of the New

Testament. Paul was a Jew by birth, a Pharisee by conviction, a Roman by citizenship, but he became a Christian by grace. He was a missionary, theologian, evangelist, pastor, teacher, preacher, leader, and more. Paul preached the gospel (1 Corinthians 9:16), loved the nation Israel and the Jewish people (Romans 9:3), suffered much persecution for Christ (2 Corinthians 11:23–27), loved the people of God (Philippians 1:8), and was fierce toward false teachers (Galatians 1:8–9). But most importantly, Paul loved the Lord Jesus Christ (1 Corinthians 16:22). One of the most wonderful verses that he penned is in Galatians 2:20 where he affirms how he was able to live such a fruitful and faithful life in Christ:

> *I have been crucified with Christ. It is no longer I who live, but Christ who lives in me. And the life I now live in the flesh I live by faith in the Son of God, who loved me and gave himself for me.*

In Paul's conversion account, I've put together the external accounts of his conversion from Acts 9, 22, and 26 as well as the internal conversion account from Philippians 3 and Romans 7:7–11. I suspect that some theologians would disagree in how Romans 7 is used regarding Paul's internal conversion account. However, the Romans 7:7–11 account delineates a time where he saw his personal sin differently than he did in his pre-conversion life; therefore, I believe we'll see how relevant this portion of Scripture is in his conversion account. We'll start by simply giving Paul's conversion account without any commentary; then we'll break down the conversion account into smaller sections and analyze it.

Paul's Conversion Story

Note: To allow Paul's story to flow as a narrative, I omitted quotation marks in this section and simply used parenthetical Scripture citations for each source. All Scripture text is taken from the English Standard Version.

Paul's Upbringing, Education, and Persecution of Christians

I am a Jew, born in Tarsus in Cilicia, but brought up in this city, educated at the feet of Gamaliel according to the strict manner of the law of our fathers, being zealous for God as all of you are this day (Acts 22:3). My manner of life from my youth, spent from the beginning among my own nation and in Jerusalem, is known by all Jews. They have known for a long time, if they are willing to testify, that according to the strictest party of our religion I have lived as a Pharisee (Acts 26:4–5). I myself was convinced that I ought to do many things in opposing the name of Jesus of Nazareth. And I did so in Jerusalem. I not only locked up many of the saints in prison after receiving authority from the chief priests, but when they were put to death I cast my vote against them. And I punished them often in all the synagogues and tried to make them blaspheme, and in raging fury against them

I persecuted them even to foreign cities (Acts 26:9–11).
I persecuted this Way to the death, binding and delivering to prison both men and women, as the high priest
and the whole council of elders can bear me witness.
From them I received letters to the brothers, and I journeyed toward Damascus to take those also who were there
and bring them in bonds to Jerusalem to be punished
(Acts 22:4–5). In this connection I journeyed to Damascus with the authority and commission of the chief priests
(Acts 26:12).

Paul's Encounter with the Risen Lord

As I was on my way and drew near to Damascus, about
noon a great light from heaven, . . . brighter than the sun,
that suddenly shone around me and those who journeyed
with me (Acts 22:6, 26:13). And when we had all fallen
to the ground, I heard a voice saying to me in the Hebrew
language, "Saul, Saul, why are you persecuting me? It is
hard for you to kick against the goads." (Acts 26:14). And I
answered, "Who are you, Lord?" And he said to me, "I am
Jesus of Nazareth, whom you are persecuting. But rise and
stand upon your feet, for I have appeared to you for this purpose, to appoint you as a servant and witness to the things in
which you have seen me and to those in which I will appear
to you, delivering you from your people and from the Gentiles—to whom I am sending you to open their eyes, so that
they may turn from darkness to light and from the power

of Satan to God, that they may receive forgiveness of sins and a place among those who are sanctified by faith in me." (Acts 22:8, 26:15–18). The men who were traveling with me stood speechless, hearing the voice but seeing no one (Acts 9:7). Now those who were with me saw the light but did not understand the voice of the one who was speaking to me. And I said, "What shall I do, Lord?" And the Lord said to me, "Rise, and go into Damascus, and there you will be told all that is appointed for you to do." And since I could not see because of the brightness of that light, I was led by the hand by those who were with me, and came into Damascus and for three days I was without sight and neither ate nor drank" (Acts 9:8–9, 22:9–11).

Paul's Internal Dialogue While Awaiting Ananias

"And I thought, 'What then shall we say? That the law is sin? By no means! Yet if it had not been for the law, I would not have known sin. For I would not have known what it is to covet if the law had not said, "You shall not covet." But sin, seizing an opportunity through the commandment, produced in me all kinds of covetousness. For apart from the law, sin lies dead. I was once alive apart from the law, but when the commandment came, sin came alive and I died. The very commandment that promised life proved to be death to me. For sin, seizing an opportunity through the commandment, deceived me and through it killed me. It was sin, producing death in me through what is good, in order that sin might be shown to be sin, and through the commandment might become sinful beyond measure'" (Romans 7:7–11, 13).

Paul's Encounter with Ananias

Now there was a disciple at Damascus named Ananias. The Lord said to him in a vision, "Ananias." And he said, "Here I am, Lord." And the Lord said to him, "Rise and go to the street called Straight, and at the house of Judas look for a man of Tarsus named Saul, for behold, he is praying, and he has seen in a vision a man named Ananias come in and lay his hands on him so that he might regain his sight." But Ananias answered, "Lord, I have heard from many about this man, how much evil he has done to your saints at Jerusalem. And here he has authority from the chief priests to bind all who call on your name." But the Lord said to him, "Go, for he is a chosen instrument of mine to carry my name before the Gentiles and kings and the children of Israel. For I will show him how much he must suffer for the sake of my name." So Ananias departed and entered the house. And laying his hands on me he said, "Brother Saul, the Lord Jesus who appeared to you on the road by which you came has sent me so that you may regain your sight and be filled with the Holy Spirit." (Acts 9:8–17). And one Ananias, a devout man according to the law, well spoken of by all the Jews who lived there, came to me, and standing by me said to me, "Brother Saul, receive your sight." And at that very hour I received my sight and saw him (Acts 22:12–13). And immediately something like scales fell from my eyes, and I regained my sight (Acts 9:18). And he said, "The God of our fathers appointed you to know his will, to see the Righteous One and to hear a voice from his mouth; for you will be a witness for him to everyone of what you have seen and heard. And now why do you wait? Rise and be baptized and wash away your sins, calling on his name" (Acts 22:14–16).

Paul's Internal Dialogue and Moment of Conversion

And then I thought about righteousness through the flesh and the law versus the righteousness of Christ and I thought to myself, circumcised on the eighth day, of the people of Israel, of the tribe of Benjamin, a Hebrew of Hebrews; as to the law, a Pharisee; as to zeal, a persecutor of the church; as to righteousness under the law, blameless. But whatever gain I had, I counted as loss for the sake of Christ. Indeed, I count everything as loss because of the surpassing worth of knowing Christ Jesus my Lord. For his sake I have suffered the loss of all things and count them as rubbish, in order that I may gain Christ and be found in him, not having a right-eousness of my own that comes from the law, but that which comes through faith in Christ, the righteousness from God that depends on faith" (Philippians 3:5–9). Then I rose and was baptized and I called on the name of the Lord (Acts 9:18, Acts 22:16, Romans 10:13).

Analysis of Paul's Conversion

Analysis of Paul's Upbringing, Education, and Persecution

> *I am a Jew, born in Tarsus in Cilicia, but brought up in this city, educated at the feet of Gamaliel according to the strict manner of the law of our fathers, being zealous for God as all of you are this day.*

> —Acts 22:3

Paul was born a Jew in Tarsus, a city of Asia Minor on the Syrian border, which would be modern-day Syria and Turkey. During this time, Tarsus was a distinguished city controlled by Rome; it had a distinguished university. Thus, although Paul had Jewish parents, he would have also had Roman citizenship since he was born in a Roman-controlled area.

It is important to note that Paul was born in Tarsus in Cilicia because Tarsus was an important trade city, and that brought many travelers, and thus, many false religions into the city. False religions in Tarsus included Mithraism, the cult of Hercules, the cult of Zoroastrianism, the cult of Cybele, the cult of Manichaeism, the cult of Isis, and the cult of Sandan. False religion was ubiquitous in this region at this time. So why is that important? It's important because it shows that though Paul may have been exposed to false religions, he didn't pursue them but was faithful to Judaism. Not only this, but this is a testimony to Paul's parents in that though they were surrounded by false religion, they still had an influence on Paul to remain in the Jewish religion, and they eventually brought him to Jerusalem to be educated under one of the most revered rabbis. Therefore, when Paul says he was born in Tarsus in Cilicia, this testifies to the devoutness that he and his family maintained amongst a panoply of false religion.

It is hard to determine how long Paul lived in Tarsus, but we know that at some point, he was moved to Jerusalem and was brought up there. The word used for *brought up* is *anatethrammenos* with the root word being *anatrephó*, which means to "rear," "bring up," "nourish," or "educate," and is used in the sense of "forming the mind." As we learned in Chapter 3, a pious Jewish father would take great care in teaching his son or sons the Bible. Regular instruction would begin at the age of five to six years of age at which time, the child would primarily learn the Bible. At ages ten to fifteen, the child was to learn the Mishnah, or traditional law. After this, the child would enter theological discussions, which occupied time and attention in the higher academies of the rabbis. Although it's not clear when Paul moved to Jerusalem, we know that his upbringing would have included instruction in the Bible as well as the Mishnah and Gemara according to Jewish culture.

Additionally, when Paul moved to Jerusalem, he was taught under Gamaliel. Scripture helps us see how Gamaliel, a Pharisee, was honored amongst the Jews where it says this in Acts 5:34: *"But a Pharisee named Gamaliel, a teacher of the*

law, who was honored by all the people, stood up in the Sanhe-
drin and ordered that the men be put outside for a little while"
(NIV). Gamaliel wasn't just honored by the people, he was
honored by the Sanhedrin, which was the Jewish ruling
council in Jerusalem. In fact, Gamaliel was so honored that
he was able to speak to the Sanhedrin and persuade them not
to put the apostles to death (Acts 5:33). Therefore, we know
that Paul studied under one of the most revered teachers,
Gamaliel. We can also safely assume that Gamaliel was not
only learned in Scripture, but also the Mishnah and Gemara,
which contained the handwashing regulations, Mikvah regulations, Sabbath regulations, and more. We can also surmise
that Paul's education in Judaism would have been some of
the best Jewish instruction during his time.

Paul was educated in the strict manner of the law of
the Jewish fathers. The word for *strict manner* comes from
akribeia, which means "strictness," "accuracy," "exactness,"
"attention to detail," or "scrupulousness." It is a strong and
precise word, indicating that his instruction would have
been right in line with Pharisaic Judaism as he was a Pharisee
(Philippians 3:5). In other words, he would have been well
acquainted with ceremonial washings. He would know, for
example, that ceremonial handwashing required a minimum
of a quarter of a log of water that was to be poured over the
hands. He knew that less than a log of water was not suffi-
cient for ceremonially washing hands. He knew that only
vessels closely covered with a lid could be used for ceremonial
handwashing. He knew that if one poured the first and the

second water over the hands beyond the joint and they flowed back to the hands, the hands remain uncleaned. Paul knew the mikvah or ritual bath laws and regulations, and he knew how to ceremonially wash dishes, utensils, and mattresses. Paul knew that you shouldn't carry enough ink to write more than two letters on the Sabbath; he also knew that you could not carry a cow's mouthful of straw or a camel's mouthful of bean stalks, or you were in violation of the Sabbath. He studied Scripture as well as the oral laws and traditions of the Pharisees. In fact, we see that he said that he was a *zealot*, meaning he pursued all this instruction and education with wholehearted devotion and enthusiasm. Because Paul was raised as a Jew and studied under one of the most prominent teachers, he was zealous for the laws of the fathers. Paul was not ignorant of what the Pharisees taught. Not at all. He was raised by devoted Jews, studied under the best Jewish rabbis, studied under Pharisees, became a Pharisee, and was a zealot for Pharisaic Judaism.

> *My manner of life from my youth, spent from the beginning among my own nation and in Jerusalem, is known by all Jews. They have known for a long time, if they are willing to testify, that according to the strictest party of our religion I have lived as a Pharisee.*
>
> —Acts 26:4–5

Paul also testified that he was not some rebel Egyptian or that he came from a pagan culture or religion. Rather, his youth was spent learning Scripture and the Pharisaic traditions and oral laws. In fact, his reputation was so well-known that he was willing to have other Jews and religious leaders testify to his zealous devotion to Pharisaic Judaism (Acts 26:5). Paul was not a novice in Pharisaic Judaism. Paul wasn't studying Pharisaic Judaism in some corner where no one knew him. Rather, Paul gives an account of how much he was advancing in Judaism: "*And I was advancing in Judaism beyond many of my own age among my people, so extremely zealous was I for the traditions of my fathers*" (Galatians 1:14). We clearly see that Paul didn't just blend in with his study of Judaism. No, he was a standout student who was on fire for the traditions of his fathers. The word *extremely* comes from *perissós*, which means "greatly," "exceedingly," "abundantly," or "vehemently." Paul didn't take his instruction lightly. On the contrary, he was boiling over in zealousness for Pharisaic Judaism. He loved to learn of the Sabbath regulations. He loved to learn of the handwashing regulations. He most likely held to a Pharisaic understanding of circumcision in salvation as he recalls being circumcised on the eighth day (Philippians 3:5). It's also important to note that Paul says that he "*lived as a Pharisee*" in Acts 26:5. Being a Pharisee wasn't a part-time job or a side hustle or something he did for fun. Not at all! Paul's life, which included his thinking, reasoning, logic, will, motivation, and purpose, was given to being a Pharisee. Paul was a hard-nosed, card-carrying, zealous Pharisee who had advanced in Judaism.

I myself was convinced that I ought to do many things in opposing the name of Jesus of Nazareth. And I did so in Jerusalem. I not only locked up many of the saints in prison after receiving authority from the chief priests, but when they were put to death I cast my vote against them. And I punished them often in all the synagogues and tried to make them blaspheme, and in raging fury against them I persecuted them even to foreign cities.

—Acts 26:9–11

Since Paul was a Pharisee, he was under the influence of the Pharisaic group who strongly opposed and rejected Jesus. It is not clear whether Paul ever heard Jesus speak or saw Him personally, but it is clear that Paul would know truths about Jesus strictly through Christ's discussions, teachings, and altercations with the Pharisees. We can know this because we read that the news about Christ was spreading from Syria, Galilee and the Decapolis, Jerusalem, Judea, and beyond the Jordan (Matthew 4:24–25). Jesus's ministry wasn't private or unknown. No, the news of his ministry was well-known as Paul said to Festus and King Agrippa that Christ's ministry has not been done in a corner (Acts 26:26). For a reminder of Jesus's teachings, ministry, claims, and miracles that the Pharisees rejected, see "Ceremonial Washings During the Life and Times of Paul" in Chapter 2. That section documents the Pharisees' constant, deliberate, and intentional rejection of Christ. Paul was a Pharisee who was influenced by other Pharisees who ultimately had Christ crucified.

The Pharisees were in direct confrontation with Jesus, and they were steadfast in their opposition. Not only were they in opposition with Jesus, but they also sought to scare and intimidate others into rejecting Christ (John 9:22, 12:42). Not only were the Pharisees against Jesus, but Jesus was against the Pharisees and their corrupt religion that damned the souls of men (Matthew 23:13). Jesus denounced them for their burdensome regulations (Matthew 23:4), self-righteousness (Matthew 23:5), and love of praise and recognition from men (Matthew 23:5–7). Jesus called them "hypocrites" or "false teachers" (Matthew 23:13), and He called their religion "damning and false" (Matthew 23:15). Jesus called them "blind guides" (Matthew 15:14, 23:16) and "blind fools" (Matthew 23:17). Jesus declared that they were defiled (Matthew 23:25-26). Jesus denounced them for their external religion and spiritual deadness (Matthew 23:27–28). Jesus called them "serpents" (Matthew 23:33) and pronounced condemnation on them (Matthew 23:33). Jesus denounced the scribes for misinterpreting Scripture (Luke 11:52). There was a great confrontation between the false teaching Pharisees and Jesus. Paul would have been heavily influenced by the Pharisaic sect that viewed Jesus as a false Messiah. Thus, he was wrongly convinced that opposing Jesus and His teaching was the right thing to do.

Although Jesus did many miracles and taught with authority that substantiated His claim to be God and the Messiah, the Pharisees had clearly rejected His works and words. Not only did the Pharisees reject Jesus, but they also opposed Him, sought to kill Him, and eventually killed Him.

Therefore, Paul believed he was doing a service to God by attacking the disciples and followers of Christ. We clearly see that Paul approved of the stoning of Stephen when Stephen gave his speech to the council and High Priest. Stephen accused the Jewish leaders of being uncircumcised in heart and ears, and Paul approved of the stoning of Stephen (Acts 7:51, 8:1). In fact, in the original language, *put to death* is written in the present tense and participle mood, which means the saints were continually being put to death and killed. And Paul was continually giving his approval to putting them to death; Paul was a Christian-killing Pharisaic zealot.

Not only was Paul putting Christians to death, but we read in Acts 8:3 that "*Saul was ravaging the church, and entering house after house, he dragged off men and women and committed them to prison.*" The word *ravaging* comes from the word *lumainomai*, which means "maltreat," "corrupt," "defile," "treat shamefully," "devastate," and "ruin." Paul wasn't just forcefully debating Christians; he was violently seeking to throw them into prison and persecute them. This is what Paul was speaking of when he told Timothy of his previous violent way of life in 1 Timothy 1:13: "*Formerly I was a blasphemer, persecutor, and insolent opponent.*" Paul was a ravaging, persecuting, Christian-killing Pharisaic zealot.

Paul even went into synagogues to look for followers of Christ, and wherever Christ was preached, he tried to compel followers to blaspheme Christ. He wasn't just taking them and putting them in prison. No, he was also trying to get them to curse, mock, and deny their faith in Christ publicly in the synagogues. It would be in the realm of possibility that he not only tried to get them to blaspheme against the Lord, but also to become an apostate to the Christian faith under the threat of persecution and death. All this he did in *raging fury*, which comes from *emmainomai*, which can mean "to act madly" or "to act in deranged fury." Paul was aggressive and violent for the cause of Pharisaic Judaism, and he went to great lengths in Jerusalem, synagogues, and foreign cities to persecute the church and destroy the Lord's people.

> *I persecuted this Way to the death, binding and delivering to prison both men and women, as the high priest and the whole council of elders can bear me witness. From them I received letters to the brothers, and I journeyed toward Damascus to take those also who were there and bring them in bonds to Jerusalem to be punished.*
>
> —Acts 22:4–5

> *In this connection I journeyed to Damascus with the authority and commission of the chief priests.*
>
> —Acts 26:12

We've come to understand that the Pharisees hated Jesus; the Sanhedrin hated Jesus (Acts 4–7), the high priest hated Jesus (Acts 4–7); and Paul hated Jesus and the church. The rulers and teachers of Jerusalem had put Jesus to death, and they were set on persecuting and killing the Lord's people. Therefore, the council of elders provided letters to Paul, so he could bring Christians back to Jerusalem and punish them. These were essentially extradition papers that he would give to Jewish brethren, which would allow him to bring the Christians back to be imprisoned and persecuted. He's essentially saying that his Pharisaic zeal for Judaism was very well-known within the ruling class of the Jews. His next stop was to Damascus to continue his persecution.

Analysis of Paul's Encounter with the Risen Lord

> *As I was on my way and drew near to Damascus, about noon a great light from heaven . . . brighter than the sun, that shone around me and those who journeyed with me.*
>
> —Acts 22:6, 26:13

> *And when we had all fallen to the ground, I heard a voice saying to me in the Hebrew language, "Saul, Saul, why are you persecuting me? It is hard for you to kick against the goads."*
>
> —Acts 26:14

> *And I answered, "Who are you, Lord?"' And he said to me, "I am Jesus of Nazareth, whom you are persecuting. . . . But rise and stand upon your feet, for I have appeared to you for this purpose, to appoint you as a*

servant and witness to the things in which you have seen me and to those in which I will appear to you, delivering you from your people and from the Gentiles—to whom I am sending you to open their eyes, so that they may turn from darkness to light and from the power of Satan to God, that they may receive forgiveness of sins and a place among those who are sanctified by faith in me."

—Acts 22:8, 26:16–18

As Paul was on his way to Damascus, the Lord stopped him in his tracks when He appeared to him in a light, which appeared from heaven that was brighter than the sun. In his first letter to Timothy, it seems appropriate for Paul to tell him about this light that was brighter than the sun:

He who is the blessed and only Sovereign, the King of kings and Lord of lords, who alone has immortality, **who dwells in unapproachable light,** *who no one has ever seen or can see. To him be honor and eternal dominion. Amen.*

—1 Timothy 6:15–16 (emphasis added)

If there was anyone who could describe the bright shining unapproachable light of the Lord, it would be Paul. On the road to Damascus, he was surrounded by the light and heard the Lord speak to him in Hebrew.

The voice asked Paul, *"Why are you persecuting me?"* and then stated, *"It is hard for you to kick against the goads."* Here the Lord is confronting Paul with his sin. Paul's actions of persecuting the church are directly tied to persecuting the Lord. When Paul is attacking Christians, he is attacking Christ. This would not be a new concept for Paul. To harm the Lord's people is the same as harming the Lord. Paul could have easily remembered Zechariah 2:8 where it says, *"For thus said the LORD of hosts, after his glory sent me to the nations who plundered you, **for he who touches you touches the apple of his eye**."* (emphasis added). The apple of one's eye is a very sensitive part of the eye. It can be easily damaged and is vulnerable. Paul would most likely know this verse, and he would certainly know that harming one of the Lord's people was to harm and attack the Lord.

The Lord's people are near and dear to Him, and He watches over them zealously. Paul would have known that persecuting the Lord's people was a serious sin and an affront to the Lord. The Lord is confronting Paul with his sin! The Lord is charging Paul with persecuting and killing His people, which is the equivalent of engaging in warfare against the Lord.

The Lord tells Paul that it is hard to kick against the goads, which means Paul's efforts are futile and only harming himself. A goad is a long stick that has long nails on one end. When the ox began to kick, the farmer would take the stick and hold it behind ox's heel in the yoke. Then when the ox would kick, it would ram its heel right up against the nails. This would teach the ox to stop kicking and submit to its master. If an ox would kick against the goad, it wouldn't hurt the goad, but it would hurt the ox. While Paul was persecuting the church and trying to get the disciples and followers of Christ to recant, it was not proving successful. The only thing that was happening was that the gospel was spreading to all nations, and the Lord's people would not recant. No matter what he did, he saw that the followers of Christ would not blaspheme or recant their faith in Christ. Paul was fighting a losing battle against Christ; that is how Paul was kicking against the goads.

The Lord tells Paul that he would be God's chosen servant and witness for Him to the Jews and to the Gentiles. Paul would be used as a witness for the Lord to turn people from the kingdom of darkness to the kingdom of light and to receive forgiveness of sins through faith in Him. What the Lord told Paul about turning people from darkness to light and from the power of Satan to God sounds like Paul's statement in Colossians 1:13–14 where he says, *"He has delivered us from the domain of darkness and transferred us to the kingdom of his beloved Son, in whom we have redemption, the forgiveness of sins."* Paul was going from being an adversary of Christ to being an ambassador of Christ; he was going to go from a servant of Satan to being a servant of the Savior. Paul's gospel ministry, which he had been given by the Lord, was going to bring deliverance to God's people. The Lord had set Paul apart for this gospel ministry in his mother's womb (Galatians 1:15–16).

Not only was Paul made aware of this foreordained plan for his life, but he also saw how mankind was to be reconciled to Christ. The Lord had just explained that mankind would be transferred from the kingdom of darkness to the kingdom of light and receive forgiveness of sins through faith in Him (Acts 26:18). Previously, this would have been absolutely devastating for Paul. As a Pharisee, Paul had been told that Jesus's body had been stolen from the tomb by His disciples, but now, Jesus was alive and confronting him with his sin (Matthew 28:11–15). Paul had been told that Jesus did not rise from the dead—that He was a false Messiah who deserved to be mocked and crucified, but now this Jesus of Nazareth had confronted Paul (Matthew 27:27–31).

Paul may have heard about Peter's message at Pentecost in which Peter proved they were in the last days (Acts 2:17); that the last days included divine judgment, wrath, and deliverance (Acts 2:19– 21); that Jesus's person and work were consistent with that of the Messiah (Acts 2:23); that the Jews were guilty of crucifying the Messiah (Acts 2:23); that God the Father raised Christ from the dead (Acts 2:24, 27, 31); that Jesus was the ascended Messiah (Acts 2:32–33); that Jesus was glorified (Acts 2:33); that Jesus was the baptizer with the Holy Spirit (Acts 2:33); that Jesus was the Christ and Lord over all authorities and equal with the Father (Acts 2:34–35); that the Jewish audience had murdered the Lord Jesus Christ (Acts 2:36); and that they needed to repent and be baptized, or rather, repent and solely identify with Jesus

Christ as Lord and Savior for the forgiveness of their sins (Acts 2:38).

Paul would have recalled the message that was preached by Peter after he healed the lame beggar and preached to the rulers and elders where Peter proclaimed that Jesus was raised from the dead by God, was the chief cornerstone that the builders had rejected, and that there was no other name given under heaven by which men must be saved (Acts 4:1–12). Paul would have remembered that Jesus was the reason why many were being healed in Jerusalem (Acts 5:12–16). Paul would have remembered Peter explaining again that God had raised Jesus from the dead and was exalted as Lord and Savior and the ruling council were the ones who had put Jesus to death (Acts 5:17–32). Paul had heard much of the life, death, and resurrection of Jesus, and now he was face-to-face with Jesus whom he had heard about. He realized that the Jesus that the apostles were preaching was the resurrected and ascended Messiah. He now realized that he had been wrong; Paul's world had just come crashing down by the visitation of the resurrected Lord and Messiah, Jesus Christ of Nazareth.

Finally, we see that forgiveness of sins comes through faith in Christ (Acts 26:18), not through physical circumcision. Forgiveness of sins would not come through a ceremonial, sacramental, ritual washing with water, or Sabbath law observance. Forgiveness of sins would not come through another burnt offering of cattle, sheep, goats, or birds. No, forgiveness of sins would come through faith in the Lord Jesus Christ.

The men who were traveling with me stood speechless, hearing the voice but seeing no one. . . . Now those who were with me saw the light but did not understand the voice of the one who was speaking to me. And I said, 'What shall I do, Lord?' And the Lord said to me, 'Rise, and go into Damascus, and there you will be told all that is appointed for you to do.' And since I could not see because of the brightness of that light, I was led by the hand by those who were with me, and came into Damascus. . . . And for three days he was without sight, and neither ate nor drank.

—Acts 9:7, 22:9–11, 9:9

The men around Paul had seen the light but did not understand the voice that had spoken to Paul. Therefore, they were unable to discern what had just taken place. Many theologians would argue that Paul had just been saved on the Damascus road as he takes direction from Christ and calls Jesus "Lord." Though it's true that Paul took the Lord's direction, we'll see that Scripture gives us the strongest indication that Paul's conversion occurs later after his discussion with Ananias. Although Paul had met the risen Christ, at this point, he was being led by the Lord. His next instructions were to go to Damascus and wait. He was unable to see due to the light. Therefore, those that were with him led him into Damascus.

We are told that Paul neither ate nor drank for three days. In other words, Paul was fasting. Biblical fasting was often tied to sorrow or lamentation. For example, when the plague of locusts came, the prophet Joel called for a holy fast, saying, "*Consecrate a fast; call a solemn assembly. Gather the elders and all the inhabitants of the land to the house of the Lord your God, and cry out to the Lord.*" Another example in which fasting is tied to sorrow or lamentation occurs when Nehemiah heard that the wall of Jerusalem was broken and that its gates had been destroyed by fire: "*As soon as I heard these words I sat down and wept and mourned for days, and I continued fasting and praying before the God of heaven*" (Nehemiah 1:4). One more example of sorrowful fasting is after David had committed adultery and killed Uriah. The Lord had said that the child conceived from David's and Bathsheba's adultery would die. The Lord afflicted David's child, and it says this about David's response: "*David therefore sought God on behalf of the child. And David fasted and went in and lay all night on the ground*" (2 Samuel 12:16). Therefore, we can strongly surmise that Paul not eating or drinking for three days was a fast out of repentance, sorrow, and lamentation. He was grasping the depth of his sin. Later we learn that he was praying, which would support the notion that he was sorrowful, repentant, and lamenting over what he had done. Paul fasted for three days, and this is where we will transition to Romans 7:7–11, 13.

Analysis of Paul's Internal Dialogue While Awaiting Ananias

What then shall we say? That the law is sin? By no means! Yet if it had not been for the law, I would not have known sin. For I would not have known what it is to covet if the law had not said, "You shall not covet." But sin, seizing an opportunity through the commandment, produced in me all kinds of covetousness. For apart from the law, sin lies dead. I was once alive apart from the law, but when the commandment came, sin came alive and I died. The very commandment that promised life proved to be death to me. For sin, seizing an opportunity through the commandment, deceived me and through it killed me. . . . It was sin, producing death in me through what is good, in order that sin might be shown to be sin, and through the commandment might become sinful beyond measure.

—Romans 7:7–11, 13

At this point, I am inserting Paul's internal dialogue from Romans 7 where he contemplates the law and sin. Although I'm sure some theologians will disagree with me, I believe that this was a time when Paul was reflecting on the law, his righteousness, and his personal sin. The man who thought he was doing the work of God was fighting against God. The man who thought he was righteous now sees his unrighteousness by attacking Christ and his people. The man who was zealous for God now sees that he was zealous for blaspheming God. Once Paul had met the risen Christ on the road to Damascus, the veil was taken off. Paul no longer saw his righteousness, but rather, his filth and personal sin against the living God. This is why I'm inserting Romans 7:7–11, 13 into Paul's conversion analysis.

In Romans 7:7–11, 13, Paul gives four accounts of how his sin killed him. In three of these accounts, Paul includes a pre-conversion account of his view of the law and his sin and then a post-conversion account of his view of the law and his sin. Paul's dialogue begins with a reflection on the law in verse 7. He understands that the law is good. This is true because the law reflects the nature and character of God. However, he starts to see that the law didn't produce righteousness within him, but rather, it made his sin known to him. When he reflected on the tenth commandment something changed. Paul looked at the law of coveting and saw that he was full of covetousness (Romans 7:8). Up until this point he was self-righteous and "*was alive*" and had not yet seen his sin. However, at some point, Paul's view changed. Rather than keeping the commandment, he states that "*I died*" (Romans 7:9). It was as if the sin came alive and plunged a knife in his heart and Paul felt every inch of the blade of sin kill him. His self-righteousness died. His pride died. His self-reliance died. Paul suffered a catastrophic and fatal heart wound when he came face-to-face with the law.

Again, in Romans 7:10, Paul had a pre-conversion, self-righteous view of himself where he thought the commandment promised life. However, in this same verse he states again that it *"proved to be death to me"* (Romans 7:10). Paul reinforces the death blow that was delivered when he was confronted with his sin. As we mentioned earlier, the burnt offering and the slaughtering of the cattle was to picture the grotesque nature of sin. Paul would surely have experienced this same feeling. The law had done the exact same thing to him. The law exposed his sin, and it is almost as if Paul was the ox that was slaughtered—the one whose throat was cut by sin. All Paul's righteousness dissolved, and sin came alive and killed him.

Again, Paul emphasizes the shock he went through in verse 11. Although he had thought he was keeping the commandment, he had been deceived. In fact, the word for deceived comes from *exapataó*, which means "deceive thoroughly," "deceived into illusion." The external commandment seemed like something he could keep, but when he grasped the true intent and requirement of the commandment, it killed him. Not only was he completely deceived by thinking he was keeping the commandment, but once he realized he was deceived, it was as if the commandment suddenly came to life out of nowhere and killed him. Thus, he says the commandment *"deceived me and through it killed me."* Once again, this is the painful realization that Paul was going through. His law-keeping was once his pride. His commandment observance was once his righteousness. Now, he found that those things just slayed him. Not only this, but the commandment also stood as a constant reminder to show him how far short he had fallen from the glory of God (Romans 3:23).

It's important to note that in Romans 7:7–11, Paul mentions three times that he died when he realized his sin. When Jews repeated something but said it in different way, it was their way of bolding, underlining, or putting in an exclamation point. The fact that Paul repeats that coming to grips with his sin was death to him emphasizes the spiritual agony and sorrow he experienced due to his own personal sin. He was experiencing the Beatitudes in the sense that he was one who was poor in spirit and recognized his spiritual bankruptcy before a holy God (Matthew 5:3); he was mourning over sin (Matthew 5:4) and had been made meek by his own sin (Matthew 5:5). As we'll see later, Ananias shows Paul how to satisfy his hunger and thirst for righteousness (Matthew 5:6). The three days of fasting was a time for Paul to reflect, repent, mourn, and lament over his sin.

Analysis of Paul's Encounter with Ananias

Now there was a disciple at Damascus named Ananias. The Lord said to him in a vision, "Ananias." And he said, "Here I am, Lord." And the Lord said to him, "Rise and go to the street called Straight, and at the house of Judas look for a man of Tarsus named Saul, for behold, he is praying, and he has seen in a vision a man named Ananias come in and lay his hands on him so that he might regain his sight." But Ananias answered,

"Lord, I have heard from many about this man, how much evil he has done to your saints at Jerusalem. And here he has authority from the chief priests to bind all who call on your name." But the Lord said to him, "Go, for he is a chosen instrument of mine to carry my name before the Gentiles and kings and the children of Israel. For I will show him how much he must suffer for the sake of my name." So Ananias departed and entered the house. And laying his hands on me he said, "Brother Saul, the Lord Jesus who appeared to you on the road by which you came has sent me so that you may regain your sight and be filled with the Holy Spirit."

—Acts 9:10–17

And one Ananias, a devout man according to the law, well spoken of by all the Jews who lived there, came to me, and standing by me said to me, 'Brother Saul, receive your sight.' And at that very hour I received my sight and saw him.

—Acts 22:12–13

And immediately something like scales fell from my eyes, and he regained his sight.

—Acts 9:18

Ananias is going to be the servant who goes to visit Paul where he is staying and speaks with him. We even see that Paul is praying and sees in a vision that Ananias will come to him. Ananias is afraid to go see Paul because of his well-known reputation for persecuting and murdering Christians. The news of Paul's murderous persecution was known even in the region of Syria, which would have been approximately 150 miles from Jerusalem. However, Ananias listens to the Lord and goes to Paul.

As mentioned earlier, the combination of Paul praying and fasting shows that he was most likely in a state of mourning and lamentation. It was a time for Paul to pray and have total dependence on God. He was no longer praying for show (Mark 12:40) or to be seen by others (Matthew 6:5). No, he was praying to God. Not only had Paul been praying, but he had also had a vision that a man named Ananias would come and lay hands on him so that he may regain his sight.

Although Ananias was hesitant to go to Paul, the Lord declared that Paul was His chosen instrument to carry His name or the gospel to everyone. Additionally, the Lord said that Paul would be shown how he must suffer for the Lord's sake. Later, Paul certainly thought of suffering in this way as he penned this statement in Philippians 1:29: *"For it has been granted to you that for the sake of Christ you should not only believe in him but also suffer for his sake."* As Christians, we are graced with the opportunity to suffer for Christ. Paul knew that suffering produced perseverance, character, and hope (Romans 5:3–5). He knew that suffering helped believers focus on the coming glory that will be revealed to us (Romans 8:18). He knew that suffering persecution drives us to prayer (2 Corinthians 1:3–11). He knew that suffering and persecution helps us grow in sanctification (Philippians 3:10). Paul was going to suffer afflictions for the sake of Christ and His gospel.

Finally, Ananias was sent to Paul as an instrument to help him regain his sight, and Paul would be filled with the Holy Spirit. Some theologians may contend that the moment Ananias laid his hands on Paul and the scales fell off, Paul was filled with the Holy Spirit. Although a case could be made for this, Scripture strongly indicates that Paul was not indwelt and filled with the Holy Spirit then because he had not yet called on the name of the Lord as we'll see in the next analysis.

Analysis of Paul's Internal Dialogue and Moment of Conversion

> *And he said, "The God of our fathers appointed you to know his will, to see the Righteous One and to hear a voice from his mouth; for you will be a witness for him to everyone of what you have seen and heard. And now why do you wait? Rise and be baptized and wash away your sins, calling on his name."*
> —Acts 22:14–16

I [Paul] thought about my old "righteousness" through the flesh and the law versus the righteousness I gained through Christ:

> [I was] *circumcised on the eighth day, of the people of Israel, of the tribe of Benjamin, a Hebrew of Hebrews;*

as to the law, a Pharisee; as to zeal, a persecutor of the church; as to righteousness under the law, blameless. But whatever gain I had, I counted as loss for the sake of Christ. Indeed, I count everything as loss because of the surpassing worth of knowing Christ Jesus my Lord. For his sake I have suffered the loss of all things and count them as rubbish, in order that I may gain Christ and be found in him, not having a righteousness of my own that comes from the law, but that which comes through faith in Christ, the righteousness from God that depends on faith."

—Philippians 3:5–9

Then he [Paul] rose and was baptized and . . . he was strengthened.

—Acts 9:18–19

Ananias laid his hands upon Paul, and Paul regained his sight. Ananias tells Paul that the God of our fathers, or rather, the God of Abraham, the God of Isaac, and the God of Jacob has appointed it that Paul would see and hear the voice of the Righteous One, Jesus Christ. The *Righteous One* was a Messianic title, so Paul would understand that he would be a witness for Jesus the Messiah.

Finally, Ananias calls Paul to *"rise and be baptized and wash away your sins, calling on his name"* (Acts 22:16). Ananias was doing the same thing that Peter did when he delivered a sermon on the day of Pentecost. In his sermon, Peter gave the gospel to the Jewish audience. In Acts 2:21, he quoted Joel 2:32 saying, "*And it shall come to pass that everyone who calls upon the name of the Lord shall be saved.*" In Acts 2:36, Peter showed that God the Father made Jesus both Lord and Christ: "*Let all the house of Israel therefore know for certain that God has made him both Lord and Christ, this Jesus whom you crucified.*" Peter then gave a gospel call to the Jewish audience, calling them to repent and be baptized for the forgiveness of sins (Acts 2:38). This would be a public acknowledgment and confession accepting Jesus as Lord and Christ; it would be a costly decision. Peter was calling them to abandon false Judaism, to count their circumcision as nothing, to count their righteous acts as nothing, and to trust completely in Christ for salvation as evidenced by a public baptism. This was an extreme call to repentance for the Jewish community; they would need to so identify with Jesus that they would deny themselves, take up their cross, and follow Him (Matthew 10:37–39, 16:24–27; Luke 9:23–26, 14:26–34; Mark 8:34–38; John 12:24–26). The people knew that it was costly to follow Christ; confessing Jesus as Lord and Christ might mean imprisonment or persecution. This was a call to unconditional surrender and trust in Christ; they knew that confessing Christ could end in crucifixion.

Let's remember that it wasn't the baptism that gave forgiveness of sins; it was faith in Christ Jesus the Lord. As we learned earlier, those that put their faith in Christ receive the Holy Spirit (John 7:38–39). A person does not receive the Holy Spirit when they're water baptized. Rather, they receive the Holy Spirit when they put saving faith in Christ (Ephesians 1:13). Paul makes this abundantly clear in Ephesians 1:13, where he says, *"In him you also, when you heard the word of truth, the gospel of your salvation, and believed in him, were sealed with the promised Holy Spirit."* Those who would come to faith in Christ would receive the Holy Spirit. Although it was costly to come to Christ for salvation, those who would put their faith in Christ would receive a gift much more precious than all creation. Those who repent and trust Christ shall never be disappointed. Let's also note that all those who give their lives for Christ and the gospel must count the cost. It is costly to follow Jesus, but it is more costly not to follow Him. Ananias was calling Paul to be baptized as a public confession of his faith in Christ.

So how can we know that Paul was not yet converted and justified by faith? How would Scripture lead us to believe that Paul was not yet saved? We see this in Acts 22:16 where Ananias says the following: *"And now why do you wait? Rise and be baptized and wash away your sins, calling on his name."*

In this verse, we can see that Paul had not yet salvifically called on the name of the Lord because Ananias commanded Paul to call on the name of the Lord. Ananias asked Paul why he has delayed and not yet called on the name of the Lord. In fact, the word *delay* comes from *melló*, which means "to be about to do" or "intending to do." Additionally, Ananias says that Paul's sins had not yet been forgiven, and they remained. This means that Paul had not yet called on the name of the Lord, and he had not been forgiven of his sins. Some may wonder whether Paul's baptism was what washed away his sins. Let's remember that the cost associated with repenting, being baptized, and identifying with the Lord was great, and came with possibility of persecution, death, ostracism, being unsynagogued, stoning, imprisonment, and more. Just as Paul had persecuted the church and killed Christians, he was now commanded to identify with Christ even if it meant being stoned, beaten with rods, persecuted, put in prison, or put to death (2 Corinthians 11:23–33). Let us remember Peter's words at the Jerusalem Council (Acts 15:9) when they debated whether believers needed to be circumcised and keep the law of Moses: "*and he* [God] *made no distinction between us and them,* **having cleansed our hearts by faith**" (emphasis added). It is not water baptism that washes away sins. When one comes to saving faith in Jesus Christ, their sins are forgiven. Let's transition to Philippians 3:5–9 to continue the analysis of Paul's internal dialogue and conversion.

If we break down Paul's internal conversion dialogue, we can classify Philippians 3:5–7 as Paul's repentance and Philippians 3:8–9 as Paul's response of faith in Christ. Recall what we've learned thus far about circumcision, ceremonial washings, Sabbath observances, and burnt offerings. Think about the upbringing of a Jewish child and Paul's knowledge of Scripture as well as the Mishnah and Gemara. Being aware of this background will help us understand Paul's theology on conversion.

As we see in Philippians 3:5, Paul looked at his circumcision and considered it dung in terms of salvation. Paul was aware that some taught that no circumcised Jew would go to hell. Although this may not have been taught by leading rabbis such as the ones mentioned in Chapter 1, the teaching that circumcision was salvific was prevalent in Judaism. So how did Paul look at being circumcised on the eighth day as it relates to salvation? Paul considered this Abrahamic Covenant sign as dung in terms of salvation. Paul's repentance included a turning away from ritualism and reliance on covenant signs for salvation. Paul put no confidence in the circumcision of the flesh.

In Philippians 3:5, we learn that Paul had previously taken comfort in being an Israelite and coming from an esteemed tribe. In the past, he took salvific comfort when he looked at his biblical knowledge as well as his knowledge of the oral law such as the Mishnah and Gemara when he says, "As to the law, a Pharisee." So how did Paul look at his heritage, ethnicity, and knowledge as it relates to salvation? After his conversion, Paul considered his Jewishness or being in the Abrahamic Covenant nation of Israel as dung in terms of salvation. Likewise, Paul considered his upbringing, his vast knowledge of Scripture and the law, which included the Mishnah and the Gemara, as dung in terms of salvation. Therefore, Paul repented of and put no salvific confidence in relying on his national heritage and knowledge of Scripture for salvation.

In Philippians 3:6 Paul says that he had been zealous for Pharisaic Judaism, so much so that he persecuted the church. Paul looked at his outward righteousness to the Ten

Commandments, handwashing, ritual purification, Sabbath observance, sacrificial offerings, adherence to the Mishnah, adherence to the Gemara, and more. He was blameless when it came to handwashing. He was blameless when it came to external washings with water. He was blameless when it came to sacrificing the burnt offering. He was blameless when it came to washing utensils, mats, and dishes. He was blameless when it came to understanding the mikvah water purification rituals. He was blameless when it came to not carrying more than a dried fig on the Sabbath. He was blameless when it came to not carrying enough ink to write more than two letters on the Sabbath. He was blameless when it came to not committing adultery externally. He was blameless when it came to not carrying a cow's mouthful of straw or a camel's mouthful of bean stalks on the Sabbath. So how did Paul look at being a Pharisee as it relates to salvation? When Paul saw Christ, he considered all the practices of Pharisaic Judaism and external religion to be dung, manure, and refuse in terms of salvation. Paul abandoned ritualism, external washings, and law-keeping as a means of salvation; he repented of and put no confidence in self-reliance, self-esteem, and self-righteousness.

In Philippians 3:7 everything that Paul mentioned in Philippians 3:5–6 was to be counted *"as loss for the sake of Christ."* These things had no value when it came to salvation. Circumcision, external washings with water, law-keeping, self-reliance, self-pride, self-esteem, dead religion, and national heritage needed to go into the loss column in terms of salvation. All these things were to be repented of and abandoned in terms of salvation. For Paul, holding onto external washings with water as a means of salvation was like holding onto dung. Holding on to circumcision as a means of salvation was like holding onto refuse. For Paul, ceremonialism, sacramentalism, ritualism, and legalism were to go in the loss column. In fact, when Paul says that these were to be *"counted as loss,"* the word *counted* is written in the perfect tense and indicative mood, which means that he counted all the ceremonialism, sacramentalism, ritualism, and legalism garbage and refuse in terms of salvation in the past and continued to consider these garbage and refuse in terms of salvation in the present.

However, in Philippians 3:8–9, we see the one thing that Paul found that was powerful to save. All the dead works, dead ceremonies, and dead religious activities would be given up and repented of for the surpassing worth of knowing Christ Jesus. Paul was more than happy to give up his reliance on such things. In fact, Paul said:

> *For his sake I have suffered the loss of all things and count them as rubbish,* **in order that I may gain Christ and be found in him**, *not having a righteousness of my own that comes from the law,* **but that which comes through faith in Christ**, *the righteousness that depends on faith.*

This was Paul's response of faith; he found the righteousness that justified him before a holy God. Paul saw the righteousness of Christ, and he responded in faith. Paul made a spiritual accounting decision, and he:

- Suffered the loss of everything yet gained everything.

- Denied himself, took up his cross, and followed Christ (Matthew 16:24, Luke 9:23).

- Responded to the gospel call of Christ to hate his own father, mother, wife, children, brothers, sisters, and yes, even his own life (Luke 14:26).

- Saved his life by losing his life (Matthew 16:25).

- Reasoned that it would profit a man nothing if he gained the whole world yet forfeited his soul (Mark 8:37).

- Hated his own life to save it (Luke 14:26–27).

- Lost his life for the sake of the gospel and Christ (Mark 8:35).

- Hungered and thirsted for a righteousness that was not his own (Matthew 5:6).

Paul was the man who found the hidden treasure in the field, covered it up, and in his joy sold all that he had to buy the field (Matthew 13:44). Paul was the man who was like a merchant in search of fine pearls and when he found the pearl of great value, went and sold all he had and bought it (Matthew 13:45–46). Paul wanted the righteousness of Christ and not a righteousness that came from the law, and he put off the old self which was his former and sinful manner of life and put on the new man which is Christ (Ephesians 4:22, 24).

Note that this was not a righteousness based on rituals, sacraments, or ceremonies. This was not a righteousness that came from law observance. No, this was the righteousness that came by faith in Christ. This was a repentant faith in Christ, not a faith that hung onto ceremonies, rituals, sacraments, law observance, or self-righteousness. This was a repentant faith that was slain by Paul's own sin. It was a repentant faith that reached out to Christ and asked for mercy. It was a repentant faith that suffered the loss of all things to gain Christ. It was a repentant faith that forsook self-will, self-righteousness, and self-love. It was a repentant faith that called out to the Lord for salvation with no merit, empty hands, brokenness, and destitution. It was a repentant faith that abandoned self and dead religion and trusted Christ for forgiveness. It was a submissive faith. It was a God-fearing faith. It was a Christ-loving faith. It was a faith that trusted Christ's perfect life and sacrificial and substitutionary death for sinners. It was a faith that saw that Christ had been raised from the dead and was the ascended Messiah who possessed all authority to judge all men. When Ananias told Paul to call on the name of the Lord, this is the response of faith in Christ he was calling Paul to. Likewise, this is what it means to call on the name of the Lord as Paul says in Romans 10:13, *"For 'everyone who calls on the name of the Lord will be saved.'"*

Acts 9:18 and Acts 22:16 say that Paul was baptized and called on the Lord. He publicly declared that he trusted in Christ Jesus the Lord even if it would cost him his life (Luke 14:26–34). If the Jewish community would stone him or put him on a cross, Paul acknowledged that this was the price he would pay for his faith in Christ.

As we close this chapter, we have gained a greater theological understanding of Paul's conversion story and his repentance and faith in Christ. When Paul gives his internal conversion account in Philippians, we are supposed to think of all the rituals, ceremonies, laws, washings, and more that Paul put no hope in for salvation. This conversion account of Paul is to demonstrate that he responded to the call of repentance and faith in Christ; his conversion was radical, but so is the conversion of anyone who is converted to Christ. In the next chapter, we will explore Paul's theology on conversion; meanwhile, let's keep Paul's conversion at the front of our minds.

Part 3

The Apostle Paul's
Theology on Conversion

Chapter 6

Paul's Theology on Conversion in Ephesians

But that is not the way you learned Christ!—assuming
that you have heard about him and were taught in him,
as the truth is in Jesus, to put off your old self, which
belongs to your former manner of life and is corrupt
through deceitful desires, and to be renewed in the spirit
of your minds, and to put on the new self, created after
the likeness of God in true righteousness and holiness

—Ephesians 4:20–24

In this chapter, we will start to understand Paul's theology on conversion. As we go through this chapter, we should come to understand that Paul believed conversion leads to radical transformation and that conversion includes both repentance and faith. Paul was unquestionably firm on his stance that salvation was by grace alone, through faith alone, and in

Christ alone. Paul defended the doctrine of justification by faith in Christ and that there was no right standing and justification before God without faith in the Lord Jesus Christ. Additionally, Paul was able to describe the gospel call and faith that justifies. Paul made declaratives statements such as in Ephesians 2:8–9 that one was saved by grace through faith in Christ and described the faith that justifies in Ephesians 4:22–24. When a person understands that justification is by grace alone through faith alone in Christ, that does not mean that they possess justifying faith. When saving grace is applied to an individual through the sovereign salvific work of the Triune God, this grace is radical, transformational, and life-changing. It is the life of God in the soul of a person.

This chapter explores Paul's theology on conversion by focusing primarily on Ephesians 4:20–24 but also by pulling in Scripture from Paul's other epistles and his accounts in Acts. By the end of this chapter, it is my hope that we'll see Paul's theology on conversion, understand that his gospel call was identical to that of the Lord Jesus Christ, and that conversion always brings about a radical transformation in one's life.

Before we transition to Ephesians 4:20–24, it would be good to get a running start and briefly review the book of Ephesians at a very high level:

- Ephesians 1:3–6: Paul explains how believers were predestined for salvation in Christ by God the Father in love.

- Ephesians 1:6–10: Paul explains that redemption and the forgiveness of sins were accomplished in Christ.

- Ephesians 1:11–14: Paul explains that in Christ, all believers have an eternal redemption and inheritance.

- Ephesians 1:15–23: Paul explains that believers have all the resources, power, and wisdom in Christ who is the Head of the church and sovereign over all things.

- Ephesians 2:1–10: Paul characterizes man's pre-salvation fallen condition as being dead in trespasses and children of wrath. As believers we're made new in Christ, raised with Christ in the heavenlies, saved through Christ, and created in Christ for good works.

- Ephesians 2:11–3:13: Paul explains how Christ brought peace for both Jew and Gentile and reconciled both groups to God, brought unity to the church, and made the Gentiles coheirs with Jews through the gospel of Christ Jesus.

- Ephesians 3:14–21: Paul prays for believers to have the fullness, strength, and knowledge to comprehend the breadth, length, height, and depth of Christ and for this knowledge to lead to maturity and the fullness of God.

- Ephesians 4:1-6: Paul explains God's plan for unity and faithful living in the church.

- Ephesians 4:7-17: Paul explains Christ's provision to build the church.

As we begin to consider our main text of interest, Paul is going to describe how the Christian is to live their life in Christ. But first, he reminds the Ephesians how the Gentiles lived, which was counter to the new life in Christ.

Paul commands the Ephesian church that they must no longer live as the Gentiles do in the futility of their minds because they are darkened in their understanding and separated from the life of God because of their ignorance and hard hearts and because they practice all kinds of sin (Ephesians 4:17–19). In other words, Paul might say that the Gentiles had uncircumcised hearts that are self-willed, stubborn, disobedient, ignorant, apathetic, indifferent, unbelieving, unregenerate, unconverted, sinful, and rebellious toward the Lord. How can we know this? We can know this because Paul states that they have minds that are *mataiotés* or rather "purposeless," "ineffective," "frail," "aimless," and minds that are *agnoia* or rather "ignorant" and "blind."

The unbelieving Gentiles weren't those who possessed the life of God or the Holy Spirit (Romans 8:9). No, they were those who were alienated from the life of God (Ephesians 4:18). They weren't those who possessed the mind of Christ (1 Corinthians 2:16). No, they were those who possessed a futile and worthless mind (Ephesians 4:17). They weren't those who had circumcised hearts (Romans 2:28–29). No, they were those who had hard and stubborn hearts (Ephesians 4:18). They weren't those who had become obedient from the heart to the teaching they received (Romans 6:17). No, they were callous (Ephesians 4:19). They weren't those who were imitators of God (Ephesians 5:1). No, they were sensual, greedy, and impure (Ephesians 4:19). As we transition into our text of interest, Paul is going to remind them of the saving gospel call they responded to when they were saved by grace and received the Holy Spirit (Ephesians 1:13, Ephesians 2:8–9).

Ephesians 4:20–21 – *But that is not the way you learned Christ!—assuming that you have heard about him and were taught in him, as the truth is in Jesus.*

Paul plainly tells the Ephesians that this is not how they learned Christ. The Ephesians didn't learn about Christ and then remain in sensuality, in a futile mind, and alienated from God. The Ephesians didn't learn about Christ and believe they were to remain in their former and sinful manner of life. No, Paul taught them the truths about the person and work of Christ before he issued a gospel call to faith in Christ. So let's note that the Ephesian church was taught the truths about Christ. One may ask the question, "What did the Ephesian church learn about Christ, or what exactly was taught about Jesus Christ?" Paul will answer this question in Ephesians 1:13 where he says, "*In him you also, when you heard the word of truth, the gospel of your salvation, and believed in him, were sealed with the promised Holy Spirit."* We can clearly see that the church in Ephesus was at least taught the gospel; they had to at least be instructed in the foundations of the Christian faith. This raise the primary question: "What is the gospel?" I will give a definition of the gospel so we understand the saving message that would have been shared with the Ephesians. However, before we get to the good news, the bad news needs to be comprehended, so we'll first start with the bad news.

The Bad News – Sin, Death, Hell

Man sinned by breaking God's law by either not doing what God's law demands (James 4:17) or doing what God's law prohibits (James 2:10) in thought (Matthew 5:28), word (Matthew 5:22), deed (Matthew 5:39), or intent (Matthew 6:1). God hates (Psalm 5:5, 11:5), abhors (Psalm 5:6), is angered with sin (Psalm 7:11), and He is ready to destroy and punish those who sin (Psalm 7:12–13) because sin is warfare against Him (James 4:4); God considers sin an abomination (Proverbs 22:12) and evil (Psalm 7:9). Because God hates sin, He must deal with sin according to who He is. God must punish sin because He is infinite (1 Timothy 1:17), loving (Psalm 136, 1 John 4:17), just (Genesis 18:25, Deuteronomy 32:4, Job 34:10, Jeremiah 17:10, Ezekiel 18:1–32), good (Psalm 25:8, Mark 10:18), faithful (Lamentations 3:22–23), omniscient (Psalm 147:5, Hebrews 4:13), immutable (James 1:17, Numbers 23:19), omnipresent (Jeremiah 23:23–24), and holy (Isaiah 44:6, 45:5). For God to leave sin unpunished would violate and act in opposition to His character. Therefore, God must punish sin. The punishment for sin is hell, which is a place of God's full wrath; it is a place of blackest darkness (Jude 13, Matthew 22:13), filled with the furious, all-powerful, concentrated, raging, and vengeful fire of God, which devours and consumes His enemies (Matthew 5:22, 5:29, 13:42, 13:50; Hebrews 10:26–31). Hell is filled with the lost who are weeping and angry against God; they are unrepentant, Christ-rejecting (Matthew 11:20–24), and Christ-neglecting sinners (Hebrews 2:1–3). The lost will spend all eternity being punished for every sin they ever committed (Revelation 20:12) with no hope of escape (Luke 16:26) and with only the expectation of excruciating torment to their body, soul, and spirit (Matthew 10:28) and an undying conscience that will haunt them day and night, forever and ever, with no reprieve (Luke 16:25).

The Good News – The Person of Christ

The gospel is the good news of salvation that God has authored and owns (Romans 1:1). God had promised His plan of salvation through His prophets and Holy Scripture and has fully revealed the good news of salvation through Scripture (Romans 1:2), which is the authoritative, inspired, inerrant, infallible, and all-sufficient Word of God (2 Peter 1:20–21; 2 Timothy 3:16-17). The good news concerns the person and work of the Lord Jesus Christ. Jesus is the Jewish Messiah and Son of the Living God (Matthew 16:16, Romans 1:1–4). Jesus is God, and He is coequal and coeternal with God the Father and God the Holy Spirit (John 5:17–18, 10:30, 10:38, 14:10). Jesus is the eternal, only begotten, one-of-a-kind, Son of God (John 3:16). Jesus is the Anointed One of God (Luke 4:18–19). Jesus is the Savior of the world (Luke 2:11). Jesus is the Creator and Sustainer of the Universe (John 1:1–14). Jesus is the King of Israel (John 1:49). Jesus is the Son of David (Matthew 1:1–16, Luke 3:23–38). Jesus was born of a virgin (Matthew 1:23, Galatians 4:4). Jesus was the Word made flesh (John 1:14). Jesus was physically born into this world as a man (Matthew 1:25). Jesus is thus truly God and truly man (Philippians 2:5–11).

The Good News – The Work of Christ

The work of Jesus is that He lived a sinless life (Matthew 26:59–60, 1 Corinthians 5:21) and fulfilled all righteousness found in the law and the prophets (Matthew 5:17–20, Luke 24:44–46). He declared Himself to be the Christ (Matthew 16:16), the only begotten Son of the living God through His teaching (John 3:16, Matthew 22:41–46), which was attested to by His miracles and display of divine power (John 10:37–38). Jesus offered himself as a spotless and blameless sacrifice for sin (John 1:29, 1 Peter 1:19) to propitiate the righteous anger of God the Father for all the sins of God's people (John 10:11, Romans 3:25, Isaiah 53, 1 Peter 2:24). Christ bore the full and omnipotent wrath of God the Father on the cross, which was due to man (Matthew 26:39, 27:45–46; Luke 22:44). His sacrifice propitiated the righteous anger of God and reconciled (Romans 5:10–11) and brought peace from man to God and God to man (Matthew 27:51–53; John 19:30; Romans 5:1; 1 Peter 2:25). His substitutionary sacrifice and death also redeemed sinful man to Holy God by forgiving man's sin (Hebrews 8:12, Ephesians 1:7) and imputing Christ's righteousness to man (1 Corinthians 5:21, Isaiah 53:1–12, Romans 4:3–5). Jesus was resurrected from the dead on the third day by His own power (John 10:18), by God the Father (Galatians 1:1) and God the Holy Spirit (Romans 8:11), which affirmed His person, His teachings, and salvific work for sinners (Romans 4:25). He ascended to the right hand of the Father (Luke 24:51) and is empowered with all authority to bring about the plan of salvation for all His people (Matthew 28:18) by causing them to be born again (John 3:1–10) and justified by His grace (John 3:16, 3:18, 3:36). He will also return to bring all His own to heaven with Him (John 6:37–40, 14:1–3) to be glorified (John 17:24) while also judging and condemning Satan, demons, and sinful man to hell (Matthew 25:31–46, Revelation 20:7–15). The benefits of the person and work of Christ are available to those who respond to the gospel call of repentance toward God and faith in the Lord Jesus Christ (Mark 1:15, Acts 20:21).

The Good News – The Response of Repentance and Faith in the Lord Jesus Christ

Repentance is a gift from God and a radical change in mind (Acts 5:31, 11:18, 2 Timothy 2:25) in which the sinner understands his sin against God and is thus, poor in spirit (Matthew 5:3, Luke 18:9–14), has godly sorrow and mourns over his sin against God (Matthew 5:4, 2 Corinthians 7:10), turns away from his sin and sinful former way of life (Ephesians 4:22), and turns toward God for righteousness and salvation (Matthew 5:5–6; Luke 3:3–17; Acts 17:30, 20:21; 1 Thessalonians 1:9). Saving faith is a gift from God (Ephesians 2:8–9) whereby a sinner has knowledge of Jesus's person and work such that a sinner will respond to Christ's person and work by denying themselves (Matthew 16:24, Mark 8:34, Luke 9:23), picking up their cross (Matthew 10:38, 16:24; Mark 8:34; Luke 9:23), and lovingly (Luke 14:26–27, James 4:7) and obediently (2 Thessalonians 1:8, Romans 1:5), submitting (James 4:6, Matthew 11:28) and committing their life to Jesus (Matthew 10:37–39, 16:24–26; Mark 8:34–37; Luke 9:23–26, 14:25–33), and trusting in Him only for salvation (Romans 10:13, John 3:16, John 3:36, Acts 4:12). Thus, conversion is the turning away from sin in repentance and turning to the Lord Jesus Christ in faith for salvation (Acts 20:21, 1 Thessalonians 1:9, Ephesians 4:22–24, Colossians 3:9–10, Mark 1:15).

Paul taught that the Scriptures were the Word of God and were thus authoritative, infallible, inerrant, and all-sufficient. Paul taught that the gospel was about the person and work of Christ, the only begotten Son of God. Paul taught that Jesus was the Creator and Sustainer of the universe. Paul taught that Jesus was the Christ. Paul taught that Jesus was born of a virgin and lived a sinless life. Paul taught that Jesus was a substitutionary atonement for sinners. Paul proclaimed the offense of the cross; that the cross is an offensive message to man. Tim Conway, a pastor at Grace Community Church in San Antonio, Texas, has these helpful insights about the offense of the cross:

> The cross did not spare our Savior. You realize this that He was alive when they hung Him on that cross and six hours later they took Him down and He was dead! He was completely dead! The cross is a killing instrument! It is an instrument of death, not of beauty! And in that cross, there is an offense. He went to the cross to die; to suffer and die and you and I do not want to empty the cross of its power. 1 Corinthians 1:17 you can see this is exactly Paul's concern; don't empty the cross of its power! Which tells me what? What does it tell us? It tells us that it's distinctly possible to empty the cross of its power. How does that happen? I'll tell you what, there's only one way it happens; only one way. It's when we make the cross something it isn't. That is the only way you empty the power of it. When you present the power of the cross as what it is, it has power. And what it is, is offensive to men.

I'll tell you what, there is power in that cross to do
what nothing else in this universe can do; to turn
away the wrath of God, to take away sin, to reconcile God and man so that there is peace, to do what
nothing else can do. . . . The cross of Christ is offensive and do you know why? Listen, you say, "I don't
see anything offensive about it." Not if you think
about it as something you hang around your neck.
Not if you look at it as a crucifix on the wall. That's
not offensive! What is offensive about it is when you
see the Son of God in all His purity having to die the
way He died. There's something in it that's offensive
because I'll tell you what it is. It leaves man no place
to hide. That's exactly what it does. Jesus Christ suffered unspeakably on a cross and died and do you
know what that thunders to men? Do you know
what it thunders in men's ears?! Sin is not trivial to
God. It says to mankind, "You are in trouble if you
do not take what My Son did for sinners on that
cross." It spells out that God has such an opinion of
sin and will deal with it in such a way and when we
see what horrors Christ had to endure on the cross,
it makes men step back and realize, "Man, my sin
isn't as trivial as I thought it was. In fact, I thought
it was hardly anything."

It wakes us up to the fact that our sin is so great we
needed to be saved by nothing less than the horrid

execution of the Son of God. I'll tell you what, men think little of their sin. Men by nature are boasters, they love to boast in their own goodness. They love to boast in their own merit. They love to boast in their own achievements. . . . You know what the cross says? It says, "Sinner, shut your mouth!" You say, "How dare you! That's offensive." Exactly. Exactly. That is the offensiveness of the cross. It tells men to shut their boasting mouths. It tells men they are bad. They are real, real, real, bad! It tells men that without the cross there is nothing but certain condemnation and death and eternal punishment and destruction. It tells men that God is not playing around with sin. It tells men that they are in dire, dire trouble![36]

This is the offensive message that Paul brought; it was a powerful message of the cross of Christ and His resurrection that validated His salvific work for sinners. This is the Christ that Paul proclaimed. This gospel of Christ and Paul demands and commands obedience. Here, we can see what Paul meant when he says the Ephesian church learned Christ (Ephesians 4:20). There is much more than can be said about everything that Paul taught regarding Christ and the gospel, but for the purposes of this book, we will be focusing on how he taught conversion, or rather, repentance and faith.

Ephesians 4:22–24 will explain the subjective response to the person and work of Christ. When one knows the truths of the person and work of Jesus, the gospel commands and demands a response. As we see in Acts 20:21, Paul was continuing to testify that the response to the person and work of Jesus Christ was repentance and faith as he describes himself *"testifying both to Jews and to Greeks of **repentance toward God** and of **faith in our Lord Jesus Christ**"* (emphasis added). What good is it if you know the objective truths about Jesus, but you don't know how to respond to Him? What good is it if you tell people the truth about the person and work of Jesus Christ, but never command them to repent and put their faith in Jesus? In the next verse, we will learn how Paul commanded his listeners to respond after they had heard the gospel truths about the person and work of Christ.

Repentance

> **Ephesians 4:22** – *To put off your old self, which belongs to your former manner of life and is corrupt through deceitful desires.*

Paul Says Put Off Your Old Self; Jesus Says Deny Yourself

Here we come to Paul's gospel invitation or call to saving faith; this is how Paul called people to come to faith in Christ. As we learned in Ephesians 4:20, the Ephesian church had a time of learning about the person of Christ—a time for them to understand the truth about sin, death, hell, and judgment.

Likewise, there needed to be a time of learning the Word and how it pointed to Christ. They needed a time of learning about the person and work of Christ, which included the truths about His deity, being born of a virgin and conceived by the Holy Spirit, living a sinless life, miracles that attested to His teaching and claims, His substitutionary atonement on the cross, His resurrection, His ascension, and His second coming. There needed to be a time to learn of Christ's attributes, which included his love, grace, mercy, justice, wrath, omniscience, omnipotence, faithfulness, and goodness. After Paul had taught of Christ and the Ephesian church had learned of Christ, Paul gave the invitation to come to faith in Christ and here is how he did it.

The first part of Paul's Invitation to come to Christ begins with a call to repentance. Paul called his listeners to "put off your old self." The word *put off* comes from *apotithémi*, which means to "lay off," "renounce," or "cast off." This word was used of runners who participated in the Olympic games who cast off their clothes and ran nearly naked in the stadium. Figuratively, this word conveys the idea of being done or finished with something. When Paul used the word *apotithémi*, he used the aorist tense, infinitive mood, and middle voice, which means that this was a call for a complete and decisive action. The middle voice means that the person who performs the action is affected by the action. When Paul writes in the aorist tense, infinitive mood, and middle voice, he is commanding someone to definitively cast off, renounce, and put off your old self. When *put off* is written in the aorist tense and infinitive mood, it commands the listener to obey the action to finality. This is clearly a call to repentance. This was a call to renounce one's sins—a call to repent of one's sin, worldly desires, pride, self-will, self-righteousness, and self-reliance. The listener was to make a decision that would put an end to one's old self and manner of life. The word *manner of life* comes from *anastrophe* and it means, "conduct," "life," "behavior," "manner of life," or figuratively "change of outward behavior from an upturn of inner beliefs." This is an extreme call to renounce everything about your former way of life that was sinful. This was Paul's call to repentance.

Paul used similar language in Colossians 3:9 where he says, *"Do not lie to one another, seeing that you **have put off** the old self with its practices"* (emphasis added). When Paul says that the Colossians had *put off the old self*, he uses the word *apekduomai*, which means "to strip," "divest," "renounce." This is a compound word with *apó* meaning "away from" and *ekdýō* meaning "go down and completely away from." The double prefix of *apó* and *ek* emphasizes and intensifies the depth of renouncing. Additionally, when Paul says that they had *put off the old self*, this was in the aorist tense and participle mood, meaning that this was a completed action that occurred at a fixed point in time. The aorist tense gives the sense that the believers in the Colossian church had made a definitive decision to once and for all put off the old self, which meant putting off and repenting of their former sinful life, putting off self-will, putting off self-righteousness, and putting off self-reliance. Therefore, we see that Paul's call to *put off the old self* was just as clear and as strong to the church in Colossae as it was to the church in Ephesus.

Paul would say it another way regarding repentance and casting off one's old life in Romans 6:11: "*So you must also consider yourselves dead to sin and alive to God in Christ Jesus.*" Putting off the old man was tantamount to dying to sin. Putting off the old man was equivalent to calling men to die to their sinful pattern of life. Paul called men to "*put off your old self*" and, as we'll see, Christ gave the same command as Paul when He said, "*deny yourself.*"

So why would Paul command that the old self be put off? He answers this question in Ephesians 4:22 where he says that the old man is, "*corrupt through deceitful desires.*" The old man possesses nothing good or meritorious. In fact, Paul would say that the old man is in a state of corruption, a state of defilement, and a state of being destroyed and brought to ruin. Why is the old man in this condition? The old man is in this condition because he is full of sin and deceitful desires. The deceitful desires of sin are what characterize the old man. The old man can be characterized by loving false religion, dead religion, and false sacramental Christianity; being moral but not loving or possessing Christ; and being immoral, amoral, worldly, and loving sin. The old man is in a state of corruption through deceitful desires, and they practice sin because they are slaves to sin (John 8:34). Therefore, the old man needs to be put off.

Paul's call to repentance is not unique. Rather, it is simply mimicking the Lord's call to repentance. In Matthew 16:24–25, Jesus told His disciples this regarding the call to follow after Him in saving faith: *"If anyone would come after me, let him* **deny himself** *and take up his cross and follow me. For whoever would save his life will lose it, but whoever loses his life for my sake will find it"* (emphasis added).

When Jesus says that a person must *deny themselves,* He is giving a strong call to repentance. The word *deny* is written in the aorist tense and imperative mood and middle voice. Once again, this is a command calling for a decisive obedience on the part of the listener. The word *aparneomai* is a compound word made up of *apó* meaning "from" and *arnéomai* meaning "deny." The prefix *apó* intensifies *arnéomai. Aparneomai* means to "deny," "disown," "repudiate," or "disregard." *Aparneomai* means "to strongly deny." It means "to utterly deny." This same word, *aparneomai,* is used when Jesus told Peter that he would deny Him three times and that it would be a strong renunciation and denial.

So, what does it mean when Jesus called for self-denial? In Jesus's ministry, He was very clear about what He meant by self-denial. Jesus called for:

- Denial of self-righteousness (Luke 18:9–14).

- Self-denial of works-righteousness salvation (Matthew 5:20).

- Self-denial of the love of money (Matthew 6:24).

- Self-denial of false religion (Matthew 15:12–14).

- Self-denial of following the world and the deceitfulness of wealth (Matthew 13:22).

- Denial of loving the world (John 15:19).

- Self-denial of living for worldly comfort (Luke 9:57–58).

- Self-denial of other relationships taking preeminence over Him (Luke 14:26, Matthew 10:34–38).

- Self-denial of running one's own life (Luke 14:26).

- Self-denial and repentance of one's sin.

Jesus's call to deny oneself is a radical call of repentance, submission, and faith in Him. Just as Peter said, "*I don't know the man*," so Jesus called people to say the same thing to their own sinful and corrupt lives, which is to say to ourselves, "I don't know the old man. I forsake my sinful self. I repudiate my sinful self. I reject my sinful self. I disaffirm my sinful self. I will lose my life, reject myself, disaffirm myself, and repudiate myself and turn to the Lord Jesus Christ for life and salvation." This is a call to be done living for yourself and to stop being the lord of your life. Jesus is calling you to deny the unholy trinity of me, myself, and I. This is a call to repent of your sins; say goodbye to your worldly desires and pride; and say goodbye to self-will, self-sufficiency, self-wishes, and self-righteousness in exchange for the Lord Jesus Christ's yoke, His will, and His rule over your life. This was a call to abdicate the rule and lordship over one's own life.

Let's also note that it is a self-denial that encompasses the whole of one's person, which includes one's mind, heart, will, soul, and body. There is not one single element of one's person that is not included in "deny himself" or "deny yourself." In Hebrew, the heart is the center of one's being. It is not merely the home of one's affections, but also the seat of the will and moral purpose. The condition of one's heart determines one's influence. Proverbs 4:23 says, "*Watch over your heart with all diligence, for from it flow the springs of life*" (AMP). In fact, Jesus said in Matthew 16:25, "*For whoever would save his **life** will lose it, but whoever loses his **life** for my sake will find it*" (emphasis added). The words *life* and *soul* come from the original word *psuché*. *Psuché* can mean "the human soul," "the soul as the seat of affections and will," "the self," "a human person," "an individual," or a "life." Jesus was calling for the whole of one's body and soul to be submitted to Him. No longer would one's personal knowledge and wisdom be the driving force, but rather, it would be replaced with the knowledge and wisdom of the Lord Jesus Christ. Christ is not calling for sinless perfection. May it never be! But Christ is calling for the renunciation, denunciation, and repudiation of one's life. Jesus is calling for commitment, submission, devotion, dedication, faithfulness, fidelity, and loyalty of one's life unto Him.

Paul Says Crucify the Flesh; Jesus Says Take Up Your Cross

Not only did Jesus give a call to *deny yourself* but He also called His followers to take up their cross and follow Him. The word *take up* is written in the aorist tense, imperative mood, and active voice. The tense, mood, and voice of this verb calls for the listener's decisive obedience to this command. Crucifixion was considered one of the most brutal and shameful modes of death. It likely had origins with the Assyrians and Babylonians and was eventually introduced to Rome by the Phoenicians in the third century BC. The Romans perfected crucifixion for five hundred years until it was abolished by Constantine I in the fourth century AD. Death by crucifixion could take from six hours to several days and was likely due to aftereffects of compulsory scourging, maiming, hemorrhage, and dehydration causing hypovolemic shock. Death could also be precipitated by cardiac arrest. The attending Roman guards only left the site after the victim had died and would either break the victim's legs, stab the heart or chest with spears, or build a fire at the foot of the cross to asphyxiate the victim. Those who were crucified included slaves, disgraced soldiers, Christians, foreigners, and very rarely, Roman citizens. The Jews knew what Jesus was talking about when Jesus said, *"Take up his cross and follow me."* There was absolutely nothing glorious about the cross. They had seen crucifixion before. They knew it was the death of deaths. They knew the cross meant agony. They knew the cross meant suffering. They knew the cross meant torture. They knew the cross meant shame. They knew the cross meant certain death.

Jesus's invitation to carry your cross is an invitation to not only deny yourself, but also to die to yourself and be identified with Christ, even if it costs you your physical life. This is a death to self-will, a death to personal sins. This is a willingness to give your life to Christ even if it calls for death. This is a death to the lust of the flesh, the lust of the eyes, and the pride of life. This is not perfection, but it is the call to die to yourself daily. In fact, in Luke 9:23, Jesus says, "*If anyone would come after me, let him deny himself and take up his cross **daily** and follow me*" (emphasis added). This is an ongoing death to self—a daily death to self. Not only is this an open invitation, but it is also a command. Notice that Jesus invites everyone, but He still requires all His disciples to bear a cross and to do it daily. This is a call to supreme loyalty and faith in Christ to give your life to Him daily, and if He so chooses for your life, to die for Him.

Christ said, "*Take up his cross and follow me.*" Likewise, Paul would give the same command but in a different way. For example, in Galatians 5:24 he says, "*And those who belong to Christ Jesus have **crucified the flesh** with its passions and desires*" (emphasis added). Just as Jesus commanded one to take up their cross, Paul called for a crucifixion of the flesh. When Paul says that "*those who belong to Christ Jesus have crucified the flesh with its passions and desires,*" he uses the aorist tense and indicative mood, which means that this is an action that the Galatians had done in the past. Paul is stating that those who belong to Christ have made a definitive decision to crucify the flesh. This word *crucify* comes from *stauroó*, which means "to fix to the cross," "crucify." This word can also figuratively mean to put the old self to death by submitting all decisions (desires) to the Lord. This utterly and decisively rejects the decision to live independently from Him. Note that Paul uses strong language when speaking about how the followers of Christ have decided to repent. They have renounced themselves. They have taken their sin, self-will, pride, self-righteousness, and violently cast it away and killed it.

Biblical repentance is frequently characterized as a violent act. Jesus describes the kingdom of heaven being taken by violence and the violent claiming it (Matthew 11:12). As we learned earlier, Paul speaks of the violence of entering the kingdom of heaven when he says that those who belong to Christ Jesus have crucified the flesh with is passions and desires (Galatians 5:24). Jesus pictures repentance as the gouging out of eyes and the cutting off of hands (Matthew 5:29–30). Jesus describes repentance as denying yourself and refusing to associate with your sinful desires, self-righteousness, and self-will (Matthew 16:24). Jesus pictures repentance as seeing your own sin and crying to God for propitiation of your sin (Luke 18:9-13). In 2 Corinthians 7:11, Paul pictures true repentance as an eagerness to turn from sin, having holy indignation and anger with your personal sin, having fear of bringing shame to God's name and God's glory, longing for godliness, and having zeal for holiness (2 Corinthians 7:11). Therefore, we see how Jesus and Paul speak of the violent and zealous nature of repentance in which an individual is radical in dealing with their own sin. The individual who has true repentance is pictured as taking sin in their life and violently killing it and maiming it. True repentance pictures an individual deliberately shunning and refusing to associate with their sin. True repentance pictures an individual hating their life of sin and turning from it. True repentance pictures the violent and aggressive attitude of killing, maiming, denying, shunning, and turning from sin in one's life and a continual turning to Christ.

Not only was this a one-time decision to repent and put one's faith in Christ, but it was also a lifelong call. As Jesus said in Luke 9:23, this is a daily walk of life to deny self and take up one's cross. Paul said the same thing in Romans 8:13 where he talks about an ongoing death to self, saying, "*For if you live according to the flesh you will die, but if by the Spirit you put to death the deeds of the body, you will live.*" When Paul says, "*Put to death the deeds of the body,*" he is talking in the present tense. Not only was there a decision to put off the old self and die to the old self, but there was also a decision in the past to live one's life in a perpetual state of putting to death the deeds of the body. The term *put to death* comes from *thanatoó*, which means to literally, "put to death," "mortify," "to make to die," or "to kill." It is a strong word. The Christian's fight with sin is a real fight, seeking to not only fight sin, but also to put it to death. Paul had this in mind with his call to repentance. It was a call to decisively and perpetually repent and crucify the flesh for the rest of one's life and trust in Christ.

Christ gave gospel calls or calls to saving faith when He said things like this in Luke 14:26: "*If anyone comes to me and does not hate his own father and mother and wife and children and brothers and sisters, yes, and even his own life, he cannot be my disciple.*" Jesus was not calling one to hate people or even hate one's self by committing suicide. Rather, Jesus was showing contrast or preference as he did in Matthew 6:24 when He said a man cannot serve two masters, for he would love one and hate the other. Jesus was pitting our affections for our dearest loved ones against our affection for Himself. Jesus was also pitting our love for our own life against our love for Him. Jesus was saying that our affections for Him must be far greater than the love we have for those in our closest concentric circle. He was saying that our affections for Him must be so much greater that, by comparison, it seems like hate toward others. Jesus was calling for our total allegiance and affection above anything and everyone else. Not only this, but He was also calling people to "hate their own life." The word *life* comes from *psuché*, which can also mean "soul." Christ is calling all people to hate their own soul. Again, to *hate one's own soul* is the same thing as *denying yourself* and *putting off your old self*. Christ was calling for total loyalty, submission, surrender, and faith in Him. Hating one's own life meant being finished with living for yourself, living for your flesh, living for your sin; it meant coming to the end of yourself and no longer being the lord of your own life.

Paul had more to say about repentance. In 2 Corinthians 7:10 he says, "*For godly grief produced a repentance that leads to salvation without regret, whereas worldly grief produced death.*" The original word for *repentance* comes from *metanoeo*, which means, "to change one's mind" or "a change of mind." Repentance is certainly a change of mind, but when this change of mind occurs, it is radical. When this change of mind occurs or when there is true repentance, the person realizes they've been wrong about sin. The person realizes they have been wrong about God; they have been wrong about salvation; they have been wrong about their standing before God; and they have had a wrong worldview and much more.

Paul describes this godly repentance in 2 Corinthians 7:11 where he says, "*For see what earnestness this godly grief has produced in you, but also what eagerness to clear yourselves, what indignation, what fear, what longing, what zeal, what punishment! At every point you have proved yourselves innocent in the matter.*" Paul pictures true repentance as being sorrowful for sinning against God, being eager and diligent to vindicate one's self by turning from sin, having holy indignation and anger with one's own personal sin, possessing the fear of the Lord and fear of bringing shame to God's name and God's glory. True repentance over one's sin is characterized by longing and desiring godliness and having zeal for holiness.

True repentance makes one poor in spirit, or rather, spiritually bankrupt before God, and the person sees their spiritual poverty before a holy God (Mathew 5:3). This change of mind causes one to mourn over one's sin against God (Matthew 5:4). This change of mind causes one to be meek and submissive to a master (Matthew 5:5). This change of mind leads one to turn to Christ and to hunger and thirst for the righteousness they don't possess (Matthew 5:6). This change of mind or repentance causes one to confess their sins before God and turn from sin.

False repentance can be characterized in several ways. False repentance has worldly grief; this is grief that is sorry for sin but doesn't turn toward God. Worldly grief may include someone being sorry for sin, but trying to be a better or more moral person. This worldly grief may include being sorry because of the consequences of sin but not being sorrowful before God.

Is true repentance some built-up exercise of the human will? It is true that man is responsible and commanded to repent (Acts 17:30); it is also taught that repentance is granted by God (2 Timothy 2:25, Acts 11:18). Repentance is not some built-up effort performed by man. May it never be! Repentance that leads to life is a gracious and merciful gift of God. Therefore, it is true that man is commanded to repent, and it is equally true that God grants repentance. True repentance is always turning away from sin and toward Christ (Acts 20:21).

The start of Paul's Christian life was a repentance and

death to self-righteousness, death to Pharisaic Judaism, death to a works salvation, and death to pride and a hope and faith in Jesus Christ as Lord and Savior. The same way Paul started his Christian life is the same way he ended it as he said Timothy:

> *For I am already being poured out as a drink offering, and the time of my departure has come. I have fought the good fight, I have finished the race, I have kept the faith. Henceforth there is laid up for me the crown of righteousness, which the Lord, the righteous judge, will award to me on that day, and not only to me but also to all who have loved his appearing.*
>
> —2 Timothy 4:6–8

Paul's faith journey began when he gave up his life to have Christ, and his faith journey ended when his life was taken away for the sake of Christ and His gospel. Paul could truly say, "*For to me, to live is Christ and to die is gain*" (Philippians 1:21).

Hence, we can understand that repentance is a gift from God in which the sinner has a radical change of mind and understands his sin against God (intellect), has godly sorrow and mourns over his sin against God (emotions and affections), turns away from his sin, puts off his old self/denies himself, and turns toward God for righteousness (will or volition).

As we transition to the next verse, let's keep Paul's call

to repentance in mind. In Acts 17:30 he said, "The times of ignorance God overlooked, but now he commands all people everywhere to repent." When Paul called men to repent, let's not forget what this call to repentance looked like.

Ephesians 4:23 – *"And to be renewed in the spirit of your minds."*

At salvation, there is transformation, and Paul states that there is to be a renewing of the mind. The word for *renewing* comes from *ananeoó*, which is a compound word with *aná* meaning *"up*, completing a *process*," and *néos meaning* "new." This word conveys the idea of being inwardly made new and transformed. Additionally, the word *ananeoó* is written in the present tense and infinitive mood, meaning that this is an ongoing process in which the mind is continually made new. So why would the mind need to be made new? The mind needs to be made new because it has been corrupted by sinful and deceitful desires. The mind needs to be continually made new and informed about sin, about the attributes of God, about salvation, about God's will, about Christ, and more. Paul helps us clarify why the mind needs to be made new at salvation and in sanctification when he says, "For the mind that is set on the flesh is hostile to God, for it does not submit to God's law; indeed, it cannot. Those who are in the flesh cannot please God" (Romans 8:7–8). Therefore, we see that the old man has a mind that is set on the flesh, set on the world, set on sin, set on self-righteousness, set on self-reliance, but it is not set on God. The old man has a mind that is set on the flesh, and it cannot submit to God. Indeed, the old man and his mind are hostile to God. Therefore, the mind needs to be made new.

The next question we should ask is this: How is the mind made new? Paul helps us answer this question in Romans 12:2 where he says, *"Do not be conformed to this world, but be transformed by the renewal of your mind, that by testing you may discern what is the will of God, what is good and acceptable and perfect."*

The first thing we learn is that the mind is not made new when it is guided, influenced, persuaded, and formed by the worldly system. The word for *conformed* comes from *suschématizó*, which conveys the act of something taking on a shape that mimics or mirrors an existing model. It is to be molded or fashioned in accordance with a set pattern or standard. Additionally, when Paul says that we are not to be conformed to this world, he writes this verb in the present tense and imperative mood, which means that this is a command that is to be continually obeyed. Paul is stressing that the mind is not to be influenced, molded, and shaped to be like the world.

So what does it mean to be conformed to the world or to have a mind that is conformed to the world? Satan is the prince of the power of the air and he controls all the ungodly systems of the world. To say that Satan is the prince of the power of the air is to say that he is the prince and lord over pornography, the LGBTQ movement, witchcraft, abortion, theft, vandalism, materialism, dirty jokes, idolatry of sports, selfishness, self-reliance, short tempers, corrupt politics, divorce, broken homes, alcoholism, drug addiction, smartphone addiction, abusive parents, rebellious children, deception, lying, false Christianity, sacramentalism, baptismal regeneration, praying to dead saints, the doctrine of purgatory, false works-righteousness Christian churches, false teachers, false doctrine, Islam, Mormonism, Christian Science, Buddhism, Taoism, Hinduism, Shintoism, Jehovah's Witnesses, and everything that is corrupt, evil, wicked, and vile. Thus, we can understand that our mind is not made new when it is conformed and influenced by the world and its deceitful schemes.

Rather than be conformed to this world, Paul tells us that we are to be transformed in our mind. This word for *transformed* comes from *metamorphoó*, which means "transfigured." This is not a change that is merely outward. Rather, it is a complete transformation that occurs in the innermost man or the mind. It is also important to note that the verb for *transformed* is written in the present tense and imperative mood, which means that this is a command that is to be continually obeyed. At salvation, we know that the Lord baptizes with the Holy Spirit and regenerates and causes sinners to be born again, and He gives them a new heart, a devoted heart, a new mind, a new spirit, and the Holy Spirit (Ezekiel 11:19–20, 36:24–28; Jeremiah 24:7, 31:31–33, 32:37–41) so man is enabled and gifted to repent and put his faith in Christ.

So not only is there a transformation of the mind at

regeneration and salvation, but there should also be an ongoing work of transformation, which occurs in progressive sanctification for the justified believer. So how is the believer continually transformed by the renewal of the mind? It's quite simple. Paul gives us the answer in 2 Corinthians 10:5 where he says, "*We destroy arguments and every lofty opinion raised against the knowledge of God, and **take every thought captive to obey Christ***" (emphasis added). The Christian is transformed in his mind because he has learned to think and see things as Christ sees them. He takes arguments, philosophies, religious talk, and worldly wisdom captive to Christ. His measuring stick is the Word of God. His mind is renewed because he has a biblical worldview. He does not get his wisdom or instruction from the world. Rather, he takes every thought captive to obey Christ. He submits every single thought and compares it against the Word of God. He is transformed because his thoughts are measured, evaluated, and submitted to God's Word. The believer possesses the mind of Christ as he understands and applies the Word of God and makes spiritual evaluations because he is not conformed to the world or circumstances of life (1 Corinthians 2:14–16).

This is what Paul means when he states that we are to be made new in the spirit of our mind. It is to flood our minds with Scripture and submit to Scripture because it is the very Word of God. How do you test and discern what is the will of God and what is acceptable and pleasing to God? It is quite simple. Submit to the Word of God because it is profitable for teaching, reproof, correction, and training in righteousness (2 Timothy 3:16). The Word of God is the weapon of the Christian's warfare (2 Corinthians 10:4–5, Ephesians 6:17). The Word of God is how we behold the glory of the Lord and are transformed into His image from one degree of glory to another (2 Corinthians 3:18).

Faith in Christ

Paul Says Put on the New Self, Christ Calls for a Submissive, Preeminent Loving, and Humble Faith in Him

> **Ephesians 4:24** – *And to put on the new self, created after the likeness of God in true righteousness and holiness.*

Paul states here that when they learned about Christ, they not only put off their old self, they were renewed in the spirit of their mind, but now we learn that they have been taught to put on the new self. Although salvation occurs in a split-second, it involves both the putting off of the old man (repentance) and putting on of the new man (faith). Putting on one's new self is Paul's way of explaining coming to faith in Christ. The term to put on comes from *enduo*, which means "to put on" or "to clothe or be clothed with." It carries with it the idea of sinking into a garment. It's important to note that "to put on" is in the aorist tense, infinitive mood, and middle voice. When written in the aorist tense and infinitive mood, this is a call for a complete and decisive action. The middle voice means that the person who performs the action is affected by the action. When Paul is writing in the aorist tense, infinitive mood, and middle voice, he is commanding them to definitively put on, embrace, and receive the new self.

Paul had called the Ephesian church to make a decisive decision to not only cast off the old self, but to also fully commit, submit, and put their faith in Christ. Coming to faith in Christ would immediately give positional righteousness, or rather, justification before God, but it would also immediately lead to practical righteousness, or rather, living out one's faith, which bears and produces good works (Ephesians 2:10).

How can we know that the new man is Christ? Paul answers this question for us in Galatians 3:26–27 where he says: *"For in Christ Jesus you are all sons of God,* **through faith***. For as many of you as were baptized into Christ* **have put on** **Christ***"* (emphasis added).

How does one become a child of God? One becomes a child of God when they put their faith in Christ Jesus (Galatians 3:26). What happens when one puts their faith in Christ Jesus? One is justified and counted righteous by faith in Christ (Galatians 3:6). What happens when one is justified by faith in Christ? They are spiritually baptized, immersed, and united with Christ (Galatians 3:27, Romans 6:3-4). What happens when one is justified by faith and united with Christ? One receives the Holy Spirit (Galatians 3:2, 3:14).

Therefore, we can know that when one has put their faith in Christ, they have been immersed into Christ and have put Christ on. Another way of saying this according to Paul can be understood through Galatians 3:14 where he says, *"So that in Christ Jesus the blessing of Abraham might come to the Gentiles, so that we might **receive the promised Spirit through faith**"* (emphasis added). And in Galatians 3:2, Paul says, *"Let me ask you only this: Did you receive the Spirit by works of the law or by hearing with faith?"* In other words, when one comes to faith in Christ, they receive the Holy Spirit (Galatians 3:2, 14); the Holy Spirit unites them to Christ (Galatians 3:14, 26–27), and they are clothed with Christ and His perfect righteousness (Galatians 3:26–27). We can know that the baptism that Paul is speaking about in Galatians 3:27 is not water baptism for the reasons we mentioned in the discussion of ceremonial washings in Chapter 2 as we traced Paul's distinction between water baptism and baptism with the Holy Spirit. We can also know that this is not water baptism because Paul condemns those who teach salvation is through a ritual or covenantal sign in the book of Galatians and throughout the New Testament. In fact, Paul consistently denounces those who teach a works-based salvation, ritual-based salvation, or ceremonial-based salvation throughout the New Testament. For example, you will find the following denunciations in the book of Galatians:

- Proclaiming that you can be saved by your works plus Christ, sacraments plus Christ, or anything else plus Christ is to proclaim that Christ died for nothing, and it is an attack on the propitiating, reconciling, expiating, and redeeming work of Christ (Galatians 2:21).

- Proclaiming that you can be saved by your works plus Christ, sacraments plus Christ, or anything else plus Christ puts you under God's curse (Galatians 3:10, 13).

- Proclaiming that you can be saved by your works plus Christ, sacraments plus Christ, or anything else plus Christ makes you obligated to keep the whole law (Galatians 5:2–3).

- Proclaiming that you can be saved by your works plus Christ, sacraments plus Christ, or anything else plus Christ makes Christ's salvific work of no benefit for you (Galatians 5:2).

- Proclaiming that you can be saved by your works plus Christ, sacraments plus Christ, or anything else plus Christ severs and completely cuts you off from Christ (Galatians 5:3–4).

- Proclaiming that you can be saved by your works plus Christ, sacraments plus Christ, or anything else plus Christ makes you a full-fledged pagan, and you may as well worship a false god because you are not a believer in Christ (Galatians 5:12).

The definition of Spirit baptism in Chapter 2 helps us understand that the baptism that Paul's speaking of in Galatians 3:27 is not a water baptism, but an element of the baptism with the Holy Spirit. Thus, we understand that putting on the new man is equivalent to coming to faith in Christ or putting on Christ.

The object of Paul's faith was the person and work of the Lord Jesus Christ. The object of Paul's faith was not a water baptism, not the Lord's Supper, not his works, and not any works done by men on his behalf. By faith, Paul lovingly embraced the reconciling (Romans 5:8–10), propitiating (Romans 3:25), expiating (Colossians 2:13–15), redeeming (Ephesians 1:7), regenerating (Titus 3:4–7), justifying (Romans 3:26), sanctifying (1 Corinthians 6:11), and glorifying work of the Lord Jesus Christ (Colossians 3:4). By faith, Paul embraced Jesus as Creator (Colossians 1:16–17), Jesus as Lord (Philippians 2:11), Jesus as Christ (Acts 17:2), Jesus as co-equal with God the Father and God the Holy Spirit (Colossians 1:15, Philippians 1:19), Jesus as truly man and truly God (Philippians 2:5–11), Jesus being born of a virgin (Galatians 4:4–5), and more. By faith, Paul lovingly, trustingly, obediently, humbly, meekly, and repentantly embraced the biblical person and work of Christ for the salvation of his soul.

The Ephesians had learned about Christ as we noted when we studied Ephesians 4:20–21. They were called to strip off their old self in Ephesians 4:22. Then they were to put on the new self, or rather, Christ. Once again, it's important to note that this is a faith that doesn't trust one's own works for righteousness before God (Romans 4:15, Galatians 2:16). This is a faith that doesn't trust ceremonies, rituals, or sacraments for salvation before God (Romans 4:9–12). This is a repentant, humble, meek, and submissive faith that has been slain and brought low by one's sin against God (Romans 7:7–11). This is faith that clings to Christ's person and work as the only means for salvation (Galatians 2:20). This is a faith that clings to Christ and trusts that His death paid for their personal sin (1 Corinthians 5:7, 2 Corinthians 5:21). This is a faith that fears God (Philippians 2:3), and it is a faith that loves God (1 Corinthians 16:22).

Paul gives the motive for Christ's sacrificial death where he says, *"And the life I now live in the flesh I live by faith in the Son of God, who loved me and gave himself for me"* (Galatians 2:20). Paul sees the motive for Christ's sacrificial death, which is love. Love is what caused the only begotten Son of God to give His life for the worst of sinners (1 Timothy 1:15). Believers have the same motive when embracing Christ in faith, which is preeminent love and trust in Christ. In fact, we can be certain that this faith is a faith that preeminently loves Jesus Christ. This is a faith that understands who Jesus is and what Jesus has done to atone for one's sin and loves Christ preeminently.

So what type of faith in Christ justifies a man? Are we to believe that someone is justified by faith in Christ when they are actively and unrepentantly committing adultery (1

Corinthians 6:9)? Are we to believe that someone is justified by faith in Christ when they are unrepentantly living and fornicating with their boyfriend or girlfriend (1 Corinthians 6:9)? Are we to believe that someone is justified by faith in Christ when they are unrepentantly teaching and preaching a false gospel and yet claim allegiance to Christ (Galatians 1:8–9, Titus 1:16)? Are we to believe that someone is justified by faith in Christ when they are actively and unrepentantly buying illegal drugs and becoming intoxicated (1 Corinthians 6:10)? Are we to believe that someone is justified by faith in Christ when they unrepentantly believe a false gospel, remain in a false church, and sit under false doctrine and false teachers (1 Corinthians 6:10, John 10:5)? Are we to believe that someone is justified by faith in Christ when they show no fruit of repentance (Acts 17:30, Luke 13:1–9)? Are we to believe that someone is justified by faith in Christ but they show no evidence of a changed and transformed life (James 2:14–26, 2 Corinthians 5:17)? Are we to believe that someone is justified by faith in Christ but the trajectory of their life is not marked by doing the will of the Father or following the teaching of Christ (Matthew 7:21–23, John 10:27–28)?

We are justified by grace through faith, but we need to explain what this saving faith is because saving faith in modern Christianity is often stripped down, redefined by man, and unbiblical. Therefore, it is crucial to understand what it means to *put on the new man* and come to saving faith in the Lord.

Jesus said in Matthew 10:37, "*Whoever loves father or mother more than me is not worthy of me, and whoever loves son or daughter more than me is not worthy of me.*" Jesus is saying that if one loves someone more than Him, they are simply not worthy of Him. Jesus also says this in Luke 14:26, "*If anyone comes to me and does not hate his own father and mother and wife and children and brothers and sisters, yes, and even his own life, he cannot be my disciple.*" Jesus is once again saying that if one loves anyone or anything more than Him, they cannot be His disciple. Paul says it this way in 1 Corinthians 16:22, "*If anyone does not love the Lord, he is to be accursed. Maranatha* (NASB2020)!" Here, Paul is declaring anathema or God's curse on those who do not love the Lord Jesus Christ. How could it be that both Jesus and Paul seem to be contradicting the doctrine of justification by faith? How could it be that Paul says we are saved by grace through faith and yet pronounce God's curse on those who do not love Christ (Ephesians 2:8–9, 1 Corinthians 16:22)? Are Paul and Jesus contradicting themselves?

We can be sure that both Paul and Jesus are not contradicting themselves. Rather, they are describing saving or justifying faith. The justifying faith that puts on the Lord Jesus Christ is not a faith which is cold, sterile, and apathetic. This is a faith that preeminently and lovingly trusts and submits to Christ over anyone and anything else. This is a faith that loves the Lord with supreme allegiance, submission, and trust.

Jesus gave a gospel invitation that emphasized brokenness, meekness, submission, and trust in which He says:

> Come to Me, all who are weary and burdened, and I
> will give you rest. Take My yoke upon you and learn
> from Me, for I am gentle and humble in heart, and you
> will find rest for your souls. For My yoke is easy, and My
> burden is light.

—Matthew 11:28–30

Jesus has a yoke for all His followers that they are to bear. As we learned earlier, a stiff-necked animal is stubborn, disobedient, and un-submissive. However, the opposite of this stiff-necked animal is an one that is meek, obedient, and submissive. When an ox that has been made meek is directed by its owner to turn left, the ox will turn left. When an ox that has been made meek is directed by its owner to stop, it will stop. Jesus gave a similar picture of the man who would bow his head and take on Jesus's yoke. It was a man who was weary and heavy-laden under the yolk of sin, shame, guilt, and a dead spiritual life. The man who was weary and heavy-laden would bow his head, submit, and take the yoke upon his shoulders; for the yoke was easy, the burden was light, and he had found the Lord and Savior who gave him rest. Paul tells his listeners to *put on the new man* that speaks of a preeminent loving and submissive faith. Jesus tells his listeners to take His yoke and learn from Him, which speaks of a preeminent loving and submissive faith. Both Paul and

Jesus spoke of saving faith as a preeminent loving, repentant, humble, submissive, and obedient faith.

Paul talks about this meek and submissive faith in another way in Romans 6:11 where he says, "*So you also must consider yourselves dead to sin and alive to God in Christ Jesus.*" Being dead to sin is tantamount to "*putting off the old self.*" Here we see that part of "*putting on the new man*" is being alive to God. The new man is alive to God in that he responds in faith to God. The new man is alive to God and His Word. The new man has embraced, received, surrendered, and submitted to Christ through faith. Jesus speaks of this submissive faith in John 10:27: "*My sheep hear my voice, and I know them, and they follow me.*" The new man or the sheep are those who are dead to sin and alive to God. They are those who possess a submissive, repentant, and preeminent loving faith in Christ. Therefore, we should understand that "*putting on the new man*" is a submissive, meek, and obedient faith in Christ.

It's also important to note that the faith that Paul speaks of has intellectual, emotional, and volitional elements. Paul notes that there is an intellectual component of faith in learning about Christ (Ephesians 4:20–21). Paul also notes that this is a faith that has an emotional/affectional component to it that preeminently loves the Lord and trusts Him over man (1 Corinthians 16:22, Galatians 1:10). Finally, Paul notes that this is a volitional faith that *puts off the old self* and *puts on the new self.* As we noted earlier, salvation and justification by faith occur in a split-second, in a moment in time, and the moment one believes the gospel, they are justified by faith and receive the Holy Spirit. In other words, when one understands the person and work of Jesus and in the split- second they repent and believe in Jesus Christ, they are justified by faith. All three intellectual, emotional/ affectional, and volitional elements of faith are present in conversion.

Additionally, just as repentance is a gift, so is faith. Faith is a gift from God and not earned or merited by man (Ephesians 2:8–9, Philippians 1:29, Romans 4:1–5). Therefore, we can understand that saving faith is a gift from God (Ephesians 2:8–9) whereby a sinner has knowledge of Jesus's person and work such that a sinner will respond to Christ's person and work by denying themselves (Matthew 16:24, Mark 8:34, Luke 9:23), picking up their cross (Matthew 10:38, 16:24; Mark 8:34; Luke 9:23), and lovingly (Luke 14:26–27, James 4:7) and obediently (2 Thessalonians 1:8, Romans 1:5) submitting (James 4:6, Matthew 11:28), and committing their life to Jesus (Matthew 10:37–39, 16:24– 26; Mark 8:34–37; Luke 9:23–26, 14:25–33) and trusting in Him only for salvation (Romans 10:13, John 3:16, John 3:36, Acts 4:12).

Paul declared in Romans 10:17, "*So faith comes from hearing, and hearing through the word of Christ.*" The faith that saves comes through hearing about Christ and the gospel. No saving faith that comes from Mormonism, which teaches that God the Father was once a man. No saving faith comes from Jehovah's Witnesses who teach that Jesus was the archangel Michael before the creation of the world. No saving faith comes from a gospel that includes a reconciliation through works or sacramentalism. A corrupt gospel message is no gospel at all. For God to save men under a false gospel would bring shame and dishonor to Himself and His Son.

The Transformed Life – Evidence of True Conversion

When one comes to faith in Christ, they are a new creation. Salvation is transformation and, as we learned earlier, conversion is the laying aside of the old pattern of life and putting on the new man or Christ. We also learned that regeneration is God giving man a new heart, new spirit, a new mind, and new affections, which enable man to repent and put his faith in the Lord Jesus Christ. Paul refers to this transformation and new creation in 2 Corinthians 5:17 where he says, "*Therefore, if anyone is in Christ, he is a new creation. The old has passed away; behold, the new has come.*" Where there is true conversion, the person has new affections and a new will to love, honor, obey, and trust the Lord Jesus Christ. Paul refers to the new creation in Galatians 6:15 where he says, "*For neither circumcision counts for anything, nor uncircumcision, but a new creation.*" There is nothing more drastic in someone's life than being converted to Christ; conversion to Christ is the most significant event in a Christian's life. It is the time when all their affections change, and their relationship with sin changes. It is a time in their life when they begin their relationship with Christ. Paul talks about the dramatic change in one's life this way:

"He has delivered us from the domain of darkness and transferred us to the kingdom of his beloved Son" (Colossians 1:13). This transformation is going from spiritual darkness and darkened understanding to possessing spiritual understanding and knowledge of Christ.

Paul talks about the spiritual darkness and blindness of an unbeliever in 2 Corinthians 4:3–4 where he says:

> *And even if our gospel is veiled, it is veiled to those who are perishing. In their case the god of this world has blinded the minds of the unbelievers, to keep them from seeing the light of the gospel of the glory of Christ, who is the image of God.*

Paul contrasts this spiritual darkness of an unbeliever to the spiritual life of a believer who is in Christ in 2 Corinthians 4:6 where he says, "*For God, who said, 'Let light shine out of darkness,' has shone in our hearts to give the light of the knowledge of the glory of God in the face of Jesus Christ.*" Paul is consistent in his message that conversion to Christ is a night-and-day transformation. It is blindness to sight. It is death to life. It is darkness to light. Although salvation occurs at a point in time, the Christian will continue in a life of repentance and faith as Paul says in Colossians 2:6, "*Therefore, as you received Christ Jesus the Lord, so walk in him.*"

Conversion to Christ is only the beginning of the Christian's sanctified walk with Christ until they die and go to be with Christ. As we close this chapter, my hope is that you have understood Paul's conversion and his theology on conversion. This understanding will draw a sharp contrast with those who teach and preach sacramental conversion, which is completely contradictory to biblical conversion and Paul's theology on conversion. My hope and goal for this chapter is that we have made it crystal clear that Paul called men to repent and put their faith in Christ. His gospel invitation was similar in nature and content to Christ's invitation to repent and believe in Him. We will end with a hypothetical example of how Paul could have called men to Christ given what he has written in Scripture.

Paul: A Hypothetical Gospel Invitation

You have been wrong in your worship of pagan gods, and you have lived selfishly for your own sinful and corrupt desires. The Living God who is the Judge of the living and the dead sees your sins and must punish and judge you with an everlasting destruction and fire away from the presence of God because of your sins. God cannot look on your sin with favor, and no man can be justified by the works of the law. For the law only makes man aware of sin, and the law brings wrath! You are alienated, hostile in mind, and cut off from God.

However, because God is rich in mercy, He sent His Son who was born of a woman, born under the law, into this world. He is the God-man, Jesus Christ, who is the mediator between God and man. Jesus, who is equal with

God the Father and God the Holy Spirit, humbled Himself and became a man and lived in total obedience to His Father. He lived a sinless life and knew no sin. His claims to deity were attested to and affirmed by His miracles and ministry. He was rejected by His people and sentenced to death, even death on a cross. On that cross, He who knew no sin, became sin for us. God laid forth Jesus Christ as a propitiation for sin to be received by faith. On that cross, Jesus suffered the wrath of God that was due to man. On the cross, His Father put man's sinfulness on Jesus Christ. There was wrath that God needed to take out on man's sin, so God could satisfy His justice and wrath against man's sin. Therefore, God would be the just and the justifier for all mankind. God would be just in condemning sinful man, and He would be the justifier of man by punishing His Son with His full unbridled wrath, which man deserves. Jesus, who knew no sin, became sin on behalf of men, so that we might become the righteousness of God. Christ became a curse on the cross, and God the Father cursed His one and only Son as if Jesus were the iniquitous, trespassing sinner though he had done no wrong. God the Father cursed Jesus on that cross with the divine wrath that man deserved, which is hell.

Jesus's substitutionary work was accepted by the Father, and Jesus was raised for our justification. Jesus rose from the dead on the third day and conquered sin, death, and the devil. He is now seated at the right hand of God, and all authority in heaven and on earth has been given to Him. He is coming again and will judge the world in righteousness. Those who do not obey the gospel will suffer divine wrath, everlasting punishment, and retribution in hell.

Those who obey the gospel will be resurrected and brought to be with God in heaven. Because Jesus took the wrath of God on the cross and was raised to life, He is the only mediator between God and man. God is kind and long-suffering, and His kindness is meant to lead you to repentance. He is the only one who can forgive you of your sins. He alone can give you His perfect righteousness. All your sins can be forgiven, and all His righteousness can be given to you so you can be reconciled to God, united to Christ, become a child of God the Father, coheir with Christ, and receive eternal life. You can be justified and saved by faith in Christ from the wrath that is to come. Not one sin will be brought up in judgment for those in Christ. Not one sin will be brought to your charge before the judgment seat of Christ if you are in Christ Jesus. There is no condemnation for those in Christ for Christ, the sacrificial Lamb, has borne the fiery divine wrath for sin. God is rich in mercy and has shown forth His great love for mankind.

You now know of your sins and that your sins are an abomination to God. You now know what Christ has done to provide reconciliation with God. None of your idol worship, works, and ceremonies will reconcile you to God. Now you know what God has done to provide pardon for your sins in His Son Jesus Christ. I am compelled by Christ's love and as an ambassador for Christ knowing the sternness and kindness of the Lord and the fear of the Lord to issue you this call: "I beg you, I plead with you, I command you to put off your old self, die to sin and repent of your sins. Put on the new self, be reconciled to Christ, call on the name of the Lord Jesus Christ, put your faith and hope in the Lord Jesus Christ, and trust in Him alone for your salvation, and he will give you the free gift of eternal life."

Chapter 7

Paul's Theology on Conversion in Romans

Therefore I urge you, brothers and sisters, by the mercies of God, to present your bodies as a living and holy sacrifice, acceptable to God, which is your spiritual service of worship.

—Romans 12:1 NASB2020

In this chapter, we'll look at how Paul gave a gospel call or invitation to the Romans in his letter to them. When exploring Romans 12:1, it may be helpful to go back and review Chapter 4 as Paul will draw language and imagery from sacrificial offerings and use this in his gospel call or invitation to come to Christ in saving faith. Although the gospel invitation language is different, it carries with it the call of repentance and faith in Christ. This verse is often tied to sanctification, and for good reason. While I wholeheartedly agree that this is a call to live a sanctified life, it is equally true that this is a call to come to faith in Christ. As we start this chapter, we'll break down smaller sections of Romans 12:1 as we work through this verse.

Romans 12:1: *Therefore I urge you, brothers and sisters, by the mercies of God* (NASB2020).

Paul is going to give an exhortation to the Romans. Paul has just laid out the majesty of the person and work of Jesus Christ in salvation. We will see that Paul's exhortation is not simply a "turn or burn" message. Although it contains the message of God's wrath, it also contains the manifold blessings of the salvific work of Christ.

We can know that Paul's exhortation to offer oneself as a living sacrifice is to be obeyed knowing the manifold blessings from the previous eleven chapters of the book of Romans as Paul begins Chapter 12 with the word *therefore*. The word *therefore* is meant to tie together the reason for Paul's exhortation. Paul expects the Roman audience look back at the doctrine he has laid out in the first eleven chapters of the book of Romans, and he will appeal to his listeners based on the doctrine he has laid out. How do we know Paul is making his appeal based on the previous eleven chapters of the book of Romans? We can see this because he uses the word *mercies* in the plural form. He's not just appealing to one aspect of God's mercy. No, he is appealing to the manifold compassions and mercies that should motivate a person to give their life to Christ and trust Christ with everything. Likewise, it is the manifold blessings of the person and work of Christ that should motivate us to continue in our sanctified walk with the Lord. We can get a very good understanding of these blessings if we perform a high-level view of just the first eight chapters of Romans. We'll start with the "bad news" and then move to the "good news" to understand the "mercies of God."

The Bad News

- **Wrath of God Against Sin** – God's wrath is revealed from heaven against all mankind's ungodliness and unrighteousness (Romans 1:18).

- **Man's Sinful Depravity** – Mankind has rejected the knowledge of God and chosen to worship created things and lead an unrighteous and sinful life (Romans 1:21–32).

- **Sinful Depravity of the Religious but Lost** – It's not just the sinful lascivious and wanton population of mankind that is subject to God's wrath, but also those who are religious and moral (Romans 2:1–5).

- **The Just Condemnation of Mankind** – All of mankind has sinned and is deserving of God's condemnation (Romans 3:10–18).

- **No Justification by Works** – The law holds man accountable to God, and that no one will be justified by works of the Law (Romans 3:19–20).

The Good News

- **God's Kindness Leads to Repentance** – God's kindness is meant to bring man to repentance (Romans 2:1–5).

- **The Righteousness of Christ** – The righteousness of God has been manifested in the person and work of Jesus Christ (Romans 3:21–22).

- **Justification is a Gift of Grace in Christ** – Justification is through the redemptive work of Christ (Romans 3:24).

- **Christ as a Propitiation for Sin** – Christ was put forward as an atonement or propitiation for sin (Romans 3:25).

- **Christ's Sacrifice to be Received by Faith** – God the Father poured out His wrath on Jesus Christ, which allows Him to be the justifier of all who come to Christ by faith and to also be just in punishing sinful man (Romans 3:25–26).

- **Faith Is Better than the Law** – God justifies by faith and not by the law (Romans 3:27–28).

- **God Saves People from All Nations** – God's plan of salvation includes Jews and Gentiles (Romans 3:29–30).

- **The Imputed Righteousness of Faith** – God imputes His righteousness to all who come to Him in faith (Romans 4:1–6).

- **The Blessing of Forgiveness** – God forgives sin and will not count man's sin against him because of God's righteousness that is credited to man's account through faith in Christ (Romans 4:7–8).

- **Faith Is Better than Rituals, Ceremonies, and Sacraments** – Righteousness or justification comes by faith and not by covenant signs, ceremonies, or rituals (Romans 4:9–12).

- **The Promise of Faith Is Better than the Law** – God is faithful to keep His Covenant with Abraham (Romans 4:13–22).

- **Justification for All Who Put Their Faith in Christ** – The promise of becoming righteous and justified by faith is not only for Abraham, but for all those who believe in Christ (Romans 4:23–25).

- **Reconciliation Through Christ** – There is peace with God through faith in Christ (Romans 5:1).

- **Promised Holy Spirit Given to Believers** – The Holy Spirit is given to those who put their faith in Christ (Romans 5:5).

- **The Love of God for Sinners** – Christ died for us while we were His enemies (Romans 5:8).

- **Peace with God Through Christ's Blood** – We are justified by Christ's blood and saved from the wrath of God (Romans 5:9).

- **Reconciled to God Through Christ's Work** – We are reconciled to God through His Son (Romans 5:10–11).

- **Christ Is Better Than Adam** – Adam's sin imputed unrighteousness to all mankind, but Christ's free gift of grace and righteousness come through Christ to all who believe in Him (Romans 5:12–21).

- **New Life in Christ** – We have new life in Christ (Romans 6:1–4).

- **Freed from the Power and Penalty of Sin Through Christ** – We have been set free from the rule of sin (Romans 6:5–11).

- **Practicing Righteousness in Christ** – Sin no longer has dominion over us (Romans 6:12–14).

- **Slaves of Righteousness in Christ** – We are now slaves to Christ and righteousness (Romans 6:15–23).

- **Freed from the Power and Penalty of Sin in Christ** – We are released from the law and the condemnation that the law brings (Romans 7:1–7).

- **The Christian's Struggle with Sin and Promise of Delivery** – The Christian will still struggle with sin, but Christ will ultimately deliver us from the body of death (Romans 7:13–25).

- **No Condemnation in Christ** – There is no condemnation for those in Christ (Romans 8:1).

- **Freedom in Christ** – The Holy Spirit has set us free (Romans 8:2).

- **Practical Righteousness in Christ** – The Holy Spirit helps us walk in righteousness, gives us peace, helps us submit to God's law, and helps us please God (Romans 8:3–8).

- **Indwelt by the Holy Spirit and Promise of Resurrection** – We are indwelt by the Holy Spirit (Romans 8:9–11).

- **Adoption Through Christ** – We are sons of God (Romans 8:14).

- **God as the Believer's Father** – God is our Father (Romans 8:15–16).

- **Coheirs and Inheritors of All Spiritual Blessings with Christ** – We are coheirs with Christ (Romans 8:17).

- **Resurrection Hope and Future Glory** – We will have redeemed bodies (Romans 8:18–25).

- **God the Holy Spirit's Intercession** – The Spirit intercedes for us according to the will of God (Romans 8:26–27).

- **God's Good Purpose for His Children** – God will work all things for the good of His children (Romans 8:28).

- **Progressive and Prospective Sanctification and Glorification** – God planned for us to be conformed to the image of His Son along with the hope of glorification (Romans 8:29–30).

- **Security of the Believer in Christ** – Those in Christ cannot lose their salvation (Romans 8:31–35).

- **Victorious and Conquerors Through Christ** – We are victorious because we are in Christ (Romans 8:37).

- **Security of Believers in Christ** – Nothing can separate us from Christ (Romans 8:38–39).

In the first eight chapters of the book of Romans, Paul laid out the manifold blessings of the person and work of the Lord Jesus Christ and what Christ has accomplished for the believer. Paul did this very same thing with the church in Ephesus when he talked about the manifold blessings of being in Christ in the first three chapters of the book of Ephesians. After explaining the blessings the Father gives through the person and work of Christ, he explained the call of repentance and faith in Christ, which is to put off your old self, and to put on the new self.

Paul's exhortation to put off the old self and put on the new self comes after he had taught about Christ. In Paul's letter to the Romans, he does this very same thing. He exhorts his listeners to come to faith in Christ or continue in their walk with Christ after he explains the manifold mercies and blessings of the gospel and Christ.

Romans 12:1: *To present your bodies as a living sacrifice, holy and acceptable to God, which is your spiritual worship.*

This is where Paul gives the gospel invitation to come to faith in Christ. As mentioned earlier in this chapter, some theologians would argue that this is a call to sanctification; especially because of Paul's use of the word *brothers*. While I agree that this is certainly a call to sanctification, I believe we'll see that this is both a call to justification and a call to sanctification. Paul was certainly speaking to Christians in this letter, but it is likely that there were unconverted listeners as well. This gospel call to come to Christ serves as both a call to faith in Christ for the unconverted and also as a call to the believer to continue walking by faith in Christ.

Paul commands his listeners to *"present your bodies as a living sacrifice, holy, and acceptable to God."* The language Paul uses in this text is reminiscent of the sacrificial, Levitical system. Thinking back to Chapter 4 of this book, we recall that the sacrifices were to be offered to God on His terms and that they were to be offered with the right heart attitude.

Therefore, the first point that we'll explore here is how Paul is calling for a decisive commitment. We can see this when we understand the phrase *"present your bodies."* The word *present* comes from *paristémi* and means to "stand close beside" or "exhibit." Paul's use of this word draws from the Levitical sacrifices. The burnt offering was to be a male without defect selected by the worshiper; it was the worshipper's responsibility to seek out the best cattle, sheep, goat, or bird without blemish to be sacrificed to God. *Paristémi* carries with it the very same idea of a sacrifice being offered up and presented to God. However, in this case, the sacrifice is one's body or life, which is to be given or offered up to God. To understand Paul's gospel call, it's important to note that *paristémi* is a verb in the aorist tense, infinitive mood, and active voice. Thus, this is calling for a single momentary and completed decision or action. We could even paraphrase Paul's words this way:

- In light of God's mercies, make a decision to present your bodies as a living sacrifice to Christ for the rest of your life.

- Now that you know of God's mercies, decide once for all that you will offer yourselves and commit your life to Christ as a living sacrifice.

- You now understand God's manifold mercies. Therefore, make up your mind that you will offer up yourself as a living sacrifice and continue to live for and trust in Christ.

- In considering God's many mercies, commit to put off your old self and put on the new self by offering yourself as a living sacrifice to God for the rest of your life.

A. W. Tozer gives an excellent illustration of what Paul is saying where he says this regarding the aorist tense of *paristémi* and the call to salvation:

Present thus speaks of a definite point of commitment to God even as a bride and groom commit themselves to each other once and for all on their wedding day. The bride does not turn to the groom and say, "I give you my cooking ability." Nor does he say to her, "I give you my bank account." (They may not have either.) No, in a marriage ceremony they vow, "I give you myself." And so the dedication of ourselves to serving God begins with a decisive commitment. But just as keeping the vows spoken in a wedding ceremony requires continual reminders and recommitment, so dedicating ourselves to the Lord involves a moment-by moment awareness of the pledge we made. These reminders are necessary because the world-system relentlessly appeals to our inherent selfishness and pride.[37]

Note that Paul is calling for the surrender of one's life to Christ. We can see this when we understand that our bodies are to be given to God. When Paul tells his audience to *present their bodies*, he is referring to the totality of a person, which includes the mind, the heart, the soul, the will as well as the physical body. For example, in Paul's letter to the church in Thessalonica, he says this, "*Now may the God of peace himself sanctify you completely, and may your **whole spirit**, and **soul** and **body** be kept blameless at the coming of our Lord Jesus Christ*" (1 Thessalonians 5:23, emphasis added). Here, we can clearly see that Paul didn't just have the external body in mind, but also the soul and spirit. In Romans 6:17, Paul explains where obedience is to come from, "*But thanks be to God, that you who were once slaves of sin have become **obedient from the heart** to the standard of teaching to which you were committed*" (emphasis added). When Paul beseeches his audience to present their bodies, he is exhorting them to commit every part of their being to God. Would Christ want external obedience with no heart commitment? That would surely be dead religion with no heart to obey God. Would it be possible to have heart commitment but no physical commitment? In other words, can you have heart agreement, but refuse to obey with your body? The answer should be a resounding "No!" We are being called to hold nothing back and to give the whole of ourselves completely to Christ and entrust our souls and our lives to Him for salvation. Christ wants us to know Him and His will (intellect). Christ wants this knowledge of Him to trigger heart affections toward Him such as fearing Him, honoring Him, and loving Him (emotions/affections). Christ wants the informed affections to stimulate the will to give oneself to Him, trust Him, and do His will (volition). Christ wants us to love Him with our entire heart, soul, mind, strength, and body (Mark 12:30, Luke 14:26–27, 33). This is no blind date. This is no arranged marriage. As Paul tells us in Ephesians, the picture of marriage between a man and a woman is the picture of Christ and the church (Ephesians 5:32). Christ gave Himself up for the church, and those who belong to the invisible or true church respond by leaving all behind and loving and trusting Christ preeminently.

Next, the word *sacrifice* should remind us that we are to offer ourselves according to God's terms. The word *sacrifice* comes to us from *thusia*, which means "a sacrifice." It carries with it the idea of an official sacrifice prescribed by God; hence, it is an offering that is accepted by the Lord because the sacrifice is offered on His terms. Therefore, we can know that the person offering up their body as a living sacrifice must present themselves to Christ on His terms. How did Paul call men to come to Christ? In Acts 20:21, Paul said he did it by "*testifying both to Jews and to Greeks of **repentance toward God** and of **faith in our Lord Jesus Christ**"* (emphasis added). Paul unashamedly contends that an offering that is acceptable to God is one who comes in repentance toward God and with faith in the Lord Jesus Christ. How did Paul tell the Ephesians to come to Christ in Ephesians? He told them to put off the old self and to put on the new self (Ephesians 4:22–24). Therefore, we understand that the sacrifice of the one coming to faith in Christ needed to come on Christ's terms. The Lord will reject a sacrifice that holds onto anything plus Christ as a means to salvation whether its circumcision, water baptism, good works, church membership, the Lord's Supper, or Mass. The Lord will reject a sacrifice that refuses to repent. Paul's exhortation calls the worshipper to offer their body according to God's terms. No true worship can be performed until one has come to faith in Christ. A sacrifice of one's body not offered in repentance and faith is a sacrifice that is not offered on God's terms and is one He will oppose and reject (James 4:6).

Furthermore, God wants this sacrifice to be a living sacrifice; He does not want a dead sacrifice. The word *living* is in the present tense and participle mood, which means that the person offering their body to God is to offer it on God's terms as a way of life. Christ said this very same thing in Luke 9:23: "*If anyone would come after me, let him deny himself and take up his cross daily and follow.*" Christ commanded all believers to follow Him daily as self-denying and cross-bearing believers. This is the call to come to Christ on His terms of repentance and faith and continue to live one's life under these conditions. The call is not about sinless perfection (Romans 7:14–25); it is about the willingness to submit one's life to Christ without reserve. Paul put it this way in Galatians 2:20:

> *I have been crucified with Christ. It is no longer I who live, but Christ who lives in me. And the life I now live in the flesh I live by faith in the Son of God, who loved me and gave himself for me.*

Paul's faith in Christ compelled him to live for Christ; he continued to trust Christ for salvation and follow Him. Paul submitted his thought life to Christ (2 Corinthians 10:4–5), and his heart allegiance was to Christ (1 Corinthians 16:22, Romans 6:16–17). Paul exercised control over his body for the sake of Christ (1 Corinthians 9:24–27). This is not saying that Paul's obedience was the ground for his salvation. May it never be! Paul would never make such a claim. However, Paul knew that a person needed to obey the gospel by repenting and putting their faith in Christ as a lifelong commitment (2 Thessalonians 1:8). Robert Murray M'Cheyne captures the essence of a "*living sacrifice*" best when he says, "Lord, make me as holy as a pardoned sinner can be!"[38] Paul talks about this pursuit to be a "living sacrifice" again in Philippians 3:12–14 where he is striving, agonizing, stretching, and pressing on toward the goal of Christlikeness:

Not that I have already obtained this or am already perfect, but I press on to make it my own, because Christ Jesus has made me his own. Brothers, I do not consider that I have made it my own. But one thing I do: forgetting what lies behind and straining forward to what lies ahead, I press on toward the goal for the prize of the upward call of God in Christ Jesus.

We should also see that when the sacrifice is offered on God's terms, it is holy and acceptable to Him. Once again, the terms *holy* and *acceptable* are used to bring us back to the Levitical sacrifices. We remember that the Lord wanted His people to be holy as He says in Leviticus 11:45: "*For I am the Lord who brought you up out of the land of Egypt to be your God. You shall therefore be holy, for I am holy.*" God wanted his people to be set apart and different. They were cut away as a nation, cut away as a people, and were to have cut away or circumcised hearts. The Lord was jealous for a people for whom He would be their God and they would be His people (Ezekiel 11:19–20, Hebrews 8:8–13). Additionally, we see that when the offering was given according to God's terms in Leviticus 1:9, it was, "*a food offering with a **pleasing aroma to the Lord**" (emphasis added). In the sacrificial Levitical system, the Lord said that the offering was a pleasing aroma when it was given to Him according to His prescribed terms. Romans 12:1 uses this same language where it describes the sacrifice as "*holy and acceptable to God.*" *Acceptable* comes from *euarestos*, which means well-pleasing because it's fully acceptable. Therefore, we can see that when one has come to faith in Christ, it is a sacrifice that is *well-pleasing*. The one offering the sacrifice of their body in repentance and faith is at peace with God. The one offering their body as a sacrifice according to God's terms, is justified and reconciled with God. Paul also mentions that sacrifices offered by believers are a fragrant offering, acceptable and pleasing to the Lord (Philippians 4:18). Thus, a body offered to the Lord as a living sacrifice on His terms is pleasing to God in justification. Likewise, the sacrifices of sanctified believers living their lives as a *living sacrifice* are a fragrant offering pleasing to the Lord.

Additionally, we should see that this is the only reasonable response to the person and work of Christ and His gospel. The word that is used for spiritual is *logikos*, which means "reasonable" or "rational." You can hear the word *logic* in *logikos*. In view of all the spiritual blessings that come through the person and work of Christ, the only rational thing to do is to give one's life and body to Christ and trust in Him alone for the salvation of one's soul. If someone knows of the condemnation they deserve, if they know of the sacrifice that Christ has given, if they know of the pardon of sin, and if they know that there is a way to have a right relationship with God forever, then the only reasonable act of service is to give one's life as a living sacrifice—to repent and put one's faith in the Lord Jesus Christ. Anything else is irrational, illogical, and unacceptable.

Next, we should see that a well-pleasing sacrifice gives way to sanctification. Our justification immediately results in positional and progressive sanctification as we are now holy to God. The word *holy* comes from *hagios*, which means "set apart," "sacred," or "different/distinguished." We know that when one has been justified by grace, the wrath of God has been settled through the blood of Christ, which was shed for that individual; Christ has fully suffered the wrath of God in their place. Paul speaks of the immediate sanctification this way in Romans 6:22: "*But now that you have been set free from sin and have become slaves of God, the fruit you get leads to sanctification and its end, eternal life.*" The immediate path of the one justified by faith is a sanctified and separated life unto God. They are a slave to God rather than a slave to sin; they are holy and separated to God. Paul says it this way in Titus 2:11–12, "*For the grace of God has appeared, bringing salvation for all people, training us to renounce ungodliness and worldly passions, and to live self-controlled, upright, and godly lives in the present age.*" Paul is confirming that the grace that saves, or rather, a saving faith is one that turns from ungodliness and lives a godly or sanctified life. It is quite true that we will spend the rest of our lives fighting sin and mortifying the flesh and will not be completely free from sin until the Christian dies and goes to be with the Lord (Romans 7:14–25, 8:13). Thus, justification leads to positional and progressive sanctification, and the believer is to be continually presenting their body as a living sacrifice as they mortify the flesh, pursue Christlikeness, and seek to obey Christ.

Next, we should see that Christ is the reason for giving and living our life for Him. Not only is He our reason to come to Him in repentance and faith at justification, He is also our reason to continue to live for Him in our sanctification. The Christian should meditate on the manifold blessings of the person and work of Christ as a source of encouragement and motivation to live every moment for Christ. The Christian can live with the comfort of knowing that Christ will always intercede for us (Romans 8:31–35). The Christian can live knowing that Christ has paid for all past, present, and future sins (Romans 8:33). The Christian can live knowing that Christ died for us while we were His enemies (Romans 5:8). The Christian can live knowing that nothing will separate us from the love of God that is in Christ Jesus (Romans 8:38–39). The manifold blessings of knowing the person and work of Christ are reasons to live every moment for Him.

Finally, we should see that a person who has not offered themselves to God as a living sacrifice, holy and pleasing to God, is an unbeliever and is no worshipper of God. Jesus is the only way to the Father (1 Timothy 2:5); there is no other way to worship God. The word *worship* comes from *latreia*, which can mean "service rendered to God" or "worship." In the New Testament the idea is to render sacred service to God in a spirit of worship. This word also carries the idea of freewill obedience that is given out of a heart of adoration. True worship is not just singing hymns or praise songs; it

284The Apostle Paul's Theology on Conversion

means living a life of obedient service to God. William Macdonald states:

> Worshipful service was not that of a religious drudge (to do hard, menial, monotonous work), going through endless rituals and reciting prayers and liturgies by rote. It was service bathed in fervent, believing prayer. It was willing, devoted, tireless service, fired by a spirit that loved the Lord Jesus supremely. It was a flaming passion to make known the Good News about God's Son.[39]

If one does not come to the Father through Christ Jesus as a living sacrifice, he is not a worshipper of God. Stated another way, if one comes to Christ with no repentance toward God or faith in Christ Jesus, he is not a worshipper of God. Let's state it yet another way: If one who has not put off his old self and put on the new self comes to the Lord Jesus Christ, he is not a worshipper of God, and he has not offered his body as a living sacrifice, holy and pleasing to God.

As we close this section, it is my hope that we can clearly see how similar Paul's call to faith is to Ephesians 4:22–24. Although Paul's conversion language in Ephesians 4:20–24 is different, the message of repentance toward God and faith in Christ is present in Romans 12:1. When we think about Paul's background and his pre-conversion experience with circumcision, ceremonial defilement and washings, Sabbath observance, sacrificial offerings, his conversion experience, and his theology on conversion, it becomes overwhelmingly clear that Paul would never have taught conversion through ceremonies, rituals, or sacraments. Paul had different ways of calling someone to faith, but the message was and is the same. It is to repent and put your faith in Christ. It is to put off your old self and put on your new self. It is to offer yourself as a living sacrifice, holy and pleasing to God.

Chapter 8

Paul's Conversion Theology in 1 Thessalonians

For they themselves report concerning us that kind of reception we had among you, and how you turned from idols to serve the living and true God, and to wait for his Son from heaven, whom he raised from the dead, Jesus who delivers us from the wrath to come

—1 Thessalonians 1:9–10

In this chapter, we'll examine how Paul describes the conversion of the Thessalonians in 1 Thessalonians 1:3–10. In just seven short verses, Paul gives us deep and rich theology on the evidence of true conversion. These marks of conversion are true of all believers, so it will serve us well to study these characteristics.

Far too often pastors, churches, and professing Christians give false assurance and false evidence or marks of true conversion. Some churches say that one is a Christian because they've been baptized in water. Some churches say that someone is a Christian because they've gone through confirmation. Some churches or pastors say that someone is a Christian because they are moral and ethical. Other churches say that someone is a Christian because they attend church on Sunday and send their children to a Christian school. Yet others may that someone is a Christian because they give offerings, participate in a church committee, affirm the 1689 London Baptist Confession, affirm the Three Forms of Unity, believe the Apostle's Creed, take Communion every Sunday, and so on. However, let's pay attention and seek to understand what Paul says about true conversion as his theology on conversion agrees with Jesus and the New Testament. We'll start by examining the text of 1 Thessalonians 1:3.

Evidence of True Conversion: Faith That Works

Constantly keeping in mind your work of faith and labor of love and perseverance of hope in our Lord Jesus Christ in the presence of our God and Father.

—1 Thessalonians 1:3 NASB2020

As Paul opens his letter to the Thessalonians, he gives thanks to God and reminds them that they are always in his prayers because he is reminded of their work of faith, labor of love, and steadfastness of hope in the Lord Jesus Christ (1 Thessalonians 1:2–3). So, the first mark of true conversion we see from Paul is an active and living faith. We see this right away when Paul thinks about the Thessalonians and remembers their work of faith. Many passages come to mind when we think of an active and living faith. In fact, when Paul described the working of their faith, this is completely in line with how Jesus and other New Testament writers spoke of a living or saving faith. Keeping in mind other portions of Scripture that describe a living faith, Paul could have described the Thessalonian's faith this way:

> I give thanks to God for you and remember your work of faith. For your faith was alive and active and is the type of faith that hears the Word and obeys the Word (James 1:22). I give thanks to God because your faith is a living faith that hears God's Word and puts it into practice (Luke 6:47, Matthew 7:24). Your faith is a blessed faith because it hears the Word of God and keeps it (Luke 11:28).

Conversely, the New Testament unashamedly talks about a non-saving faith that is a foolish or moronic faith that hears the Word of God but does not obey it (Matthew 7:26). There is a demonic and foolish faith that knows the truth of God's Word, trembles at God's Word, but does not obey God's Word (James 2:19–20). There is a practical atheist faith that hears the Word of God but does not obey God and acts as if God doesn't exist (Luke 6:46). There is a dead faith that does not do the will of God (Matthew 7:21–23, James 2:26). There is a lukewarm faith that disgusts the Lord and is marked by being wretched, pitiable, poor, blind, and naked (Revelation 3:14–22). The Thessalonians were not marked as those who had a dead faith, lukewarm faith, demonic faith, or a non-submissive faith. No, we see that Paul remarked that the Thessalonians were marked by a living and working faith.

Evidence of True Conversion: Labor Done and Motivated by Love for God

Not only were the Thessalonians marked by a living and active faith, but they were also marked as those who labored in love. This word for *labor* comes *kopos*, which means "to labor," "to grow weary," or "to toil." This word conveys the act of laboring to the point of exhaustion with diligent effort and perseverance. It implies not just the act of working, but the accompanying fatigue and weariness that result from the exertion. The term does not stress the amount of work, but rather the effort. But this wasn't just cold and apathetic labor. No, this labor was done in love. The Ephesian church was rebuked because they had abandoned their first love (Revelation 2:4), but this was not true of the Thessalonians; they had love for God and His people because God had first loved them (1 John 4:9–21). They also abounded in love for one another (1 Thessalonians 3:12).

In fact, the word used here for love comes from *agape*, which is the self-sacrificial love of the will. The Thessalonians were marked as those who labored to the point of exhaustion out of love for Christ and for God's people. They were a people marked by a self-sacrificial love for God (1 Corinthians 16:22, Luke 14:26, Matthew 10:37). Though they had not seen the Lord, they loved and believed in the Lord Jesus Christ with inexpressible joy and labored for Him (1 Peter 1:8). They were marked as those who loved the Lord their God with all their heart, with all their soul, with all their mind, and with all their strength.

Evidence of True Conversion: Persevering Hope in the Lord Jesus Christ

Moreover, the Thessalonians were marked as those who had steadfast hope in the Lord Jesus Christ. The word used for steadfast is the word *hupomoné* and it conveys the idea of remaining faithful and patient under pressure and maintaining one's faith and hope despite challenges. This characteristic reflects a trust in God's character and promise. The Thessalonians weren't characterized as false Christians who receive the Word with joy, but fall away during the time of testing (Luke 8:13); they weren't characterized as false Christians who are choked out by the cares and riches and pleasures of life and bear no fruit (Luke 8:14). No, they were characterized as those who heard the Word, held it fast, and bore fruit with endurance (Luke 8:15).

Not only did they persevere, but they did so while hoping for the Lord's return (1 Thessalonians 1:10). We can be sure that they were hoping for resurrection bodies (1 Corinthians

15), and they were hoping to hear the Lord say, "*Well done good and faithful slave. . . . enter into the joy of your master*" (Matthew 25:23 NASB2020). We can also be sure that they were hoping to be made perfect like Christ (Philippians 3:12–14) and to receive the crown of righteousness that the Righteous Judge would aware them on that day (2 Timothy 4:8). We can be sure that they were hoping for the Lord's return and to be delivered from the wrath to come (1 Thessalonians 1:10). The Thessalonians had persevering hope in the Lord and His promises. Thus, they were characterized as those who persevered in the faith and held fast the confession of their hope in the Lord Jesus Christ without wavering (Hebrews 10:23).

Evidence of True Conversion: Living and Walking in the Presence of God

The Thessalonians were marked as those who lived and worked out their faith before the presence of God; they self-sacrificially labored in love for God and His people, persevered in the hope of the Lord Jesus Christ, and did all this in the presence of God the Father. We see this when Paul says, "*in the **presence** of our God and Father*" (emphasis added). The word for *presence* comes from *emprosthen*, and it conveys the idea of being in the presence of or being right in front of something or someone. This is quite a statement considering that the Thessalonians knew that all their thoughts, words, deeds, and intents were done before the watchful eyes of the Lord. They weren't like those who had hypocritical faith, practiced dead religion, or justified themselves before men. Not at all. They knew that the Lord tests the heart (Proverbs 17:3) and that the Lord watches over all the ways of His children (Psalm 1:5). They were those who, like Enoch, walked with God (Genesis 5:24); they walked humbly with God (Micah 6:8). They lived in the presence of God as those who offered up their bodies as living sacrifices before the watchful eyes of God as holy and pleasing to the Lord (Romans 12:1). Thus, Paul remembered that the Thessalonians were marked as living their Christian lives in the presence of God the Father; no hypocrisy or duplicity marked the Thessalonians.

1 Thessalonians 1:4: "*For we know, brothers loved by God, that he has chosen you.*"

In verse four, Paul affirms to the Thessalonians that they are chosen and loved by God. In fact, Paul is certain that the Thessalonians were true converts and believers. When Paul says, "*for we know, brothers loved by God, that he has chosen you,*" Paul uses the words *know* and *beloved* in the perfect tense and participle mood, which means that he was sure that their salvation took place in the past, and he was just as sure of their salvation up to the present. When he states that they are loved by God, the word *loved* is written in the perfect tense and participle mood. But why would this be so special and important for the Thessalonians to know? It means that they were chosen in Christ before the foundation of the world (Ephesians 1:4). It means that God, who is eternal, loved them in eternity past with an unconditional love, that they are loved in the present age, and that God will love them into eternity future because God's unconditional election does not change (Romans 8:29–30). This is a marvelous statement confirming God's immeasurable love for the Thessalonians.

So, how did Paul know that the Thessalonians were chosen by God and that they were loved by God? Paul could give these assurances because he believed that the Thessalonians were saved, converted, born again, and regenerated. In fact, we could ask several questions of Paul regarding the salvation of the Thessalonians. We could ask, "Paul, how did you know that the Thessalonians were saved?" "Paul, how did you know the Thessalonians were converted to Christ?" "Paul, how did you know the Thessalonians had been born again?" "Paul, how did you know that the Thessalonians had saving faith?" Not only do we have overwhelming evidence of the Thessalonian's salvation in verse three, but we will see Paul continue to give the evidence as to why he was sure the Thessalonians were converted to Christ.

Evidence of True Conversion Power: Salvation Brings Transformation, Which Is the Result of Regeneration

1 Thessalonians 1:5: *For our gospel did not come to you in word only, but also in power and in the Holy*

Spirit and with full conviction; just as you know what kind of men we proved to be among you for your sakes.

Another mark of true conversion that Paul mentions is that the gospel came to the Thessalonians in power. In fact, the word *power* comes from *dunamis*, which is where we get the word dynamite. Yes, it is true that when the gospel is preached, some neglect the gospel (Hebrews 2:3), some do not believe the gospel (Luke 8:12), some believe that the gospel is foolish (1 Corinthians 1:18), some hear the gospel and think that it is the stench of death (2 Corinthians 2:15–16), some hear the gospel but do not repent (Matthew 11:20), and some hear the gospel and make excuses why that cannot accept the gospel invitation (Luke 14:16–20). However, for the Thessalonians, the gospel came with power. As Paul said, this gospel did not come as a message that was neglected, rejected, scorned, or ignored. Rather, the gospel was received amongst the Thessalonians as the power of God for salvation to everyone who believes (Romans 1:16). It was received as the sweet fragrance of Christ to God for those who are being saved (2 Corinthians 2:15–16). It was received as the wisdom and power of God for those who are being saved (1 Corinthians 1:18–24). So, what kind of power was this? William Macdonald gives a helpful statement regarding God's supernatural power: "This is the **power** which God used in our *redemption*, which He uses in our *preservation*, and which He will yet use in our *glorification*" (emphasis added).[40]

Therefore, we can be certain that the gospel came in the power of redemption and regeneration. The greatest evidence of salvation is transformation, which is the result of regeneration. We can be certain that the gospel came to the Thessalonians and that they were regenerated and transformed by it. For the purposes of this book, we can describe regeneration as follows: Regeneration is the sovereign monergistic work of God the Holy Spirit in giving spiritual life to spiritually dead and sinful man so that man is enabled to repent and respond in saving faith to Jesus Christ.

Jesus discusses regeneration with Nicodemus in John 3:1–10. In one of the most poignant explanations of the powerful, life-giving, and monergistic work that is done in regeneration, Jesus states that *"unless one is born of water and the Spirit, he cannot enter the kingdom of God."* (John 3:5). In this statement, Jesus is pointing Nicodemus to the New Covenant promise of Ezekiel 36. Although the text of Ezekiel 36 is being spoken to Israel, it is true for every believer. Ezekiel 36:24–27 (NASB2020) says:

> *For I will take you from the nations, and gather you from all the lands; and I will bring you into your own land. Then I will sprinkle clean **water** on you, and you will be clean; I will cleanse you from all your filthiness and from all your idols. Moreover, I will give you a new heart and put a new spirit within you; and I will remove the heart of stone from your flesh and give you a heart of flesh. And I will put my **Spirit** within you and*

*bring it about that you walk in My statutes, and are
careful and follow My ordinances.* (emphasis added)

Nicodemus should have been aware of this passage of
Scripture as it pointed to Israel's restoration, and he should
have been familiar with the personal pronouns in this portion of Scripture. In these four short verses, the Lord uses
the personal pronoun *"I"* seven times. He is indicating that
salvation will strictly be a work of God; that is this work of
salvation will be a one-sided affair. The Lord God is going
to perform a mighty act of salvation for His name's sake.
To understand Jesus's statement of being born of water and
the Spirit and the powerful work of regeneration, let's look
at Ezekiel 36:25–27 for insight into how the Thessalonians
were powerfully transformed.

*I will sprinkle clean water on you, and you shall be clean
from all your uncleannesses, and from all your idols I
will cleanse you.*

—Ezekiel 36:25 NASB2020

In Ezekiel 36:25, notice the personal pronoun "I" and
notice that this work is going to be a powerful work of God
to forgive, cleanse, and purify the sinner from his sins and
idolatry. For God says, *"I will sprinkle clean water on you and
I will cleanse you."* The question to ask is this: What does
this reference to water mean? It is a reference to forgiveness
of sins and an ongoing cleansing and purging of sins and
idolatry out of one's life. After David had been confronted

by the prophet Nathan for his sin of adultery and murder, he penned Psalm 51, which gives us insight into this reference to water and cleansing. In Psalm 51:1–2, he says, "*Be gracious to me, God, according to Your faithfulness; According to the greatness of Your compassion, wipe out my wrongdoings.* **Wash me thoroughly from my guilt and cleanse me from my sin**" (NASB2020, emphasis added). In verse 7, David says, "**Purify me with hyssop, and I will be clean; cleanse me, and I will be whiter than snow**" (NASB2020, emphasis added). No theologian would exposit, or try to reason, that David is asking the Lord for a bath, a shower, or a ceremonial washing. No, the washing that David is asking for is the washing away and cleansing of sins. He is asking for personal forgiveness from the Lord. He is asking that the Lord would not look at his sins but turn away from them and forgive them. He is asking the Lord for mercy and compassion and not to deal with him according to justice. He is also asking to be cleansed. In the Hebrew, this word is *taher*, which means "to be clean or pure." In other words, David is saying:

"Cleanse me and purge me from my immorality. Only You can make me morally clean. Only You can cleanse my murderous and adulterous heart. I don't need a physical bath, Lord! I need You to cleanse the filth in my heart and forgive me."

In Ezekiel 36:25, the Lord says much the same thing; He says that He is the one who will act to forgive sins. He is the one who will purify us from our sins and cleanse us from our filthiness and idols. Note here that this is not just a reference to forgiveness of sins. This is also a promise to purify us morally from our sins and idols. Again, what the Lord is saying is that this cleansing and purification is not just forgiveness of sins, but a continual work of God to rid the person's life of sin and idolatry. Nicodemus should have known this. You can almost hear Jesus saying: "Nicodemus, don't you know that it is God who forgives sins? Nicodemus, don't you know that it is God who cleanses people from their sins? Don't you know that unless God cleanses someone from the inside, he cannot be clean before God? Nicodemus, don't you know that external water cannot take away the stain of sin and that only God can remove the stain of sin? Nicodemus, won't you learn from David and see that the cleansing you really need is from the heart? Nicodemus, God is the one who sprinkles the clean water and who cleanses you."

And I will give you a new heart, and a new spirit I will put within you. And I will remove the heart of stone from your flesh and give you a heart of flesh.

—Ezekiel 36:26 NASB2020

Remember that Jesus just told Nicodemus that a person must be born of water and the Spirit. In our passage from Ezekiel, verse 25 captures the water, and verse 27 captures the Spirit; sandwiched in between the water and the Spirit is verse 26, which talks about the Lord giving a new heart and a new spirit. So, what does it mean for the Lord to give man a new heart and a new spirit? The Lord is saying that He isn't going to help man be a better person or become more moral or love Him just a little more. This isn't the Lord slapping lipstick on a pig and calling the pig a transformed man. No, He is saying that He is going to change man's very nature and who man is. Oftentimes, the heart and the spirit encapsulate man's intellect, emotions or affections, and will (i.e., his whole being). The Lord is saying that He is going to transform man's intellect so man will know the Lord. He will transform man's emotions and affections so that man's preeminent affections will be toward the Lord and what the Lord loves. Mankind will be so transformed that they will hate what the Lord hates and love what the Lord loves. The Lord will also transform man's will so that man's disposition will be inclined to do the will of the Lord.

But what is "a *heart of stone*"? It is an inanimate object—a heart that has no life. You can kick a stone, you can shock a stone, you can scream at a stone, but the stone will not respond. The heart of stone does not respond to divine stimuli or God's Word. However, a heart of flesh is a heart that is alive and responsive. The heart of flesh has a pulse, and it responds to divine stimuli or God's Word. What then is the spirit? The spirit is the innermost part of man. Genesis 6:5 says, "*The Lord saw how great the wickedness of the human race had become on the earth, and that every inclination of the thoughts of the human heart was only evil all the time*" (NIV).

Genesis 6:5 captures the inclination of man. Man's heart and spirit is only evil and inclined toward evil all the time. It's not that man acts the wickedest every single second of his life. However, it is to say that man's intellect, affections, and will are inclined toward sin, self, false religion, and idolatry rather than serving, worshipping, loving, obeying, and trusting the living God. That is, man's spirit is inclined to evil all the time.

In Jeremiah 13:23, the Lord says, "*Can an Ethiopian change his skin or a leopard its spots? Neither can you do good who are accustomed to doing evil*" (NIV). Once again, the Lord is saying man cannot change his evil disposition any more than a leopard or an Ethiopian can change his skin. It is not possible. The Lord says of man's heart in Jeremiah 17:9, "*The heart is deceitful above all things and beyond cure. Who can understand it*" (NIV)? Jesus is drawing Nicodemus to this sovereign and powerful act of God, which changes a man's very being and imparts spiritual life.

Ontology is the study of being or the nature of being. A man will follow his nature. A pig will always lay in its filth. A migratory bird will fly south when winter comes. A man will always choose evil because that is his nature. A change of one's being is only accomplished by the sovereign work of God; man can't change his nature. However, God can change man's intellect, emotions, affections, will, and nature so that man is inclined to repent and trust in Jesus Christ (Ezekiel 11:19–20, 36:24–27 and Jeremiah 24:7, 31:33–34, 32:38–40). These verses contain "*I will*" statements that highlight God monergistically acting on His own to save. These verses describe God changing the "spirit," "heart," and "mind," which means that God changes man from the inside. These verses contain the new covenant language of *"they will be my people, and I shall be their God."* These verses speak of God giving man a devoted heart, a God-fearing heart, and an obedient heart.

It is as if Jesus was saying: "Nicodemus, don't you know that in your fallen nature, you are only prone to evil? Nicodemus, don't you remember that your heart is only wicked all the time? Nicodemus, don't you understand that your heart is deceitful and beyond cure? Nicodemus, God needs to remove your heart of stone from your flesh and give you a heart of flesh and a new spirit. Nicodemus, you don't perform this work, God does it. Nicodemus, don't you remember that God is the one that writes His law on your heart and mind? Nicodemus, don't you realize that when you receive this new heart and new spirit, God's laws will be written on them as well? Nicodemus, what can you do to earn a new heart and a new spirit? Nicodemus, don't you see that the old covenant was written on stone tablets and the promised new covenant will be written on the heart of flesh? Nicodemus, don't you know that it is God who must completely change your intellect, affections, and will?"

And I will put my Spirit within you, and cause you to walk in my statues and be careful to obey my rules.

—Ezekiel 36:27

As part of the new covenant, the Lord promises that He will put His Spirit in us to walk in His ways. So let's recap. The Lord is saying that He will forgive our sins and cleanse us from our impurities and sins. The Lord will write His law on our heart and mind, give us a new heart and spirit, and completely change us. Finally, the Lord will give us His Spirit so that we will be careful and able to obey Him. This is the regeneration that leads to transformation. God changes the mind, heart, and will of man. God gives spiritual life to spiritually dead men.

It is as if Jesus is saying: "Nicodemus, it is God who forgives our sins. It is God who cleanses us from our sin. It is God who gives us a new heart and new spirit and completely changes our nature and will. It is God who writes His law on our heart and mind. It is God who gives us a heart of flesh and who puts His Spirit in us. It is God who gives us a heart to fear Him. It is God who gives us the new heart to return to Him wholeheartedly. Nicodemus, don't you know that salvation is from the Lord and not from ceremonies, rituals, law observance, ceremonial washings, and the like? Nicodemus, it is God who causes you to be born from above. It is God who gives you the gift of faith and the gift of repentance. It is all about God monergistically saving man." Jesus emphasizes that salvation and regeneration are the sovereign monergistic work of God for Nicodemus, and He reminds Nicodemus of this by drawing him to the new covenant promise in Ezekiel 36.

Thus, we see the regenerating work of God the Holy

Spirit that was at work in the Thessalonians. The greatest evidence of salvation is transformation, which is the result of regeneration. This is the power that Paul is speaking of. The all-powerful God who created the universe is recreating man, changing him, and then dwelling in his heart. The gospel went forward to the Thessalonians, and the Spirit caused the Thessalonians to be born from above through the living and enduring Word of God (1 Peter 1:23). This powerful saving act of God transforms a pilfering, money-loving tax collector into a philanthropist (Luke 19:1–10). This powerful saving act of God transforms the sexually immoral, idolaters, adulterers, homosexuals, thieves, greedy people, drunkards, revilers, and swindlers into imitators of Christ (1 Corinthians 6:9–11, 11:1). This powerful saving act of God transformed a self-righteous, false teaching, double son of hell, inwardly dead, child of wrath, blaspheming, murderous, and false teaching Pharisee into an apostle, pastor, shepherd, evangelist, missionary, and truth teaching child of God, the Apostle Paul. This is the saving and transforming power of the gospel. It takes dead religious church-going people and turns them into people who love the Lord Jesus Christ with an incorruptible love (Ephesians 6:24). Likewise, the gospel came to the Thessalonians in power and transformation as they turned from idols to serve the living and true God (1 Thessalonians 1:9). Where there is no power of transformation, there is no evidence of salvation, and thus no reality of regeneration.

Evidence of True Conversion: In the Holy Spirit – Conviction of Sin, Righteousness, and Judgment

In discussing true conversion, Paul mentions that the gospel came to the Thessalonians in the Holy Spirit. We've learned about the power of regeneration and how the Holy Spirit transforms man. So how did the gospel come in the Holy Spirit? This seems to be a vague statement. However, when we learn more about the work of the Holy Spirit, we get a better understanding of what Paul is saying. In John 16:8, Jesus says this regarding the work of the Holy Spirit: "*And when he* [Holy Spirit] *comes, he* [Holy Spirit] *will convict the world concerning sin and righteousness and judgment.*"

Here, we can see that one of the works that the Holy Spirit performs is convicting the world of sin. This word *convicting* comes from *elegchó*, which means to "reprove," "refute," or "correct"; it conveys the idea of convincing someone of their sin, error, or wrongdoing with the aim of leading them to repentance and truth. Refuting or reproving carries the idea of convincing with solid, compelling, biblical evidence. So how does the Holy Spirit work in convicting the world of sin? The Holy Spirit convicts the sinner that God hates his sin (Psalm 5:5, 11:5). The Holy Spirit convicts the sinner that God abhors his sin (Psalm 5:6). The Holy Spirit convicts the sinner that God is angered with his sin (Psalm 7:11). The Holy Spirit convicts the sinner that God is ready to destroy and punish those who sin (Psalm 7:12–13). The Holy Spirit convicts the sinner that his sin is warfare against

Him (James 4:4). The Holy Spirit convicts the sinner that his sin is an abomination to God (Proverbs 22:12). The Holy Spirit convicts the sinner that his sin is evil (Psalm 7:9).

Not only does the Holy Spirit convict the sinner that God hates his sin, but He also convicts the sinner that because God is just and holy and He must deal with the sinner's sin according to who He is. Because God is infinite, loving, just, good, faithful, omniscient, immutable, omnipresent, and holy, He must punish the very sin that violates His law and character. Therefore, the Holy Spirit convicts the sinner that God must his punish sin. Not only this, but the Holy Spirit convicts the sinner that God will punish the sinner by sending him to hell, which is a place of God's full wrath; it is a place of blackest darkness (Jude 13, Matthew 22:13), filled with the furious, all-powerful, concentrated, raging, and vengeful fire of God that devours and consumes His enemies (Matthew 5:22, 5:29, 13:42, 13:50, Hebrews 10:26–31). Hell is filled with the lost who are weeping and angry against God; they are unrepentant, Christ-rejecting (Matthew 11:20–24), and Christ-neglecting sinners (Hebrews 2:1–3). The lost will spend all eternity being punished for every sin they ever committed (Revelation 20:12) with no hope of escape (Luke 16:26) and with only the expectation of excruciating torment to their body, soul, and spirit (Matthew 10:28) and they will have an undying conscience that will haunt them day and night, forever and ever, with no reprieve (Luke 16:25).

This is the work of the Holy Spirit to convict the sinner

of sin against God and the punishment they deserve. This conviction of sin brought on by the Holy Spirit is what causes poverty of spirit, mourning over sin, sorrow for sinning against God, hatred of sin, eagerness to clear one's self of their sin, confession of sin, and a turning from sin to God (Matthew 5:3, 5:4; 2 Corinthians 7:10–11; Luke 3:3–13).

The Holy Spirit also convicts the sinner of righteousness. In John 16:9, Jesus said that the Holy Spirit would convict the world of righteousness because He would go to the Father (John 16:10). So what does it mean that the Holy Spirit convicts the world of righteousness because Christ goes to His Father? In John the Baptist's ministry, he made many claims about Jesus that included Jesus being the baptizer with the Holy Spirit and fire, or rather, the Savior and the Judge (Luke 3:15–17). John the Baptist also claimed that Jesus was the Lamb of God who took away the sins of the world (John 1:29). God the Father testified that Jesus was His beloved Son with whom He was well-pleased (Matthew 3:17). Jesus made claims that He and the Father were one and that He did the works of His Father (John 5:18, 10:37–38). Jesus did many miracles that attested to His claims and proved that He was sent by God and was the Son of God (Acts 2:22). Jesus also predicted that He would die and then be raised to life (Matthew 16:4, John 2:18–22). However, there were towns and religious leaders who rejected Jesus, and many of Jesus's disciples no longer walked with Him. There was widespread rejection of Jesus as the Messiah.

So, when Jesus says that He would convict the world of righteousness because He would go to the Father, He was saying that all His teaching, all His claims, all His miracles, and all His salvific work would prove that He was who he said He was. If Jesus could not resurrect Himself, it would prove He was not one with the Father (John 5:17–18). If Jesus could not resurrect Himself, He would be a lying prophet (Matthew 16:21–22, 17:22–23, 20:17–19; Mark 8:31, 9:30–32, 10:32–34; Luke 9:21–22, 9:43–45, 18:31–34). If Jesus could not resurrect Himself, it would be evidence that He was not the Son with whom the Father was well-pleased (Matthew 3:17). If Jesus could not resurrect Himself, it would be evidence that He was not anointed by the Holy Spirit (Luke 4:18–21).

However, all Jesus's works, teaching, and life were validated by His resurrection, which proved that He is the Christ, the Son of the Living God. Without the Resurrection, Christ's claims and work would have meant nothing. If Jesus had died and not risen, He would not have been the Resurrection and the Life (John 11:25). If Jesus had not risen, He would have been like any other man who dies and does not come back to life (Psalm 90:1–12, Ecclesiastes 7:2). If Jesus had not risen, all His claims and miracles would have amounted to nothing as even Moses and Elisha were able to perform miracles but could not raise themselves from the dead. Without the resurrection, Jesus's claims and work would have been invalidated. Without the resurrection, Jesus would have lied when He said

He had authority to lay down His life and take it back up (10:17–18). Without the resurrection, Jesus would not be the Way, the Truth, and the Life and the only way to the Father (John 14:6).

Therefore, we can see that the work of the Holy Spirit is to convict the sinner of the righteousness of Christ. The work of the Holy Spirit is to convict the sinner that Jesus is who He says He is and that He accomplished what Scripture says He accomplished. The work of the Holy Spirit is to convince the sinner that there is no other righteousness that commends the sinner to God except the righteousness of Christ. The work of the Holy Spirit glorifies Christ as the all-sufficient propitiation for sinners. The work of the Holy Spirit convicts sinners that Jesus Christ speaks the truth about eternal life and that the way to the Father is through Him (John 14:6). Thus, we see that the Holy Spirit convicts the sinner of the righteousness of Christ.

We also see that the Holy Spirit convicts the sinner of judgment. Most specifically, the Holy Spirit convicts the sinner that Satan was defeated at the cross. This has massive implications for the Christian, for it shows that Christ was victorious over sin, death, and the devil (Colossians 2:13–15). It shows the Christian that Christ was the fulfillment of prophecy to crush the head of the serpent (Genesis 3:15). It shows the Christian that though Satan was defeated at the cross even though he is still active in this world, that there is coming a final fatal blow that will crush Satan, and he will be thrown in the lake of fire (Romans 16:20,

Revelation 20:10). This is the work of the Holy Spirit to convict sinners of judgment and that the evil one has been defeated.

However, unbelievers have a different response to the Holy Spirit when it comes to sin, righteousness, and judgment. In Acts 7, Stephen gives a sermon to the Sanhedrin and when he finished, he rebukes them for being hard of heart and not believing the gospel as he says in Acts 7:51: *"You stiff-necked people! Your hearts and ears are still uncircumcised. You are just like your ancestors:* ***You always resist the Holy Spirit"*** (NIV, emphasis added)! How did the unbelieving Jews respond to the gospel truths? They remained obstinate, stiff-necked, unrepentant, unregenerated, and uncircumcised in heart. They resisted the Holy Spirit by refusing to repent and believe the gospel truth.

Therefore, we can see what it means when Paul says the gospel came to the Thessalonians in the Holy Spirit. The Holy Spirit convicted them of their sin and condemnation. The Holy Spirit convicted them of righteousness and that the only way to be righteous before God is through Christ. The Holy Spirit convicted them of the judgment of Satan and Christ's victory over Satan. The Holy Spirit did a work in the hearts of the Thessalonians to believe the gospel truths of sin, death, hell, the person and the work of Christ, and man's responsibility to repent and trust in the Lord Jesus Christ for salvation.

Evidence of True Conversion: Full Assurance

True conversion is full assurance of the gospel. We see that when the gospel was preached, it came to the Thessalonians with full assurance. The word for *"full assurance"* comes from the word *plérophoreó*, which means "fully persuaded" or "fully convinced." This word conveys the idea of bearing the work of God to the fullest extent. In this context, it would mean that the Thessalonian believers were fully convinced of the gospel truth that they had heard. There was no doubting, hesitancy, or debating. Unlike those in the Areopagus who wanted to hear more from Paul, but did not follow him, the Thessalonians were fully convinced of the gospel that was shared with them and believed that it was the Word of God and not the word of men (Acts 17:32–34, 1 Thessalonians 2:13). Unlike the unbelieving Pharisees who tested the Lord and demanded a sign from heaven, the Thessalonians were fully convinced, received the gospel, and suffered the same persecution for the sake of Christ that the churches in Judea suffered (Matthew 16:1, 1 Thessalonians 1:6, 2:14). Unlike the authorities who knew the truth about Jesus but would not confess Him for fear of being put out of the synagogue, the Thessalonians were fully persuaded of the gospel, turned from idols to serve the living God, and mimicked Paul and the Lord Jesus Christ (John 12:42–43). The Thessalonians were marked as those who were transformed, convicted of gospel truths, and fully believed and received these truths.

Evidence of True Conversion: Imitators of the Apostles and Imitators of Christ

You also became imitators of us and of the Lord, having received the word during great affliction with the Joy of the Holy Spirit

—1 Thessalonians 1:6 NASB2020

Another mark of truth conversion is becoming an imitator of the Lord Jesus Christ. We see this as the Thessalonians became imitators of Christ. The word *imitators* comes from *mimétés,* which means to "mimic" or "be a follower." So how is becoming an imitator of Christ a mark of true conversion? In Matthew 16:24, Jesus commanded that if anyone were to come after Him in a salvific way, they needed to, *"deny himself and take up his cross and **follow me**"* (emphasis added). The word *follow* comes from *akoloutheó,* which means "to follow the one who precedes," "to join one as an attendant," or "to accompany one." This means "to be in the same way with." It carries the idea of cleaving steadfastly to one and to conform wholly to that one's example in living and, if need be, in dying also. It is a strong word that gives the idea that the one following is not following begrudgingly but is willfully following step for step with Christ. The one following isn't resentfully following, but rather, is seeking to follow Christ wholeheartedly. The self-denying, cross-bearing follower is conforming their mind to that of Christ to mimic Christ in thought, word, deed, and intent. Additionally, *akoloutheó* is written in the present tense and imperative mood in Matthew 16:24, which means it is a command that is to be continually followed. Therefore, we can be sure that this call to salvation was to be a self-denying and cross-bearing repentant, preeminent loving, and submissive faith.

This was the result of the transforming work of the Holy Spirit. The Thessalonians became self-denying and cross-bearing followers of the Lord Jesus Christ. This is what it means to mimic Jesus; to be an imitator or mimic Jesus is to be a follower of Jesus. A follower of Jesus is going to cleave steadfastly to Him and follow where He goes. One who follows Jesus will begin to mimic and imitate Christ because they are following Christ. Jesus promised that His sheep would hear His voice and follow Him (John 10:3–4, 10:27). Jesus affirmed that those who hate their life and keep it for eternity are those who follow Him (John 12:24–26). Jesus pronounced blessing on those who hear His Word and keep it (Luke 11:28). As we can see, to mimic and imitate Jesus is to listen to Him, obey Him, and follow Him. In fact, the apostle John says it this way in 1 John 2:5–6: "But whoever keeps his word, in him truly the love of God is perfected. By this we may know that we are in him: **whoever says he abides in him ought to walk in the same way in which he walked**." (emphasis added). A true mark of conversion is simply one who walks as Jesus walked, who mimics Christ, and who listens to His word and submissively trusts, obeys, and follows Him.

Those who are Christ's true disciples will be like Christ

and will be treated like Christ. Jesus affirms this in Matthew 10:24–25 when he says:

> *A disciple is not above his teacher, nor a servant above* *his master.* **It is enough for the disciple to be like** **his teacher, and the servant like his master.** *If they* *have called the master of the house Beelzebul, how much* *more will they malign those of his household.* (emphasis added)

Evidence of True Conversion: Received the Word Joyfully Amongst Affliction and with Much Joy

Receiving the gospel joyfully amongst persecution is another mark of true conversion. Jesus warned that some would hear the saving Word and receive it with joy, but would fall away during the time of testing (Luke 8:13). He also warned that some would hear the saving Word, but they would be choked out by the cares, riches, and pleasures of the world and would not bring forth fruit (Luke 8:14).

However, the Thessalonians were those who received the gospel in great tribulation. The word *tribulation* comes from *thlipsis*, which can mean "anguish," "persecution," or "distress." This word conveys the idea of pressure and constriction that is pressed upon someone and causes them to feel confined with no way out. Did the Thessalonians wilt under the tribulation? Did the gospel message get choked out and bear no fruit among them? Did the Thessalonians receive it with shallow hearts and fall away when tested? Not at all! They were the good soil that heard the gospel with honest and good hearts and bore fruit with patience (Luke 8:15). They received the Word of God not as the word of men, but as the Word of God (1 Thessalonians 2:13).

Jesus spoke about this kind of love and inexpressible joy in coming to Him with saving faith in two parables: the Hidden Treasure and the Pearl (Matthew 13:44–46). In Matthew 13:44, He says, "*The kingdom of heaven is like treasure hidden in a field. When a man found it, he hid it again, and then in his joy went and sold all he had and bought the field*" (NIV). This is speaking of a man who finds Jesus Christ, the forgiveness of sins, eternal life, and reconciliation and a relationship with the Living God. The man who finds this treasure of infinite worth is filled with joy inexpressible and sells everything to buy the field. This more specifically talks about the joy and price people are willing to pay to enter the kingdom of God when they find the infinite worth of Christ. This is the most valuable possession in the world that is worth the cost of a personal cross, denying yourself, and submitting, and trusting in Christ.

In Matthew 13:45–46, Jesus says, "*Again, the kingdom of heaven is like a merchant looking for fine pearls. When he found one of great value, he went away and sold everything he had and bought it*" (NIV). There are differences in these parables, but the underlying theme is that those who have found the forgiveness of sins, Jesus Christ, and eternal life will pay the price because what they have found is of infinite value, and everything else is of no value compared to having Christ. Just like the man who found the treasure hidden in the field and sold everything to get the treasure or the merchant who found the fine pearl and sold everything to get the pearl, so too were the Thessalonians who accepted the gospel with great joy under duress and affliction. They received and joyfully stood firm in the gospel amid great affliction, and they counted it all joy (James 1:2–4).

We get a picture of what their persecution looked like when we read that the Thessalonians were treated like the believers in Judea who were being killed, driven out, and persecuted (1 Thessalonians 2:14). As we read earlier, the Christians were pursued, persecuted, imprisoned, and put to death by the ruling Jews. Paul's testimony confirms that the price of being a Christian was costly. However, we can be sure that though the Thessalonians were persecuted for righteousness' sake, reviled, and spoken evil of on account of the Lord, they were blessed because they were being persecuted just as Jesus and the prophets had been persecuted, and their reward in heaven was great (Matthew 5:10–12). Thus, we see that a mark of true conversion is embracing the gospel and joyfully holding steadfast in faith with the joy that is found in the Lord while enduring hardship, affliction, and persecution.

Evidence of True Conversion: Becoming an Example – A Light to the World

So that you became an example to all the believers in Macedonia and Achaia. For the word of the Lord has sounded forth from you, not only in Macedonia and Achaia, but in every place the news of your faith toward God has gone out, so that we have no need to say anything.

—1 Thessalonians 1:7–8 NASB2020

The Thessalonian believers became an example of what it means to be a true believer in the Lord Jesus Christ. In fact, the word for example comes from *tupos*, which conveys the idea that the Thessalonians were a reliable precedent for others to follow. So how were they a proper pattern of what a mature Christian looks like? To answer that question, we can just sum up what we've learned thus far. They had an active and living faith; they labored to the point of exhaustion and did this all motivated by love for God and love for His people. They persevered in difficult circumstances and great afflictions while hoping on the Lord. The gospel came to them in power, and they were born again and had transformed lives. They became fully convicted by the Holy Spirit of the truths of the gospel. They became imitators of Paul and the Lord Jesus Christ. They received the gospel amid afflictions and tribulations. It wasn't just that the Thessalonians had excellent doctrines, creeds, or confessions, it was the report of their faith that was an extraordinary example.

Not only were they models of what it meant to be a believer in Macedonia and Achaia, which were the regions they resided in or were next to, they were like a trumpet blast testimony to all other regions. Alexander MacLaren says this about the Thessalonians' faith, which resounded to all places:

> The Apostle employs a word never used anywhere else in the New Testament to describe the conspicuous and widespread nature of this testimony of theirs. He says, 'The word of the Lord sounded out' from them. That phrase is one most naturally employed to describe the blast of a trumpet. So clear and ringing, so loud, penetrating, melodious, rousing, and full was their proclamation, by the silent eloquence of their lives, of the Gospel which impelled and enabled them to lead such lives. A grand ideal of a community of believers! If our churches to-day were nearer its realization there would be less unbelief, and more attraction of wandering prodigals to the Father's house. Would that this saying were true of every body of professing believers! Would that from each there sounded out one clear accordant witness to Christ, in the purity and unworldliness of their Christlike lives![41]

Therefore, we see that the faithful testimony of the Thessalonians was widespread. They didn't have a powerful testimony because they homeschooled their children or because they agreed to some creed or confession. They didn't have a powerful testimony because of their music program, children's program, outreach program, or any of the like. Not at all! They had a powerful testimony because of the witness of their faith in God. They were identified with Paul who had turned the world upside down, and so they participated in the trumpet call of turning the world upside down (Acts 17:6). Jesus said that all true believers would stand out and that they would be "the light of the world." Jesus stated that true believers would let their light shine before others so that the world would see their good works and give glory to the Father (Matthew 5:15–16). The Thessalonians were a light to the world, a city on a hill, a lamp on a stand, and a powerful testimony of the saving grace and gospel of the Lord.

Evidence of True Conversion: Turned from Idols – Repentance

> *For they themselves report about us as to the kind of reception we had with you, and how you turned to God from idols to serve the living and true God*
>
> —1 Thessalonians 1:9

A mark of true conversion that we is a turning away from idols. The word used for *turned* comes from *epistrephó*, which is a compound word with the prefix *epi* intensifying the root word. *Epistrephó* can also mean to "convert." This word depicts a pivotal act of reorientation away from sin, darkness, error, falsehood, and evil and a turn toward God.

In this verse, it's also important to note that the word *idols* is written in the plural form. In Thessalonica, there was much idolatry and worldliness. There were gods such as Cabirus, Dionysus, Aphrodite, Zeus, Asclepius, and the worship of Caesar. Not only was there worship of false gods, but the Thessalonians were surrounded by rampant worldliness and sexual immorality (1 Thessalonians 4:1–8). In fact, we learn from Paul that those who are sexually immoral, impure, and covetous are idolaters (Ephesians 5:5). So what did they turn from? They turned from false Greek gods, from serving the prince of the power of the air (Ephesians 2:2), and from serving their own selfish and idolatrous desires.

Just as there were many idols in Thessalonica, there are many idols that are being served today. There are idols such as sports, money, pornography, jobs, homes, family, wives, husbands, children, and cars. There are false idols such as Buddhism, Taoism, Shintoism, Confucianism, Hinduism, mysticism and many other false religions. There are idols in false Christianity such as Lutheranism, Roman Catholicism, Eastern Orthodoxy, United Methodists, Episcopalians, Church of Christ, and many other churches that teach that Jesus and the apostles say that water baptism saves. Many false teachings about Christ and His gospel are propagated and spread today. These are all idols that are either false gods or represent an unbiblical Jesus who is not the true Jesus of the Bible (2 Corinthians 11:4).

If the Thessalonians were here today, what would they do? Would they partner with lawlessness (2 Corinthians 6:14)?

Would they fellowship with darkness (2 Corinthians 6:14)? Would they find harmony with Belial (2 Corinthians 6:15)? Would they seek to find commonality with false religion (2 Corinthians 6:15)? Would they seek to find agreements with idols and God (2 Corinthians 6:16)? What is the resounding testimony and mark of true conversion of a true Christian? It is one that turns from idols to serve the living God. Thus, a true Christian is one who turns away from idols, including false Christianity to serve the living God. This is putting off the old man. This is denying oneself. This is crucifying the flesh. This is true repentance.

Evidence of True Conversion: Turning to and Serving the True and Living God – Submissive, Loyal, and Preeminent Loving Faith in the Lord Jesus Christ

True conversion is marked by a submissive, loyal, and preeminent loving faith in the Lord Jesus Christ. This is exactly what happened with the Thessalonians. They were surrounded by a panoply of false gods and idols. However, they turned from the idols (plural) to the living and true God (singular). They did not give their allegiance, loyalty, love, devotion, and trust to the idols. No, their allegiance, loyalty, love, devotion, and trust were given to the Lord.

Additionally, we see that they turned to "**serve** the living and true God." The word for *serve* comes from *doulos*, which can mean "slave" or "servant." Many of the New Testament writers identified themselves as a *doulos* or slave of Christ.

Today, the idea of being a slave has negative connotations, but that term doesn't bear that stigma when it comes to being a slave of Christ in the New Testament. A *doulos* in the New Testament, as used by Peter and Paul, was one who willingly committed himself to serve a master he loves and respects. The *doulos* had no life of his own, no will of his own, no purpose of his own, and no plan of his own. All things were subject to his master. Every thought, breath, and effort were subject to the will of his master. The *doulos* was one who was absolutely surrendered and totally devoted to his master. The existence of the *doulos* was for the will and purpose of his master and nothing else.

Paul referred to himself as a slave or *doulos* of Christ (Romans 1:1, Philippians 1:1, Titus 1:1). Paul referred to Timothy as a *doulos* of Christ (Philippians 1:1). James referred to himself as a *doulos* of Christ even though he was half-brother to Jesus (James 1:1). Peter referred to himself as a *doulos* of Christ (2 Peter 2:1). Jude referred to himself as a *doulos* of Christ even though he was half-brother to Jesus (Jude 1:1). John referred to himself as a *doulos* of Christ (Revelation 1:1). Jesus referred to a true believer who did His will as His faithful *doulos* (Matthew 25:21). Jesus said that those who were a true *doulos* of His would do the things He commanded (Luke 17:10). Jesus told the Jewish leaders that there was a *doulos* to sin, but if the Son sets one free, they would be free indeed, or rather, a child of God (John 8:34–42).

The *doulos* was one who had no vote. Jesus becomes the exclusive Lord of the believer's life. Jesus is not following the believer. Jesus is not the copilot of the true believer's life. Jesus is not sitting in the back seat and following where you go. No, at salvation, the believer denies self, dies to self, and takes the leap of saving faith to follow and trust Christ. The believer does not know where the Lord will lead, but the believer will obediently and submissively follow the Lord regardless of where He leads them. The world, the flesh, family, friends, and one's own understanding are not being followed. The Lord Jesus Christ is the one being followed. This is what it means when it says the Thessalonians turned to serve the living God. It means they came to saving faith in the Lord. It means they became true worshippers of God (Romans 12:1). It means they put off the old self and put on the new self (Ephesians 4:22–24). It means they were slaves and servants to Christ.

Evidence of True Conversion: Hope in Jesus Who Delivers His Own from the Wrath to Come

True conversion causes one to hope in the return of the Lord. The Thessalonians were marked as those who were hopeful for the return of the Lord to deliver them from the wrath of God. How do people who hope in the Lord's appearing live? The apostle John gives us this answer where he says in 1 John 3:2–3:

> Beloved, we are God's children now, and what we
> will be has not yet appeared; but we know that when

he appears we shall be like him, because we shall see him as he is. **And everyone who thus hopes in him purifies himself as he is pure.**" (emphasis added)

As those who had been redeemed and saved, the Thessalonians were living sanctified and holy lives in anticipation of the Lord's return. They imitated Paul and the Lord Jesus Christ by living holy, righteous, and blameless lives to walk in a manner worthy of God (1 Thessalonians 1:10–14). They were like those in the parables who remained ready and continued to serve the Lord in anticipation of His coming (Matthew 25:1–30). They were like those who, with great endurance, sought glory, honor, and immortality from God (Romans 2:6–7, 10).

As we close this chapter, we see the many marks of true conversion that mark the true believer. Is conversion brought on by covenant signs, ceremonies, rituals, or sacraments? Paul would vehemently oppose such a thought. Rather, it is the gospel that saves and converts men. It is the Holy Spirit that convicts sinners of the gospel truths. It is the Holy Spirit that regenerates and transforms the sinner through the message of the gospel. It is the sinner responding in repentance and faith to the gospel and turning from idols to the living and true God. This is true conversion. Preaching conversion and salvation by covenant signs, ceremonies, rituals, or sacraments is an abomination, a false gospel, and it is to be accursed. The gospel is the wisdom and power of God to save sinful men.

Chapter 9

Paul: Seeking the Favor of Men, or of God?

For am I now seeking the approval of man, or of God? Or am I trying to please man? If I were still trying to please man, I would not be a servant of Christ.

—Galatians 1:10

The Apostle Paul asked the Galatians whether they thought he was living to win the favor of men or living to please God with regard to preaching the gospel and living for Christ. The same question could be asked of us today. Do you find it easier to not confront false teaching and go along to get along, or are you living to please God? Is it easier to thin down the gospel and not identify those who have a corrupt gospel or to preach the gospel and identify those that have a corrupt gospel? To be sure, Christians are to love our enemies (Matthew 5:43–48), we are to bear one another's burdens (Galatians 6:2), we are to let no debt remain out-standing except the debt to love another (Romans 12:8), we are to do nothing out of selfish ambition or vain conceit but to value others above ourselves (Philippians 2:3), and more. Paul deeply loved the Lord, the people of the Lord, and the nation Israel, and he had a heart for the lost.

However, when it came to dealing with false teaching, false teachers, and false gospels, Paul was fierce. How did Paul deal with those that would teach a works salvation? How did Paul deal with those that taught that a person was saved through a ritual such as circumcision? What kind of things did Paul say about false teachers? Was Paul seeking to appease the false teachers? Was Paul seeking to see what he had in common with the false teachers? Or rather, did Paul confront false teachers that gave a false gospel?

The following is a workable definition of a false teacher: A false teacher is one who unrepentantly and persistently holds to, teaches, and preaches a false gospel that damns men's souls by attacking, twisting, misinterpreting, adding to, or leaving out the essential components of the gospel or essential components of the bad news of sin, death, and hell. A false teacher could also be one who teaches the true gospel but lives a life in contradiction and opposition to the gospel and thus, blasphemes the gospel through their life (Galatians 1:6–9; Matthew 15:14, 23:13–15; 2 Peter 2:1–22, 3:16; Luke 11:52; Jude 4; Titus 1:16).

Certainly, those that teach sacramental conversion or sacramental salvation are the same people that Paul would have considered to be false teachers and propagating a false gospel. Sacramental conversion or salvation strikes at the heart of the gospel and is a false gospel. If a man, church, or denomination teaches sacramental conversion or salvation through chrismation, baptismal regeneration, the Lord's Supper, last rites, confirmation, matrimony, or any of the like, he is to be accursed. A person who teaches a ceremonial, sacramental, or ritualistic gospel does not know God (2 John 9), is warped and sinful (Titus 3:11), is self-condemned (Titus 3:11), is a false teaching gate closer (Matthew 23:13), is outside the kingdom of God (Matthew 23:13), is a twister of Scripture (2 Peter 3:16), is a hypocrite (Matthew 23:13), is bringing destruction upon themselves (2 Peter 2:1). Such people will be caught and destroyed (2 Peter 2:12) for they are under God's condemnation (2 Peter 2:3) and accursed by God (Galatians 1:8–9).

If one is to take any of Paul's letters and actions seriously, it becomes painfully clear that he identified (Philippians 3:2), confronted (1 Timothy 1:3), sharply rebuked (Titus 1:13), warned (Titus 3:10), silenced (Titus 1:11), taught when possible (2 Timothy 2:24–26), and when necessary, shunned false teachers (Romans 16:17, 2 Timothy 3:5, Titus 3:10). Paul mimicked Jesus. Just as Jesus confronted and denounced false teachers, so did Paul. It would do all believers, especially pastors, good to observe and mimic Paul who followed Christ's example.

Today, there are too many men who hold the title of pastor, but are cowardly and afraid to speak out against these false gospels. There are too many men who fear man more than God (Proverbs 29:25). There are too many men who have the title of pastor but who have the spiritual spines of a jelly fish, who have weak spiritual hearts akin to someone with congestive heart failure, who have dumb mouths that cannot speak the truth, who have spiritually weak eyes who cannot see spiritual realities, and who are chocolate soldiers who melt in the face of opposition, adversity, and persecution.[42]

Let us close with this statement from Paul in 1 Corinthians 11:1: *"Be imitators of me, just as I also am of Christ."*

Now to him who is able to do far more abundantly than all that we ask or think, according to the power at work within us, to him be glory in the church and in Christ Jesus throughout all generations, forever and ever. Amen.

—Ephesians 3:20–21

Acknowledgments

Laura: Thank you for your companionship and faithfulness in our marriage. Thank you for giving yourself to understanding God's Word. Thank you for your tireless efforts in taking care of the boys. Thank you for being virtuous, honest, loving, faithful, kind, good, merciful, and strong. I love you. Here is my encouragement and exhortation to you: Be steadfast, immovable, always abounding in the work of the Lord. Love the Lord your God with all your heart, and with all your soul, and with all your mind, and with all your strength. Stand firm and let nothing move you. Always give yourself fully to the work of the Lord, because you know that your labor in the Lord is not in vain.

Pax and Keryx, my dear sons: My deepest desire for you is to come to a saving knowledge and relationship with Jesus Christ. Your mother prays for both of you every night that God would grant you both saving faith in His Son, Jesus Christ. It is one thing to know doctrine, but it is quite another thing to know the Lord. You could understand my books, the *1689 London Baptist Confession*, the *Three Forms of Unity*, and Reformed theology, but still be lost and unsaved. These sources are only to help you in your understanding of the Bible. They are never to be a substitute for studying and understanding God's Word.

As I see you both grow up, I look forward to teaching you God's Word and about the Lord Jesus Christ. I look forward to the day when I can tell you of how the Lord saved me as Matthew 1:21 says, "*And you shall call his name Jesus, for he will save his people from their sins.*" I was saved from a life of adultery, pornography, lying, manipulation, idolatry, and more. I was a false Christian who was on his way to hell. However, God saved me and gave me new life. He caused me to be born again through His glorious gospel. He gave me the gift of repentance and saving faith. He alone is to be worshipped and glorified. Trust in Jesus Christ alone with all your heart and with all your soul and with all your might and with all your strength.

In writing my books, I have decided to make my unconverted life public because I have become convinced that the Lord Jesus Christ receives the greatest honor and glory by demonstrating His love to save the worst of sinners, of whom I should be considered foremost (Mark 5:19–20, 1 Timothy 1:15). I consider both of you miracle children—gifts from God. God spared my life when I wanted to end it, and He sovereignly blessed your mom and me with both of you. I love both of you. I have given both of you exhortations in the books I have written, and I will do so again in this book out of love:

> Be watchful, stand firm in the faith, act like men, be strong. Let all that you do be done in love. Love the Lord your God with all your heart, and with all your soul, and with all your mind. Whatever you do, whether you eat or drink, do all to the glory of God. Lastly, deny yourselves, pick up your cross, and follow after the Lord Jesus Christ. Put off your old self and put on the new man. Repent and put your faith in the Lord Jesus Christ.

I'll Be Honest Ministries, Grace to You Ministries, and Ligonier Ministries: Thank you for being faithful pastors, able to handle the Word of Truth. Our family has been built up in the faith by your ministries.

Notes

1 John MacArthur, "Act Like Men," sermon at Grace Community Church (Sun Valley, California), June 21, 2020.

2 John MacArthur and Richard Mayhue, *Biblical Doctrine: A Systematic Summary of Bible Truth* (Crossway, 2017), 269.

3 MacArthur and Mayhue, 289.

4 MacArthur and Mayhue, 270.

5 MacArthur and Mayhue, 273.

6 MacArthur and Mayhue, 276.

7 MacArthur and Mayhue, 279.

8 MacArthur and Mayhue, 284.

9 MacArthur and Mayhue, 290.

10 MacArthur and Mayhue, 291.

11 MacArthur and Mayhue, 292.

12 MacArthur and Mayhue, 293.

13 MacArthur and Mayhue, 288.

14 MacArthur and Mayhue, 294.

15 MacArthur and Mayhue, 294.

16 MacArthur and Mayhue, 296.

17 MacArthur and Mayhue, 387.

18 Steve Lawson, "Circumcision: True and False" Bible Study, Trintiy Bible Church, Dallas, Texas, May 2, 2017.

19 *Book of Jubilees* 15:29. (n.d.), https://www.sefaria.org/Book_of_Jubilees.15.29?lang=bi.

20 Ibid.

21 "Abraham as the Great (Un)Circumciser," The Torah.com, *Genesis Rabbah Volume II,* translation taken from Jacob Neusner, ed. (Scholars Press, 1985), 182, https://www.thetorah.com/article/abraham-as-the-great-un-circumciser.

22 "Romans 2:24–26 Commentary," Precept Austin, accessed July 7, 2025, https://www.preceptaustin.org/romans_224-29.

23 "Circumcision of the Heart," Precept Austin, accessed July 7, 2025, https://www.preceptaustin.org/circumcision_of_the_heart.

24 "Sermon on the Mount 1 – Inductive Study Guide," Precept Austin, accessed July 7, 2025, https://www.preceptaustin.org/sermon_on_the_mount_1.

25 Robert L. Thomas and Stanley N. Gundry, *The NIV Harmony of the Gospels* (Harper & Row, 1988).

26 "Commentaries, Matthew 15:2," Bible Hub, accessed July 7, 2025, https://www.biblestudytools.com/commentaries/gills-exposition-of-the-bible/matthew-15-2.html.

27 "Commentaries, Matthew 15:2," https://biblehub.com/commentaries/matthew/15-2.htm.

28 "Commentaries, Matthew 15:2," https://biblehub.com/commentaries/matthew/15-2.htm.

29 MacArthur, "Understanding the Sabbath," sermon at Grace Community Church (Sun Valley, California), September 20, 2009.

30 Alfred Edersheim, *The Life and Times of Jesus the Messiah* (Longmans, Green Co., 1923).

31 Edersheim, *Life and Times of Jesus.*

32 J. H. Hertz, *The Babylonian Talmud* (Soncino Press, 1953), https://www.sefaria.org/ Mishnah_Mikvaot?tab=contents.

33 Steve Lawson, "The Perfect Sacrifice of Christ, Part 1," sermon, January 2, 2005.

34 Steve Lawson, "The Perfect Sacrifice of Christ, Part 2," sermon, February 6, 2005.

35 "Romans 12:1 Commentary," Precept Austin, accessed July 7, 2025, https://www.preceptaustin.org/romans_12_word_studies.

36 Tim Conway, "The Power of the Offensive Cross," Grace Community Church, San Antonio, Texas, February 14, 2010.

37 "Romans 12:1 Commentary," Precept Austin, accessed July 7, 2025, https://www.preceptaustin.org/romans_12_word_studies.

38 "The Treasury of Robert Murray M'Cheyne," Banner of Truth, https://banneroftruth.org/us/resources/articles/2006/

the-treasury-of-robert-murray-mcheyne-1813-1843/?srslti-
d=AfmBOoo_biIUW7EealTl4C8K5vXaGejDdUDhr2ud-
PYsVkDMzZY058fp9.

39 William Macdonald, "Greek Word Studies: Worship (3000),
latreuo, SermonIndex.net, accessed July 7, 2025, https://
www.sermonindex.net/modules/articles/index.php?view=
article&aid=36100.

40 "Ephesians 3:16–17 Commentary," Precept Austin, accessed
July 7, 2025, https://www.preceptaustin.org/ephesians_
316-17.

41 "1 Thessalonians 1:8 Commentary," Bible Hub, Accessed July
7, 2025, https://biblehub.com/commentaries/1_thessaloni-
ans/1-8.htm.

42 C. T. Studd, *The Chocolate Soldier* (Deeper Christian Press,
1914), 9.

www.ingramcontent.com/pod-product-compliance
Lightning Source LLC
Chambersburg PA
CBHW051412090426
42737CB00014B/2634